booksonline

Read SAP PRESS online also

With booksonline we offer you online access to leading SAP experts' knowledge. Whether you use it as a beneficial supplement or as an alternative to the printed book – with booksonline you can:

- Access any book at any time
- Quickly look up and find what you need
- Compile your own SAP library

Your advantage as the reader of this book

Register your book on our website and obtain an exclusive and free test access to its online version. You're convinced you like the online book? Then you can purchase it at a preferential price!

And here's how to make use of your advantage

1. Visit www.sap-press.com
2. Click on the link for SAP PRESS booksonline
3. Enter your free trial license key
4. Test-drive your online book with full access for a limited time!

Your personal **license key** for your test access including the preferential offer

rzdj-s9k7-a8b2-uiyq

Implementing and Configuring SAP® Event Management

 **PRESS**

SAP PRESS is a joint initiative of SAP and Galileo Press. The know-how offered by SAP specialists combined with the expertise of the Galileo Press publishing house offers the reader expert books in the field. SAP PRESS features first-hand information and expert advice, and provides useful skills for professional decision-making.

SAP PRESS offers a variety of books on technical and business related topics for the SAP user. For further information, please visit our website: *www.sap-press.com*.

Brian Carter, Frank-Peter Bauer, Joerg Lange, Christoph Persich, Tim Dalm
SAP Extended Warehouse Management: Processes, Functionality, and Configuration
2010, 415 pp.
978-1-59229-316-2

Shaun Snapp
Discover SAP SCM
2009, 384 pp.
978-1-59229-305-6

Balaji Gaddam
Capable to Match (CTM) with SAP APO
2009, 273 pp.
978-1-59229-244-8

Nancy Muir, Ian Kimbell
Discover SAP
2009, 440 pp.
978-1-59229-320-9

Sandeep Pradhan

Implementing and Configuring SAP® Event Management

Galileo Press

Bonn • Boston

Galileo Press is named after the Italian physicist, mathematician and philosopher Galileo Galilei (1564–1642). He is known as one of the founders of modern science and an advocate of our contemporary, heliocentric worldview. His words *Eppur se muove* (And yet it moves) have become legendary. The Galileo Press logo depicts Jupiter orbited by the four Galilean moons, which were discovered by Galileo in 1610.

Editor Erik Herman
Copyeditor Ruth Saavedra
Cover Design Jill Winitzer
Photo Credit Image Copyright zhu difeng. Used under license from Shutterstock.com
Layout Design Vera Brauner
Production Editor Kelly O'Callaghan
Assistant Production Editor Graham Geary
Typesetting Publishers' Design and Production Services, Inc.
Printed and bound in Canada

ISBN 978-1-59229-316-2

© 2010 by Galileo Press Inc., Boston (MA)

1st Edition 2010

Library of Congress Cataloging-in-Publication Data
Pradhan, Sandeep.
  Implementing and configuring SAP event management (EM) / Sandeep Pradhan.
    p. cm.
  Includes bibliographical references and index.
  ISBN-13: 978-1-59229-316-2 (alk. paper)
  ISBN-10: 1-59229-316-6
  1. SAP Event Management. 2. Business logistics — Computer programs. I. Title.
  HD38.5.P73 2010
  658.500285'53 — dc22

                              200905427

Contents at a Glance

Contents

5 Architecture in SAP Event Management 5.1 .... **95**

6 Setting Up a Procure-to-Pay Scenario **117**

Preface

Supply chain visibility is the ability of a company to track its products and business processes in a supply chain towards building operational excellence. The goal of supply chain visibility is to improve and strengthen the supply chain by making critical information in the form of business events be readily available to all stakeholders and external business partners. Supply chain event management solutions go beyond just providing status visibility to actually responding to the critical events with proactive business actions. As companies supply chains continue to grow across geographies and enterprises, the capabilities of supply chain event management solutions will soon become central elements of these extended supply chains. With SAP Event Management, an application within the SAP Supply Chain Management (SAP SCM) suite, SAP not only supports supply chain event management concepts, but also provides pre-configured visibility scenarios that customers can leverage for their own supply chain event management implementations.

This book uses the Supply Chain Council's SCOR model to guide readers in explaining the visibility scenarios, business benefits, solution architecture, and technical configurations of five critical supply chain processes. Each chapter starts with an overview of a business process and then drills into the technical configuration aspects and closes by explaining how the SAP Event Management capabilities can be used for business operations monitoring and performance measurements. The book also highlights the implementation framework and the role of service-oriented architecture (SOA) in providing a platform for exchanging information in collaborative business environment.

Lastly, I would like to offer very special thanks to my wife Imelda, daughter Jessica and my parents for giving me the time and encouragement to write this book.

Sandeep Pradhan
San Francisco, January 2010

What is this book about? Who is it intended for? How is the book structured, and what is the best way for the reader to read and interpret the topics well?

1 Introduction

Supply chain event management (SCEM) is defined as an application supporting control processes for managing events within and between companies. This integrated software functionality supports five major business processes including the ability to monitor what's happening within the supply chain, notify the right person in case of a delay or critical event, simulate activities, control your processes, and measure your supply chain activities so that you can adapt your business process and make it more effective and efficient.

The goal of supply chain event management is to introduce a proactive control mechanism in managing supply chain business events via exception management. This process allows customers to define business rules to detect operational issues in their supply chain and route notifications to the appropriate individuals or groups for remediation and resolution.

Companies that deploy supply chain event management can expect to achieve the following operational and economic benefits:

▶ **Lower inventory levels**
  Increasing the visibility of supply chains, makes it possible to place the right product at right time at the right amount. This ensures that the company carries buffer inventory for market demand variations.

▶ **Increased customer satisfaction**
  Visibility provides comfort to business partners to track and trace their orders. This increases customer service levels and order fulfillment metrics.

▶ **Reduced transportation costs**
The ability to see any operational issues upfront and be informed proactively reduces the number of rush orders or expedite shipments performed in the company. If the delays are identified well in advance, alternative options can be accommodated in the supply chain.

▶ **Reduced manufacturing costs**
The stability of the production plan with seamless integration between planning, manufacturing, and plant maintenance ensures that the production plans runs smoothly as planned.

▶ **Reduced labor costs**
There is less need for overtime to address unplanned events in the supply chain.

SAP Event Management provides real-time visibility into a company's supply chain at a granular level — around planned and unplanned events — with near real-time status reporting, event overdue, alert notification, follow-up activity workflow, and analytics to measure supply chain metrics. The tool set helps companies identify business priorities, escalation paths, and guidance in resolving variations in supply chain business operations. Companies can take advantage of preconfigured visibility scenarios provided by SAP as a template in accelerating their implementation efforts.

This book provides you with a comprehensive explanation of the implementation and configuration of SAP Event Management in today's adaptive supply chain environment. Using business process maps and the Supply Chain Operations Reference model (SCOR®) methodology, readers will learn the SCEM concept and SAP customization steps required for setting up SAP Event Management in an efficient and effective manner.

1.1 Who Is This Book For?

This book is aimed at supply chain practitioners who are concerned with learning the concept of supply chain event management and would like to implement and configure SAP Event Management functionality.

This book will teach you about the implementation framework and how to configure SAP Event Management. Using the SCOR framework and business process maps, the book explains visibility scenarios related to procurement, manufacturing, order fulfillment, transportation, and returns to give a complete picture of supply chain business SCOR processes. In addition, we explain system architecture, integration with other SAP solutions, and monitoring procedures when setting up SAP Event Management system.

Basic knowledge of supply chain management business processes and a sound understanding of material management, production planning, sales and distribution, and transportation in SAP ERP is required to fully understand the visibility scenarios explained in this book.

1.2   How Is This Book Structured?

The book consists of 12 chapters:

Chapter 2, Supply Chain Event Management, describes the concept and implementation framework. It also highlights the SCOR methodology, which can be integrated while deploying the concept and functionality.

Chapter 3, SAP Event Management, provides an overview of the functionality and its key definitions and capabilities. The chapter also details how to leverage SAP Event Management in a service-oriented architecture (SOA).

Chapter 4, Visibility Processes Supported in SAP Event Management 5.1, details the supply chain visibility processes that SAP provides as preconfigured templates. The chapter highlights the business processes mapping and business benefits of implementing supply chain event management.

Chapter 5, Architecture in SAP Event Management 5.1, deals with the technical landscape, deployment options, communication, and connectivity options available in SAP Event Management. The chapter also provides details on the hardware sizing for SAP Event Management.

Chapter 6, Setting Up a Procure-to-Pay Scenario with SAP Event Management, details the customizations required in SAP ERP Central Component (ECC) and SAP Supply Chain Management (SCM) environments and how to use the functionality capabilities in a purchasing environment.

Chapter 7, Setting Up a Manufacturing Scenario with SAP Event Management, details the customizations required in SAP ECC and SAP SCM environments and how to use the functionality capabilities in a manufacturing environment.

Chapter 8, Setting Up an Order-to-Cash Scenario with SAP Event Management, details the customizations required in SAP ECC and SAP SCM environments and how to use the functionality capabilities in an order management environment.

Chapter 9, Setting Up a Transportation Scenario with SAP Event Management, details the customizations required in SAP Transportation Management (TM) and SAP SCM environments and how to use the functionality capabilities in a transportation environment.

Chapter 10, Setting Up a Returnable Transportable Scenario with SAP Event Management, details the customizations required in SAP ECC and SAP SCM environments and how to use the functionality capabilities in a returnable transportable items environment.

Chapter 11, Integrating SAP Event Management with Other SAP Solutions, deals with the possibility of integrating SAP Event Management with other SAP products. Examples are used to show how the integration provides benefit to the supply chain visibility processes.

Chapter 12, Monitoring Procedures for SAP Event Management, provides details about the monitoring process, routine background jobs, and archiving and deleting of data in SAP Event Management.

Appendices A – C list SAP Event Management transactions, rule set activity functions, and important SAP notes related to SAP Event Management implementations.

1.3   Summary

This chapter introduced supply chain event management and the functionality provided by SAP Event Management to support the supply chain visibility concept. The process and toolset allows companies to manage supply chain exceptions and build business rules for proactive monitoring of critical events and routing of exception notifications for remediation and resolution. The book serves as technical guide for supply chain practitioners interested in implementing and configuring SAP Event Management.

The next chapter explains supply chain event management concepts in detail with example and provides a implementation methodology.

Supply chain event management (SCEM) is a set of processes and applications that support control processes for managing business events within and between companies. This chapter introduces the concept of supply chain event management and a framework for the implementation of SAP Event Management.

2 Supply Chain Event Management

Supply chain event management (SCEM) is the management of information regarding a multitude of business events across a company's supply chain. SCEM collects real-time data from multiple business partners and sources across a supply chain. This data is converted to information that gives business managers a clear picture of how their supply chains are operating. If a problem requires immediate attention, the application can launch workflows and issue alert notifications to business partners to initiate proactive business actions.

The objective of this chapter is to provide some standard definitions that business managers can use to evaluate the use of SCEM for their business operations and to present a process-based approach for implementing SCEM. This chapter also introduces Supply Chain Council's Supply Chain Operations Reference model (SCOR) to map the supply chain visibility scenarios explained in this book.

2.1 Understanding Supply Chain Event Management

The concept of SCEM has evolved as an extension of process control. Companies manage their business processes with planning, but even the best-laid plans can be interrupted by unexpected events in supply chain operations. The purpose of SCEM is to serve as a supply chain visibility tool for the monitoring of supply chain events in a proactive manner. Let's now look at some fundamental definitions related to SCEM.

▶ **Supply chain event**

Any happening or occurrence within a supply chain function or business process that can be monitored or reported upon.

▶ **Supply chain event management**

The application of statistical process and technology identification and control application to planned and unplanned supply chain events.

▶ **Event management plan**

A documented process or set of procedures that outline the steps to be taken to control or react to an event.

▶ **Planned or expected event**

An event that tends to occur within the supply chain. An event for which a documented event management plan exists.

▶ **Unplanned or unexpected event**

An event that tends not to occur within the supply chan. An event for which a documented event management plan may not exist.

Supply chain event management does not plan, source, make, deliver, or return a product, but rather conveys information regarding those supply chain processes at a specific event level, for example:

▶ Fulfillment of purchase orders or sales orders per defined business transaction milestones

▶ Movement of shipments between two logistic network nodes

▶ Tracking of equipment or assets

Supply chain events carry with them documentation (increasingly electronic) that enable systems to be developed to capture and respond to their occurrence in the supply chain. It is the establishment and documentation of these recordable supply chain events and deployment of technology tools and software that monitor and report on those events that constitutes and creates a supply chain event management system.

After defining SCEM, the next step is to understand its goal: *to improve supply chain process effectiveness and reduce supply chain costs by managing events*. This goal can be achieved to a large extent by reducing the number of variations in the supply chain and reducing the number of surprises in the supply chain by changing the unplanned events to planned events. The SCEM concept enables companies to respond rapidly and sometimes automatically to unplanned events — without having to completely regenerate supply chain plans. This is accomplished by proactive notification to supply chain managers when specific events occur (e.g., when inventories are depleted, shipment delayed, etc.). Data that represents deviations from planned events are red-flagged and need attention. Often, automated responses can resolve these issues, but in all cases the supply chain managers have the opportunity to analyze the problem and determine solutions.

Below are the core process elements of supply chain event management as identified by AMR Research (Source: *The Report on Supply Chain Management*, February 2002).

▶ **Monitor**
Provides ongoing information about supply chain events, including the current status of inventory, orders, shipments, production, and supply.

▶ **Notify**
Helps support real-time exception management through alert messaging, proactively warning decision makers if an action must be taken or if a trend is emerging.

▶ **Simulate**
Supports decision-making by assessing what will happen if specific actions occur or recommends that an action be taken based on the response to an event or trend analysis.

▶ **Control**
Lets a decision maker change a previous decision or condition, such as diverting a shipment or expediting an order.

▶ **Measure**
Provides a measurements, often key performance indicators (KPIs) and metrics, for assessing how well the supply chain performs in the past and present.

Visibility is SCEM's core benefit. Seeing a business problem is 90% of fixing it. With SCEM capabilities, supply chain managers can leverage and continually fine-tune business processes and supply chain planning. Figure 2.1 shows the control process flow between the planning and operational execution of supply chain business process. This transforms unplanned events and exceptions into opportunities to accelerate manufacturing schedules, prevent missed shipments, and contain costs. The benefits are two-fold, improving process efficiency and increasing customer satisfaction.

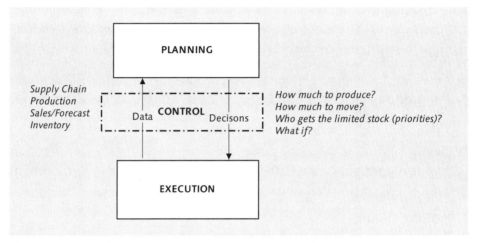

Figure 2.1 SCEM Helps Manage Control Processes in a Business Environment

The most effective usage of SCEM comes into play when the exception notification alert reaches the managers most capable of resolving the issue, regardless of their position in the supply chain or their location inside or outside the organization. Besides notification, what makes SCEM robust is its resolution capabilities that suggest a solution to the people who have been alerted to issue. A example is the automatic creation of a purchase requisition when inventory falls below a defined threshold by triggering an event to run material requirement planning in an SAP ERP system.

To illustrate an example of supply chain event management, it's best to consider the mapping and deployment of SCEM for a manufacturing and distribution company, where the SCEM solution is designed for monitoring the completion of an order-to-delivery, end-to-end business process. The business events and systems that might be included in this scenario are:

- ▶ Order management systems
  - ▶ Capture of sales order entry
  - ▶ Performance of inventory availability for order fulfillment
- ▶ Purchasing system
  - ▶ Procurement of raw materials from suppliers
  - ▶ Delivery confirmation and receipt acknowledgment from suppliers
- ▶ Production management system
  - ▶ Scheduling production for the sales order to meet delivery date
  - ▶ Production start
  - ▶ Monitoring production at events steps where adherence to plan can be confirmed or changes
  - ▶ Postproduction quality inspection
  - ▶ Product packaging and labeling
- ▶ Warehouse management system
  - ▶ Warehouse processing steps
  - ▶ Scheduling timing and placement of product in the staging for vehicle loading
  - ▶ Load into carrier's vehicle
- ▶ Transportation management system
  - ▶ Truck loading and dispatching
  - ▶ Post-shipment in transit trace updates from carrier
  - ▶ Proof of delivery confirmation from customer

Figure 2.2 shows how the integrated end-to-end business process can be captured in the SCEM for monitoring and drawing key supply chain metrics. It's in the management of the above granular event information where companies can utilize SCEM applications to enhance customer satisfaction and improve operational performance. The ability to assure customers that their orders will be fulfilled increases customer satisfaction. In addition to being reassured by this capability, customers can reduce the cost to serve because the inquiry can be done online via a self-service web portal model. When a deviation occurs from the planned event, the SCEM application enables the supply chain managers to sense and respond in a way that ensures customer satisfaction due to early detection and putting into motion an action plan for remedy. The proactive action avoids the past actions of supply chain managers when they had to wade through reams of reports (after the fact) and attempt to mitigate the damage of a lagging production schedule, missed shipments, and/or spiraling costs.

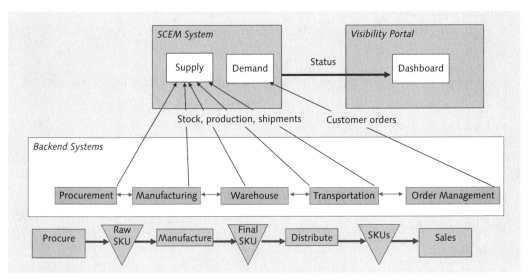

Figure 2.2 SCEM System in Action Providing Supply Chain Visibility

To summarize, the key to effective supply chain management is to close the gap between day-to-day changes in the supply chain and a company's ability to recognize and respond to them dynamically. Companies must be able to *identify* these changes as they occur in business operations, to quickly *understand* their potential impact, and to *act* immediately to deal with them. Companies must leverage their broad base of corporate knowledge, industry best practices, and established processes while evaluating these changes to choose the best course of action on any planned or unplanned supply chain event.

2.2   Implementing Supply Chain Event Management

Implementation of supply chain event management follows a business initiative sequence that is similar to activities such as Six Sigma or business process reengineering. The success of implementation is high when you take a process-based approach rather than a technology-focused approach. Whereas supply chain visibility and intelligent responses to events in a supply chain are the salient features of efficiency and velocity in the supply chain, the fundamentals of sound data collection and business process rationalization remain prerequisites to effective SCEM implementations.

During the early stages of SCEM deployment, it's important that a company identify the critical steps in their business process and, specifically, those that would cause ripple effects up and down the supply chain when schedules do not run as planned. After defining the business processes and specific events within the process, the next logical step is to document and identify the company entities that will serve as source points for recording the business event. The key to defining the business events is to establish the proper level of granularity such that SCEM output yields actionable and valuable information, but not to such a granular level that the supply chain manager in charge of the business process is inundated with exception notifications. One way to manage this is to provide tolerance ranges that monitor events, so business managers aren't notified unless an event falls outside the tolerance ranges.

A framework that works successfully for SCEM implementations should follow the methodology of assessment, implementation, and reporting. The SCEM implementation can be broadly broken down into three phases (Figure 2.3):

▶ Supply chain event assessment

▶ Supply chain event transition

▶ Supply chain event measurement

The assessment phase starts with the completion of a supply chain event management capabilities diagnostic. This assessment can focus on a single plant, a single function, or an entire supply chain organization. This is done by:

▶ Listing all of the available event candidates that currently exist within the supply chain (If we can't capture the information, we can't manage the associated business process.)

▶ Assigning more weight to event types that carry definite and known up- and downstream ripples in the supply chain

▶ Determining the severity of events in terms of cost, quality, and service and identifying the bottleneck processes that need monitoring

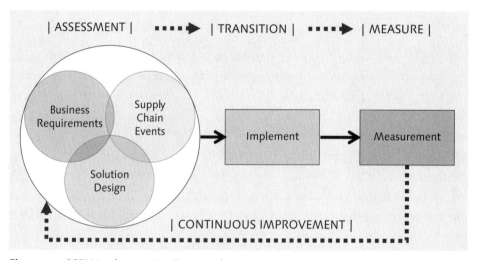

Figure 2.3 SCEM Implementation Framework

The next step toward implementation is to identify the source of supply chain event data and define an action plan for reacting to each event for the organization. These plans are then implemented according to their risk-impact priority — high, medium, or low. It's imperative to establish tolerance levels for business events and determine what actions should be taken and which business process owners should be notified when an event outcome exceeds a threshold or tolerance range. The important part of implementation involves cockpit design, as opposed to dashboard design, because the latter gives only information, whereas former can initiate notifications or workflows. SCEM systems can be powerful tools but run the risk of overwhelming users if the business process models and the alert mechanisms aren't properly calibrated.

Once implemented, the event data can be extracted as analytics for performance improvement. With SCEM, companies can break down the activities and do a root cause analysis of where the problems are in the supply chain. It also provides visibility of performance over time, so customers can perform trend analysis, drive continuous improvement, and attain corporate objectives. Figure 2.4 shows an example of supply chain metrics created in an SAP BusinessObjects application for measuring vendor performance.

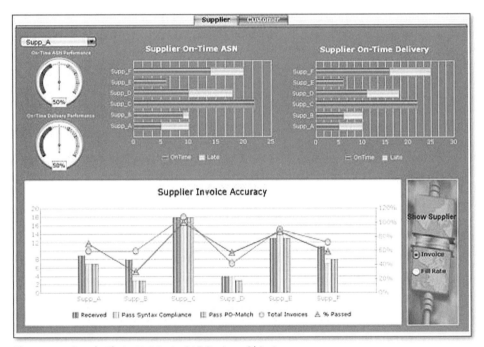

Figure 2.4 Supply Chain Metrics in SAP BusinessObjects

To summarize, SCEM can yield high benefits for companies that need to:

▶ **Balance supply and demand**
  As companies improve their sales and operations planning process, SCEM can help monitor those plans. Organizations are looking for means to reduce their

shrinking profits by monitoring their product surpluses or shortages proactively.

▸ **Support product launches**
New products bring sales and marketing campaigns, which determine the success of a product. SCEM can help organizations track production and replenishment to help meet orders on time and increase service levels and customer satisfaction.

▸ **Monitor large numbers of products, markets, customers, and vendors**
Supply chain managers can be overwhelmed by the sheer volume of data they need to manage and monitor. SCEM offers exception management tools to notify businesses of exceptions outside business thresholds.

▸ **Track key performance indicators**
Supply chain managers use key performance indicators (KPIs) for controlling and managing their supply chain. SCEM offers a measurement mechanism for recording the planned and actual event occurrences in supply chain business processes.

2.3   Integrating SCOR within Supply Chain Event Management

The Supply Chain Operations Reference model (SCOR) is a process reference model developed by the management consulting firm PRTM and AMR Research. SCOR is endorsed by the Supply Chain Council (Source: *www.supply-chain.org*) as the cross-industry de facto standard diagnostic tool for supply chain management. SCOR enables users to address, improve, and communicate supply chain practices within and between all interested parties in an extended enterprise.

SCOR is a management tool, spanning from customer to supplier. The model has been developed to describe the business activities associated with all phases of satisfying a customer demand. The model is based on three major pillars:

- ► Process modeling
- ► Performance measurement
- ► Best practices

2.3.1   The Process Modeling Pillar

The process modeling pillar describes supply chains using process modeling building blocks. The model can be used to describe supply chains that are simple or complex, using a common set of definitions. As a result, disparate industries can be linked to describe the depth and breadth of virtually any supply chain.

SCOR provides standard business process definitions, terminology, and metrics. It enables companies to benchmark themselves against others and influence future application development to improve business processes in five distinct functional areas: plan, source, make, delivery, and return (Figure 2.5).

- ► **Plan**
  Processes that balance aggregate demand and supply to develop a course of action that best meets sourcing, production, and delivery requirements.

- ► **Source**
  Processes that procure goods and services to meet planned or actual demand.

- ► **Make**
  Processes that transform product to a finished state to meet planned or actual demand.

- ► **Deliver**
  Processes that provide finished goods and services to meet planned or actual demand, typically including order management, transportation management, and distribution management.

- ► **Return**
  Processes associated with returning or receiving returned products for any reason. These processes extend into post delivery customer support.

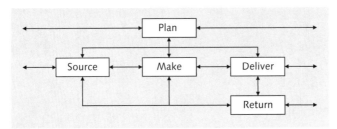

Figure 2.5   Functional Areas of SCOR

SCOR provides three levels of process detail (Figure 2.6). Each level of detail assists a company in defining scope (level 1), configuration or type of supply chain (level 2), or process element details, including performance attributes (level 3). Below level 3, companies break down core and sub business process elements into operational activities and tasks and start implementing specific supply chain management practices. It's at this stage that companies define practices to achieve a competitive advantage and adapt to changing business conditions.

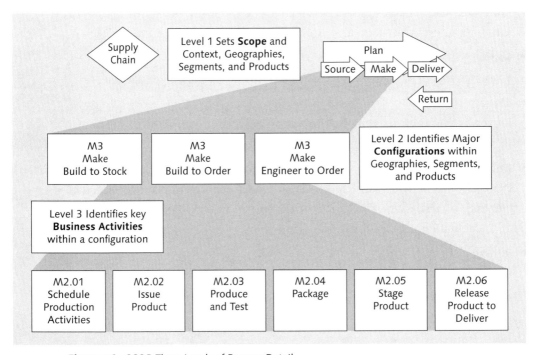

Figure 2.6   SCOR Three Levels of Process Detail

2.3.2   The Performance Measurement Pillar

SCOR contains metrics to measure supply chain business operations. The metrics are associated with the performance attributes. The performance attributes are characteristics of a supply chain that permit it to be analyzed and evaluated against other supply chains with competing strategies. The metrics in the model are hierarchical, just as the process elements are hierarchical. Level 1 metrics are created from lower-level calculations. Level 1 metrics (Figure 2.7) are primary, high-level measures that may cross multiple SCOR processes. They do not necessarily relate to a SCOR level 1 process (plan, source, make, deliver, return). Lower-level calculations (level 2 metrics) are generally associated with a narrower subset of processes. For example, delivery performance is calculated as the total number of products delivered on time and in full, based on a commit date.

	Attribute	Metric (level 1)
Customer	Reliability	Perfect Order Fulfillment
	Responsiveness	Order Fulfillment Cycle Time
	Agility (Flexibility)	Supply Chain Flexibility
		Supply Chain Adaptability
Internal	Cost	Supply Chain Management Cost
		Cost of Goods Sold
	Assets	Cash-to-Cash Cycle Time
		Return on Supply Chain Fixed Assets
		Return on Working Capital

Figure 2.7   SCOR Level 1 Metrics

2.3.3   The Best Practices Pillar

The SCOR model defines a best practice as a current, structured, proven, and repeatable method for making a positive impact on desired operational results.

▶ **Current**
   Must not be emerging and must not be antiquated.

▶ **Structured**
   Has clearly stated goal, scope, process, and procedures.

- ▶ **Proven**
  Success has been demonstrated in a working environment.

- ▶ **Repeatable**
  The practice has been proven in multiple environments.

- ▶ **Method**
  Used in a broad sense to indicate business process, practice, and organizational strategy, enabling technology, business relationship, business model, and information or knowledge management.

This book guides you through implementation and configuration in the five functional business process areas of SCOR. Using SAP pre-delivered visibility templates, companies can accelerate their SCEM implementation in each of these areas:

- ▶ **Procure-to-pay (source)**
  The procurement visibility process for production materials covers events from purchase order creation to payment, including order acknowledgement, shipping notifications, goods receipt, and invoice functions. This process can be combined with the transportation visibility process to cover shipment-related events. Role-based access for suppliers and buyers is available. Key performance indicators (KPIs) are provided on the supplier cycle time, on changes to purchase orders, and on the percentage of specific attributes.

- ▶ **Production malfunction (make)**
  The production malfunction process describes the visibility within production. It covers events from the release of the manufacturing order to the related goods receipt, including machine breakdowns. This process closes the gap between the planning and execution by notifying the planner in the event of machine breakdown and combines production- and plant–maintenance-related information. Role-based access for production planners and supervisors is available. Provision of key performance metrics on manufacturing orders affected by machine breakdown including rescheduled orders can also be measured.

▶ **Order-to-cash (deliver)**

The fulfillment visibility process monitors the delivery process and provides active tracking of the delivery for the customer. Events are reported within the company and to internal and external business partners. Follow-up activities are triggered in the form of email notification to the customer in case of order delays. Fulfillment processing covers events from warehouse activities to the proof of delivery at the customer site. Metrics such as delivery performance can also be measured in this process.

▶ **Transportation (deliver)**

The transportation visibility process is similar to the fulfillment process but focuses on transportation for inbound and outbound shipments. It covers international sea shipments, including customs and road transportations. This visibility process also deals with complex transportation networks using transportation chains. Role-based access for customers and forwarding agents can be provided. Metrics to measure the adherence to planned durations and customs processing are available.

▶ **Returnable transport item (RTI) (return)**

Returnable transport items (RTIs) include crates, pallets, containers, and industry-specific transport items varying in size and value that are reused. The tracking and tracking of company's assets provides visibility across a closed-loop RTI process covering the outbound, inbound and return process.

2.4 Supply Chain Event Management – Future Outlook

Current developments occurring in the following supply chain areas are propelling the use of SCEM by companies toward supply chain visibility.

▶ **Visibility solutions for the development of adaptive supply chains**

SCEM combines both process visibility and decision elements through electronic connectivity and application capability to seamlessly extract and create valuable real-time information for appropriate stakeholders along the supply chain. This improvement in adaptive supply chains creates real economic value by better identifying opportunities and managing orders, inventory, and shipments properly in a supply chain.

▶ **Radio frequency identification (RFID) and mobile technology**
These technologies will have a positive effect on the visibility solution. The emergence of RFID and mobile technology makes possible real-time information collection for building true adaptive supply chains.

▶ **Enhanced performance measurements**
Broader boundary-spanning metrics will be possible. An example of this is *perfect order* metrics, which consists of four attributes: on-time delivery, order shipped complete, accurate invoice, and no loss of damage. The automated control, management, and utilization of the visibility data allows businesses to adapt rapidly to change and respond to immediate requests, avoiding costly errors.

▶ **Agent-based supply chain optimization**
After companies have implemented SCEM, they look for proactive optimization technologies to improve their supply chain cost effectiveness and performance. This generates a set of options for the best method to respond to issues with a supply chain. These optimization technologies, coupled with a workflow, survey customer supply chains to understand account constraints to present alternatives and provide options to manage costs and maintain customer demand.

▶ **Focus on cost reductions that improve customer service and increase revenue**
In the current economic downturn, most companies are heavily focused on cost reduction opportunities and see supply chain visibility as way to increase customer satisfaction.

Figure 2.8 shows the various business bottlenecks in current environments affecting company's supply chain performance and the need for supply chain visibility across company boundaries.

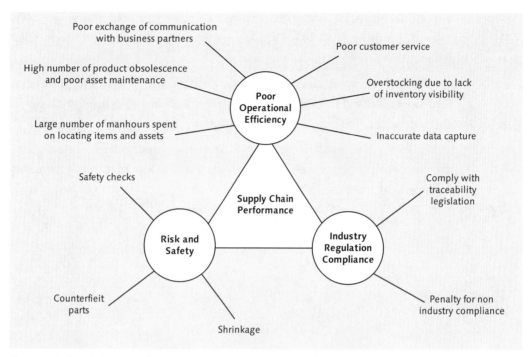

Figure 2.8 Supply Chain Performance Bottlenecks Impacting Visibility

2.5   Summary

Supply chain event management provides real-time visibility into the supply chain at a granular level, focused around events and exceptions (anticipated or otherwise) with workflows and/or analytics to identify priorities, escalation paths, and guidance in resolving variations. This chapter defined supply chain event management, highlighted its capabilities, and provided a framework for the implementation of the concept. SCEM systems do not buy, make, move, or sell products, but rather provide information around supply chain business operations. SCEM can serve as a tactical solution in the management of business-critical events and provide proactive notifications on any unplanned deviations from the supply chain plans. The key summary points in this chapter were:

▶ Use SCEM information to react to unplanned events and as a guideline or set of procedures that should be present in an organization to reduce the impact of exceptions. Business partners do realize that not everything always works as planned, but they don't like surprises, particularly when it's too late to react and make adjustments in the supply chain.

▶ Monitor critical supply chain events and notify management of exceptions that need to be managed to run operations smoothly. Define tolerance ranges on an alert mechanism for business user notification.

▶ Use the event data for statistical analysis at a tactical and strategic level to identify business process weakness and root causes to pursue for continuous improvement and identify strategic trends on supply chain operations.

The next chapter introduces SAP Event Management, key definitions, and visibility capabilities gained by implementing SAP Event Management.

*This chapter introduces SAP Event Management and provides key defini-
tions and capabilities supported by SAP Event Management. This chapter also highlights how service-oriented architecture creates collaborative
platforms for SAP Event Management, enabling adaptive supply chain
visibility.*

3 SAP Event Management

Achieving supply chain visibility is a primary step for companies seeking to
improve their supply chain maturity. Having supply chain visibility provides business managers with information necessary to proactively develop a response to an
unplanned event. SAP Event Management is a key capability within the SAP SCM
application. The objective of this chapter is to introduce you to SAP Event Management, identify its key components and capabilities, and explain how service-
oriented architecture (SOA) is helping to evolve SAP Event Management.

3.1 SAP Event Management Overview

The SAP Event Management application provides visibility within supply chain
business processes, comprising both planning and execution. The application
is flexible and can map and control any defined business process. A role-based
approach makes it possible to view the same business processes from different
business partner's points of view.

SAP Event Management provides real-time visibility into the supply chain at a
granular level, based on expected events and/or exceptions, via a web status portal, overdue list, alert framework, and workflow and analytics to identify business
priorities, escalation paths, and guidance in resolving variations. This ensures that
the right information is available for the right product at the right time and place,
allowing effective decision-making and efficient running of business processes.

The goal of SAP Event Management is to introduce a proactive control mechanism for managing business events (in particular, exceptions) and responding to them dynamically. This process and tool set help improve a company's customer service and delivery performance by managing exceptions to business processes. SAP Event Management allows you to define business rules to detect exceptions and route alerts to the appropriate individual or groups for remediation and resolution.

3.2 Using SAP Event Management to Achieve Supply Chain Visibility

SAP Event Management offers great visibility advantages over traditional, supply chain operations. This visibility can be broadly broken into three core areas of visibility: process, product, and performance.

3.2.1 Process Visibility

Process visibility concerns looking at the lifecycle status of business processes from an end-to-end perspective. Innovative companies are looking for options to getting visibility into their supply chain processes that allow them to better manage information over heterogeneous systems, and across extended supply chains, and to detect, evaluate, and solve problems in real time. An increase in collaboration with internal and external business partners increases customer satisfaction and reduces costs.

This visibility introduces real-time event alert mechanisms and means of effectively understanding the supply chain mechanics. Supply chain managers' focus must evolve from managing the *expected* outcome of business processes to managing by *exceptions*.

3.2.2 Product Visibility

Visibility into the outcomes or output of the processes (i.e., stock items, physical assets, and inventory) is also critical. Visibility is required not only at the aggregated global level, but also at a granular level (i.e., individual equipment levels). Tracking and tracing asset items across a supply chain allows companies to be made aware of exceptions with enough time to effectively act on unexpected supply chain events. The use of supply chain metrics is also essential to ensuring that supply chain assets are moving according to business expectations.

3.2.3 Performance Visibility

Performance visibility concerns empowering business users to know more than simply where their products and assets are or what happened to them. They need to know about the performance of their business processes, so they can not only manage the supply chain, but also look at improvement opportunities.

Process, product, and performance visibility addresses the market need to quickly respond to lean and agile supply chain networks. It opens up SAP Event Management capabilities in the following areas:

▶ **Extended connectivity**
Allows suppliers, logistics service providers, and customers to share supply chain event transactions. This consists of integrated platforms that support an information backbone, cross-division and cross-enterprise integration, and a centralized data repository to collect, store, organize, and cross-reference extended value supply chain data.

▶ **Enterprise transparency**
Allows distributed business users to see near real-time orders, inventories, and shipment information. These users can be suppliers, customers, or logistics service providers.

▶ **Exception-based alerting**
Allows for focused attention to the transactional data lifecycle completion. Exception-based alerting is rules-based management by exceptions, which allows managers to focus on exceptions to the process, rather than monitoring every single event. A key in this process is that the business users define the rules to deal proactively or reactively with the business events.

▸ **Performance metrics**
Leverages a centralized data repository to provide enhanced supply chain and internal performance metrics of the entire supply chain. Provides the stakeholders with the tools needed to evaluate supply chain performance.

▸ **Event-based response**
Provides the decision support and optimization capabilities to dynamically respond and re-plan to alerts on a near real-time basis. It generates and provides feasible actions to the users and provides information to the business on the supply chain impact.

▸ **Enabled control**
Builds an organization to react to changes automatically. Provides visibility of the problems and a series of feasible solutions to the users. When the alert is within a certain specified tolerance (cost, time, or service levels), the solution automatically re-optimizes and takes corrective action.

3.3 SAP Event Management Components

Based on SAP Web Application Server 6.20 with its exchange infrastructure, SAP Event Management offers a broad range of functions for tracking, proactive notifications, and alert creation with an alert framework. SAP Event Management is able to track and control business processes along the entire supply chain by integrating with supply chain planning, execution, sales and marketing, and product lifecycle management in both SAP and non-SAP applications.

SAP Event Management has four major components (Figure 3.1), which serve as an engine for management and monitoring of business events:

▸ **Event processor**
Receives incoming messages with one or several events, logs and validates events, decodes data using mapping definitions, and correlates the messages with active event handlers representing supply chain objects.

▸ **Event controller**
Creates changes, activates and deactivates event handlers, processes events, and forwards events to the rule processor and the expected event processor.

▶ **Expected events processor**

Monitors expected and unexpected events, checks that the events to ensure that they match stored rules and dates, recognizes the delay of events, and provides a profile list of expected events.

▶ **Rule processor**

Applies a set of rules to an event, coordinates the reaction to an event, calls up downstream monitoring functions, and transfers alerts and responses to target systems or users via the alert framework.

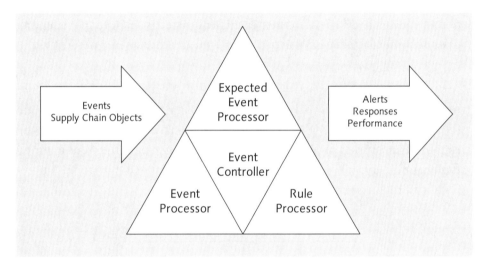

Figure 3.1 SAP Event Management Components

3.4 Types of Events in SAP Event Management

SAP Event Management can process different types of events (Figure 3.2) based on the business scenario. Within a business process, we have events that are expected to happen and actual events that do happen. Metrics can be calculated on the actual events versus planned events. Four primary types of events are reported in SAP Event Management:

▶ **Expected event**

Events that we expect to occur within the particular time frame and that do occur as planned.

▶ **Early/late event**

Events that we expect to occur within a particular time frame but that actually occur outside the tolerance date range. These events can cause subsequent rescheduling of events or can be remain as early/late events.

▶ **Unexpected event**

Events related to exceptions in a supply chain business scenario. Some activity needs to be rescheduled on another event because it has changed the milestone dates. An unexpected event can trigger an alert or other type of notification.

▶ **Unreported event**

An event expected to occur within a particular tolerance level but that's not reported at all. Similar to an unexpected event, some activity that has a timeline set needs to occur following this event, following which the event can be classed as unreported or overdue. SAP Event Management offers a monitoring tool that monitors all events at the backend of the planned milestone. A tolerance level can be set on this planned milestone.

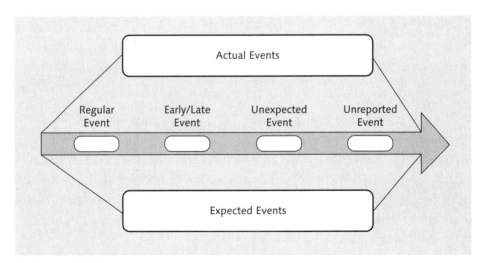

Figure 3.2 Types of Events in SAP Event Management

3.5 SAP Event Management Definitions

SAP Event Management design requires understanding three main objects: application object type, event handler and event message. Figure 3.3 shows the linkage between the three objects.

3.5.1 Application Object Type (Application System)

An application object type residing on an application system helps answer the following design questions (the associated SAP Event Management objects are in parentheses):

▶ Under what conditions does an application object need to be considered for SAP Event Management? (event management relevancy)

▶ Where does the planned event data come from?
(expected event date and time)

▶ Where do the information and control parameters come from?
(event attributes)

▶ How are query and tracking IDs determined?
(event handler searching and identification)

▶ From which tables in the application systems does the data come?
(business process type)

▶ What is the key that connects the application object and the event handler?
(application object ID)

3.5.2 Event Handler (SAP Event Management)

The event handler residing on an SAP Event Management system helps answer the following design questions (the associated SAP EM objects are in parentheses):

▶ Which events do you want to manage using the event manager?
(expected/planned and unexpected/exception events)

▶ How do you identify your event handler? (tracking ID or query ID)

▶ What additional information or data is required? (parameters)

▶ What data do you need to get a quick overview of the status of an event handler? (event handler status)

▶ Under what conditions does an event handler need to be created? (event handler condition)

▶ To build a complete business process, which event handler types should be grouped together? (event handler sets)

3.5.3 Event Message

An event message provides the means to report relevant event observations (planned or unplanned) to SAP Event Management. The event message communicated to SAP Event Management contains the following information:

▶ **Event/status**
What happened and who reported it?

▶ **Tracking ID**
Which objects are affected?

▶ **Locations**
Where did the event take place?

▶ **Partners**
Who is involved in what function?

▶ **Estimated time**
When will a subsequent event occur?

▶ **Subsequent status**
Which unplanned events might be caused?

▶ **Measurement result**
Confirmation of measurement results.

▶ **Reason**
Text message.

The posting of an event message into SAP Event Management may trigger activities such as a status update (to reflect the current situation) or an alert notification for any unplanned events.

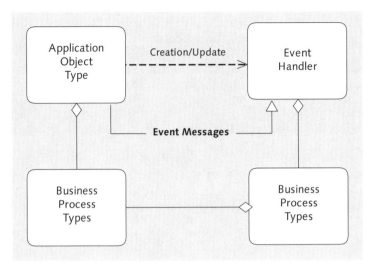

Figure 3.3 SAP Event Management Objects

The commonly used SAP Event Management terminology you need to understand (from both a business and application perspective) is listed below:

▶ **Business process type**
Classification of business objects or business processes in the application system for which you want to manage events in SAP Event Management.

▶ **Application object type**
Determines when the event handler needs to be created in SAP Event Management. Determines the data (e.g., planned events, attributes, tracking ID) that is handed to SAP Event Management.

▶ **Event type**
Determines the posting of an event message into the event handler via a tracking ID.

▶ **Event handler**
Lists the business process events that you want to manage. Also includes the attributes and the status information with a tracking ID. Figure 3.3 shows the creation of Event Handler from Application Object Type via Business Process Type.

▶ **Event**

A business incident that occurs in a business process.

▶ **Status attribute**

Provides a quick overview of the status of the event handler.

▶ **Parameter**

Used to store the attribute of the event handler.

▶ **Rule sets**

Defined rules that determine how SAP Event Management reacts to reported or unreported events.

▶ **Event handler set**

Represents an entire business process, including data from different event handlers.

▶ **Web Communication Layer (WCL)**

Web capabilities that let your business partners view the supply event to track the status of transactions or enable your business partners to input important information's directly into the WCL.

3.6   SAP Event Management Capabilities

The core capabilities of SAP Event Management lies in visibility, notification, response, collaboration, and analytics. This section explains how SAP delivers these core capabilities in a business environment.

3.6.1   Visibility

Providing supply chain visibility is a core capability of SAP Event Management. The ability to provide near real-time status and progress of end-to-end business processes and products is a huge benefit for companies. SAP Event Management helps provide transparency in the attainment of a company's corporate goals, business processes, and assets.

SAP Event Management helps provide visibility in supply chain events as follows:

▶ Proactively monitors planned events as milestones and provides current status.

▶ Sends notifications to business partners to remedy supply chain issues.

▶ Documents the process for contractual (service level agreement) or legal (FDA, dangerous goods shipments) purposes.

▶ Triggers follow-up activities after the completion of a successful supply chain events.

SAP has designed their visibility processes to correlate with common SCEM processes. The visibility processes are building blocks that you can use to formulate a complete end-to-end scenario. These processes can help customers reduce implementation efforts an average of 40%.

SAP Event Management also provides predefined visibility scenarios that include expected events, statuses, follow-up activities, and web layouts for reporting event data and enabling the global visibility of supply chain processes among business partners.

The components of these visibility scenarios include (Figure 3.4):

▶ Documentation

  ▶ Scenario descriptions that describe the business scenario and the procedure in a step-by-step guide.

  ▶ A configuration guide that lists the configured customizations and describes changes that have to be made to implement the process.

▶ Scenario-specific setup in an SAP application system

  ▶ Configured customization and process-related functions for an SAP application system.

▶ Scenario-specific setup in SAP Event Management

  ▶ Configured customization and scenario-related functions for SAP Event Management.

- ▶ All customizing settings in SAP Event Management for the particular business process, such as expected event profiles, rule sets, alerts, and responses.

- ▶ Preconfigured user interface connection to web application for event reporting and status retrieval.

- ▶ Data extraction routines for SAP Event Management data extraction events from SAP Event Management to SAP NetWeaver® Business Warehouse (BW).

▶ SAP NetWeaver Portal and SAP NetWeaver BW content

  - ▶ Key performance indicators in SAP NetWeaver Business Warehouse

  - ▶ iViews and roles based on SAP NetWeaver Portals

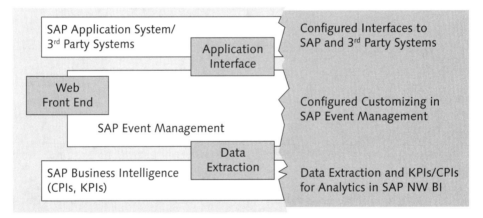

Figure 3.4   SAP Event Management Visibility Scenario Templates

3.6.2   Notification

An effective supply chain control system offers an easily usable system of notification that allows users to identify a subset of critical events and conditions to be monitored. SAP Event Management offers capability for managing and monitoring business transactions and informing business users only when an exception occurs.

SAP Event Management monitored conditions include anything from a drop of excess inventory to a rise in delivery data rescheduling. SAP Event Management can monitor high data volumes and evaluate large amounts of operational data to detect any significant changes. As the state of the supply chain changes, SAP Event Management periodically reevaluates the monitoring conditions and updates the status display.

In addition to monitoring key events, supply chain control requires the ability to alert the user to critical conditions or events requiring immediate action. Alerts are occurrences of specific business events outside a defined tolerance level. SAP Event Management, through its alert framework, delivers these notifications via reports, emails, or pages, assigning them to high, medium, or low urgency categories. With these alerts, supply chain managers located anywhere can be made aware of any significant changes in the supply chain and react appropriately.

3.6.3   Response

SAP Event Management provides responsive capabilities in the form of activities that can be easily configured to suit business requirements. These activities include the triggering of a workflow and sending automated alerts to broadcast overdue or expected event reports to business partners.

3.6.4   Collaboration

From capturing event information to analyzing it against preset milestones and then alerting appropriate parties when there is a discrepancy, SAP Event Management supports real-time responsiveness and adaptive collaboration across the business network. For collaboration, two components are critical for managing supply chain events: application building blocks and technology building blocks. The application includes an SAP ERP transactional backend system, whereas the technical blocks should include a distributed, Internet-enabled messaging architecture and prepackaged collaborative business process.

Figure 3.5 gives an example of a prepackaged collaborative business process where the two business partners exchange transactional data and trigger events to initiate either workflow or a shared web portal to provide supply chain visibility.

The architecture is flexible enough to support the level of supply chain event management required by the supply chain business process and the level of trust that exists between the business partners. Two examples provided below illustrate how to leverage SAP Event Management accordingly.

▶ A company offers vendor-managed inventory services as part of a customer value proposition. The scenario is modeled to keep inventory low across customer locations. Prepackaged collaborative business processes deliver daily information on inventory and consumption at customer locations. They use SAP Event Management to trigger real-time alerts to the warehouse, manufacturing, and suppliers if the predicted inventory drops below safety limits.

▶ A company issues discrete purchase orders to suppliers on a daily basis. A collaborative business process delivers electronic data interchange (EDI)-based purchase orders to each supplier and processes the suppliers acknowledgments. If the delivery due dates are not met, alerts go out to internal users, who follow up with the suppliers.

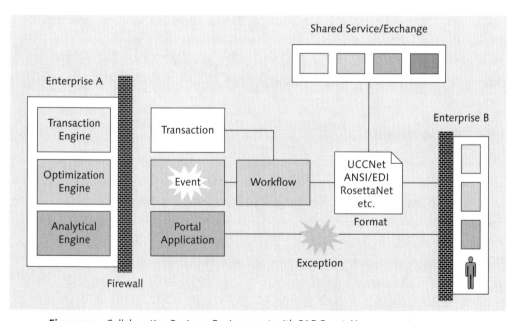

Figure 3.5 Collaborative Business Environment with SAP Event Management

3.6.5 Analysis

Analytic dashboards are available to monitor the health of customer supply chains and send notifications when exceptions occur. These dashboards also track key performance indicators, both financial and operational, which provide the information customers need to create a real-time performance management environment for making the right decisions.

3.7 SAP Event Management in Service-Oriented Architecture (SOA)

The evolution of service-oriented architecture (SOA) has enabled opportunities for companies to expand their existing solutions without having to make substantial investments in the infrastructure. SOA creates a collaboration platform with business partners that makes integration viable for companies to create end-to-end business process visibility. SOA is a blueprint for an adaptable, flexible, and open IT architecture for developing service-based, enterprise-scale business solutions. With SAP NetWeaver as a technical foundation, SOA moves IT architectures to higher levels of adaptability — and moves companies closer to the vision of real-time enterprises by elevating Web services to an enterprise level.

The characteristics for enabling SOA for a SAP SCM application include:

▶ **Configuration templates**
These allow enterprises to reduce deployment time by subscribing to common global business processes. These customers can log in, collaborate with their business partners, load master data, and plan collaboratively with suppliers. After the system or process has been set up, customers can execute processes.

▶ **Ease of integration**
To help customers leverage existing backend systems, software as a service (SaaS) solutions need to make their business process libraries available as part of an SOA application programming interface (API). The intention is to allow

customers and third-party solution providers to leverage this API as a supply chain platform.

▶ **Business process library**
To feed the configuration templates and to allow extension through the SOA API, there needs to be a set of process solutions and functional enhancements such as self-service reporting.

SAP delivers SOA enterprise services, which are typically a series of Web services combined with business logic that you can access and use repeatedly to support a particular business process. Aggregating Web services into business-level enterprise services provides a more meaningful foundation for the task of automating enterprise-scale business scenarios.

For supply chain visibility, SAP delivers the Business Event Handling for Process Tracking bundle, which you can use to create, update, and retrieve detailed information about tracked processes in SAP Event Management and thus allows for tracking and monitoring of collaborative supply chain networks.

The business objects and the operations supported by this bundle are:

▶ **Tracked process (event handler)**

  ▶ Maintain tracked process (post–event handler, asynchronous)

  ▶ Confirm tracked process

  ▶ Find tracked process by elements (search event handler by attribute, synchronous)

  ▶ Read tracked process (get event–handler-related data, synchronous)

▶ **Tracked process event notification (event message)**

  ▶ Create tracked process event notification (send event message, asynchronous)

  ▶ Confirm creation tracked process event notification

Figure 3.6 shows the Process Component View of the process tracking with subprocess decomposition. Tracked process is the business object that provides operations that are used to create, change, or delete a tracked process or tracked object.

The tracked process or the tracked object is used to monitor business processes, real world objects, or logical objects.

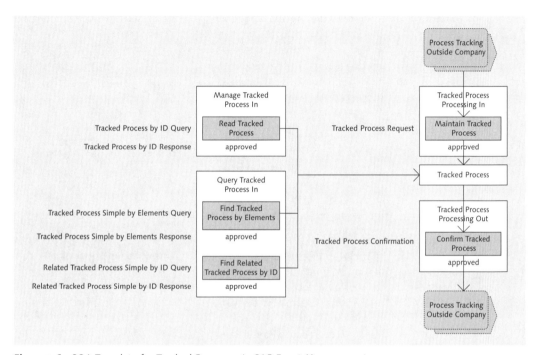

Figure 3.6 SOA Template for Tracked Processes in SAP Event Management

Table 3.1 lists the business context for the use of these different processes.

Process Component	Business Context and Use	Key Features
Read tracked process	This inbound operation sends a request to SAP Event Management to retrieve detailed information about a tracked process or tracked object. In addition, this inbound operation is used to respond to such a request.	This inbound operation processes the following message types: `TrackedProcessByIDQuery Message_sync` `TrackedProcessByIDResponse_ sync`

Table 3.1 Structure Overview for Tracked Process (Event Handler) in SOA

Process Component	Business Context and Use	Key Features
Find tracked process by elements	This inbound operation sends an inquiry to the process component to retrieve instances of the type tracked process and to receive the response to this inquiry. This includes the selection criteria of the business document that is send in an event message.	This inbound operation processes the following message types: `TrackedProcessSimpleBy ElementsQueryMessage_sync` `TrackedProcessSimpleBy ElementsResponseMessage_ sync`
Maintain tracked process	This inbound operation requests the creation or update of an existing tracked process or tracked object in SAP Event Management. This includes all business information necessary to send a business document in an event message.	This inbound operation processes the message type: `TrackedProcessRequest`
Confirm tracked process	This outbound operation confirms a request for a tracked process or tracked object and sends a notification to business partners about the result of a previous creation or update of a tracked process or tracked object. It enables the application to use the business information that is relevant for sending a business document in an event message.	This outbound operation processes the message type: `TrackedProcessConfirmation`

Table 3.1 Structure Overview for Tracked Process (Event Handler) in SOA (Cont.)

Figure 3.7 shows the process component view of the tracked process event notification with sub-process decomposition. Tracked process event notification is the business object that provides operations that are used to create and send tracked process event notifications for the business process, real-world objects, or logical events that SAP Event Management tracks. These tracked process event notifications contain information about the events that occur during the execution of the business processes, the lifetime of real-world objects, or the lifetime of the logical objects.

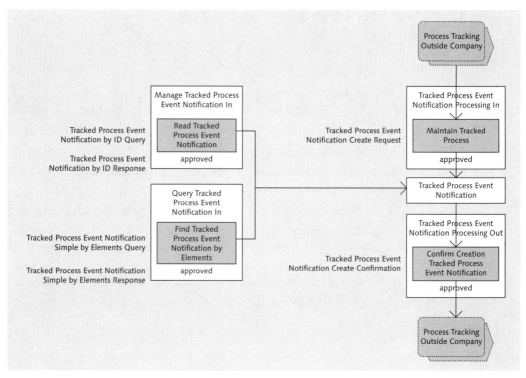

Figure 3.7 SOA Template for Event Messages in SAP Event Management

Table 3.2 lists the business context for the use of different processes.

Process Component	Business Context and Use	Key Features
Track process event notification	This inbound operation is used to report an event and therefore receive all necessary information.	This inbound operation processes the message type: `Tracked Process Event Notification Create Request`
Confirm create tracked process event notification	This outbound operation sends all relevant data for a tracked process event notification as a response of a previous request.	This outbound operation processes the message type: `Tracked Process Event Notification Create Confirmation`

Table 3.2 Structure Overview for Tracked Process Event Notification (Event Message) in SOA

3.8   SAP Event Management Example

In this section, we'll see how to integrate SAP Event Management with SAP's automotive industry solution, SAP Vehicle Management. The SAP Vehicle Management) is an application in SAP Industry Solution (IS) Automotive. VMS supports, in the area of sales and services, the business processes that you require as vehicle importer when dealing with your original equipment manufacturers (OEMs) and your dealers in new and used vehicle sales. VMS offers customers complete integration of all relevant processes such as procurement, sales, rework, returns processing, trade-in, and service processing. In addition, it allows you to react flexibly to customers' requirements in the area of production (using the pull strategy) and fast delivery times with reduced warehouse stock and sales and distribution costs.

Figure 3.8 shows the complete business process among various business partners and the business events that are recorded in SAP Event Management for this business scenario.

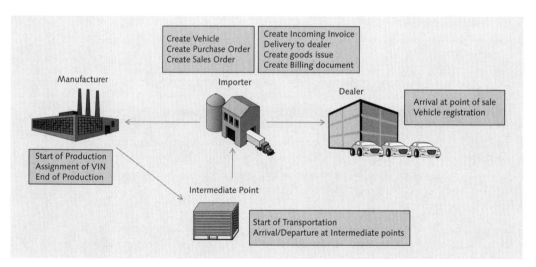

Figure 3.8   Events Recorded in SAP Vehicle Management and SAP Event Management

The process starts with a car importer configuring a car in the SAP system. The following are created with the configuration entry: a sales order from the dealer, a purchase order for the car manufacturer, and an internal vehicle number. A car manufacturer then produces the car, and it's transported to the car importer and booked on stock. The car importer delivers the car to a dealer. After a change to the sales order, the dealer gets a purchase order confirmation from the OEM.

With SAP Event Management system integration with IS Automotive Vehicle Management (Figure 3.9) and its web user interface, the production and transportation process is tracked as customers get acknowledgments from the car manufacturer. Different documents are also created during this business process, such as an invoice or a billing document. At the end of the process, the car arrives at the dealer and gets a registration number from the registration office. All of the major steps in this business process are tracked in SAP Event Management.

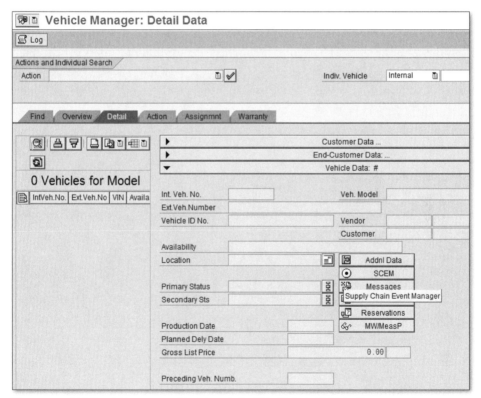

Figure 3.9 SAP Event Management is Integrated within IS-Auto Vehicle Management Functionality

3.9 Summary

SAP Event Management allows companies to manage processes, inventories, assets, and partners by exception rather than monitoring processes that are running smoothly. Its capabilities span from the ability to recognize and react to unplanned events in the supply chain to providing visibility to outside business partners with collaborative business processes and measuring supply chain performance by metrics. This chapter introduced SAP Event Management, provided key definitions, and described SAP Event Management capabilities in visibility, notification, response, analysis, and collaboration. We also looked at how SAP supports service-oriented architecture (SOA) initiatives related to supply chain event management by providing the enterprise services bundle templates for implementing any processes in SAP Event Management.

The next chapter looks at the supply chain visibility processes delivered by SAP Enterprise Service 5.1. The chapter highlights each visibility business process map and business benefits.

This chapter describes the supply chain visibility business processes supported in SAP Event Management 5.1. We explain the individual business processes, their steps, and business benefits in detail.

4 Visibility Processes Supported in SAP Event Management 5.1

In this chapter, we'll learn about the generic visibility processes delivered in SAP Event Management 5.1. Visibility processes are preconfigured parts of a business scenario that each focus on only one part of a complete business process. You can easily obtain various visibility processes in SAP Event Management to represent specific end-to-end business processes for the enterprise.

We'll explain each visibility process using the Business Process Modeling Notation (BPMN) diagram, which highlights the event-driven supply chain processes, the business benefits for each process achieved by implementation of SAP Event Management area.

4.1 Business Process Modeling Notation

The Business Process Modeling Notation (BPMN) is a standard for business process modeling and provides a graphical notation for specifying business processes in a diagram. The objective of BPMN is to support business process management for both the business user and the technical user, by providing notation that is simple to interpret. BPMN is meant to serve as a common language for all of the stakeholders in a company who constantly work to improve the business processes. The stakeholders include business analysts who create and refine processes, technical analysts who implement the processes, and business managers who monitor and manage the business processes.

Figure 4.1 lists the BPMN symbols we'll use in this chapter to describe the various business process maps.

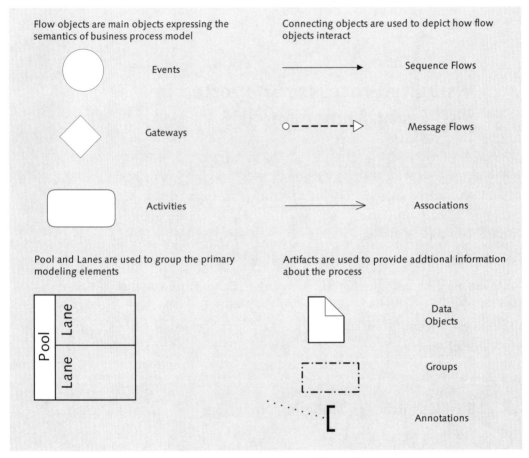

Figure 4.1 Business Process Modeling Notation Symbols Used to Map Processes

4.2   Procurement (SCOR - SOURCE)

The procurement business process falls under SCOR - Source functional area supporting sourcing of goods from external suppliers. This visibility process covers procure-to-pay in a company. SAP Event Management offers the opportunity for companies with an increased number of suppliers and/or trading partners to view, respond to, and measure the sourcing side of supply chain.

In today's business environment, both strategic and operational buyers face various business challenges:

▸ **Unpredictable consumer demand**
Forecasting end-user demand is becoming increasingly difficult. Inaccurate forecasts make it extremely difficult to manage the procurement of long–lead-time products.

▸ **Constrained supply**
Companies need as much forewarning as possible to react quickly and be able to adjust plans when a supplier is unable to meet a schedule or respond to changing needs.

▸ **Obsolescence risk**
Many products or parts which the companies market may have small shelf life and fluctuating demand. To minimize the amount of obsolescence at the component or finished goods level, organizations need to identify the slow-moving ones, to ease or eliminate future orders.

▸ **Global outsourcing variability**
A significant portion of the products may be built in low-cost manufacturing locations. This increases the need for visibility of the goods availability on time for fulfilling customer orders.

4.2.1 Process Overview

The process starts with the creation of a purchase order for a planned material, which is then followed by order acknowledgment from the supplier, confirming the delivery date and quantity of the purchase order. Subsequently, the supplier delivers the goods on the delivery date and sends an invoice. The process ends with payment by the buyer for the purchase order. The business communication is primarily between the buyer and supplier in a procurement scenario. The tracking of the purchase order can be at the purchase order line-item level. Figure 4.2 shows the standard procurement business process flow diagram.

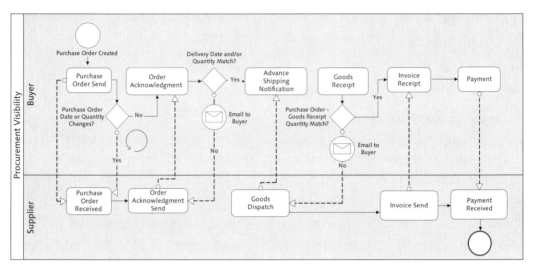

Figure 4.2 Procurement Processing Visibility Scenario in SAP Event Management

Table 4.1 captures the supply chain events for the purchasing scenario.

Business Process Event	Type of Event	Event Status	Notification
Purchase order created	Expected event	Procurement status: sent	
Order acknowledgment received without any changes	Expected event	Order acknowledgment status: received	
Order acknowledgment received with changes	Unexpected event	Order acknowledgment status: pending	Email to buyer
Advanced shipping notification received	Expected event	Procurement status: in transit	

Table 4.1 Procurement Business Events

Business Process Event	Type of Event	Event Status	Notification
Advanced shipping notification not received (detected by overdue event monitoring	Unexpected event	Procurement status: shipment delayed	Email to buyer
Goods receipt posted in SAP ERP system	Expected event	Procurement status: partly or completely arrived	
Invoice posted in SAP ERP system	Expected event	Invoice status: invoiced	
Payment created	Expected event	Invoice status: invoice paid	
Quantity changed in existing purchase order	Unexpected event	Procurement status: quantity changed Order acknowledgment status: pending	Email to buyer and supplier
Date changed in purchase order	Unexpected event	Procurement status: date changed Order acknowledgment status: pending	Email to buyer
Both date and quantity changed in purchase order	Unexpected event	Procurement status: date and quantity changed Order acknowledgment status: pending	Email to buyer

Table 4.1 Procurement Business Events (Cont.)

The related SAP Event Management procurement solution features are:

▶ **Forecast order visibility**
Integrates forecasted demand and actual sales orders as they materialize. The buyers immediately know about any deviation in supply requirements resulting from forecast changes or inaccurate forecasts.

▶ **Purchase order management**
Tracks the status of purchase orders and replenishment requests. Alert notifications occur when there is a change in the supply plan or when there is a need to generate a new replenishment.

▶ **Dynamic sourcing**
Sources the parts dynamically from the supply chain in a manner that meets customer needs while minimizing total delivery cost.

▶ **Supplier score-carding**
Monitors and measures the performance of suppliers against contracted service levels.

4.2.2 Business Benefits

The business benefits to an organization implementing a procurement visibility process are:

▶ **Reduced inventory safety stock**
Overall reduction in inventory costs with integrated demand and supply view to detect any problems such as supply disruptions. This allows a company to maintain appropriate inventory levels to meet customer expectations and minimize product obsolescence.

▶ **Reduced overall component sourcing**
Measures a supplier's ability to meet contract requirements by furnishing them with detailed scorecards. It also provides the ability to measure a supplier's ability to meet their commitments.

▶ **Reduced expedited freight costs**
Stability in the plan will reduce the rush shipments done to meet customer delivery dates.

▶ **Decreased production disruptions**
With less variance on planned and execution orders, the production will run stably and allow for proper planning of materials and resources.

▶ **Improved planner productivity**
With the primary focus on exceptions management, the system provides proactive notifications of disruptions and improvement opportunities.

4.3   Production Malfunction (SCOR - MAKE)

The production malfunction process falls under SCOR - Make functional area focusing on the manufacturing process of finished goods. This visibility scenario integrates the production scheduling, production execution, and plant maintenance teams in a manufacturing company. Several people are involved in managing the process when a machine (work center) breakdowns on the shop floor.

Providing a visibility process for this area, allows the control mechanisms that already exist in the individual areas (production planning and asset management) to be linked together more closely than has ever previously been possible. In this way, processing can be optimized. If a machine breaks down, an alert informs the production planner that one of the manufacturing orders that has been scheduled (released) for this work center could be at risk of not being processed. Moreover, processing of the malfunction notification is tracked until the machine breakdown has been repaired. Customers can evaluate (at a later time) how many orders were rescheduled (change to the planned start or end date and/or work centers) and, by taking machine breakdowns into account, draw conclusions about the quality of the original planning.

4.3.1   Process Overview

During the execution of manufacturing orders, if a machine breaks down, a notification is sent to the production scheduler and plant maintenance personnel. The scheduler then looks at opportunities for scheduling a different date and time, and the plant maintenance personnel start working on remedying the issue. Once the malfunction is rectified, both teams are informed, and the production order is further executed and delivered. Figure 4.3 captures the business process flow diagram between the manufacturing and plant maintenance team.

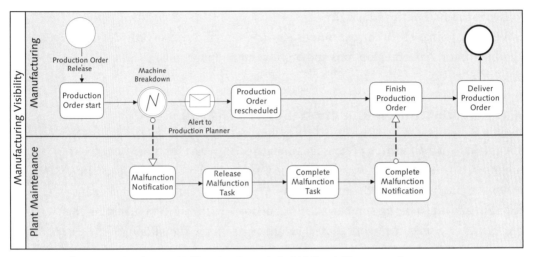

Figure 4.3   Production Malfunction Scenario in SAP Event Management

Table 4.2 captures the supply chain events for the production malfunction scenario.

Business Process Event	Type of Event	Event Status	Notification
Release manufacturing order	Expected event	Order status: released	
Start manufacturing order	Expected event	Order status: started	
Machine breakdown	Unexpected event	Order status: affected by breakdown	Production Planning and Detailed Scheduling Alert to production planner

Table 4.2   Production Malfunction Business Events

Business Process Event	Type of Event	Event Status	Notification
Reschedule manufacturing order	Expected event	Order status: rescheduled	
Malfunction in process	Expected event	Notification status: in process	
Release malfunction task	Expected event		
Complete malfunction task	Expected event	Notification status: started	
Finish manufacturing order	Expected event	Order status: finished	
Deliver manufacturing order	Expected event	Order status: delivered	

Table 4.2 Production Malfunction Business Events (Cont.)

4.3.2 Business Benefits

The business benefits to an organization implementing a production malfunction visibility process are:

▶ **Decreased cycle time**
   The ability to identify the down resource work center and switch to an alternative resource reduces the downtime.

▶ **Increased productivity and throughput**
   The integration of planning and plant maintenance streamlines the operational efficiency with stable, planned downtimes for machine maintenance.

▶ **Decreased inventory level**
   Keeping product delivery commitments reduces any cancellation of original orders from the customers.

▶ **Increased customer service reliability**
The stability of planned events ensures that the product will be manufactured and delivered on time to customers.

4.4   Order Fulfillment (SCOR - DELIVER)

The order fulfillment business process falls under SCOR-Deliver functional area supporting the order management and distribution process. Numerous sourcing points, increased customer delivery requirements, and incomplete data complicate the order delivery process in today's global supply chain. SAP Event Management visibility process offers a single comprehensive order management system and provides functionality to view, respond to, and measure your supply chain activity.

In today's business environment, a company's order management team faces many business challenges, including:

▶ **Multiple distribution channels**
Distributing products through various channels such as retailers, wholesalers, and directly to consumers poses challenges in managing product demand, customer service, and fulfillment.

▶ **Complex orders with distributed line items**
Multiple sourcing points in an order make delivering an order on time as requested challenging. Companies struggle with awareness, such as knowing when each item for that order is expected to arrive, lack of notification of any item that may not arrive with others, and then being unable to respond most effectively to maintain customer satisfaction levels.

▶ **Increased need to consolidate customer orders**
In an effort to reduce transportation costs, shippers consolidate goods while shipping goods to multiple customers. Maintaining visibility and being able to coordinate final delivery is becoming a more frequent requirement.

▶ **International logistics variability**

Huge numbers of products are built in low-cost manufacturing locations. The management of international inbound logistics is crucial in maintaining the fluidity of a company's supply chain.

4.4.1 Process Overview

Figure 4.4 shows the visibility process for covering the delivery process, from creating sales orders to outbound delivery and shipment. The process also tracks and traces goods that leave the warehouse. It can also be extended to report on proof of delivery at customer sites.

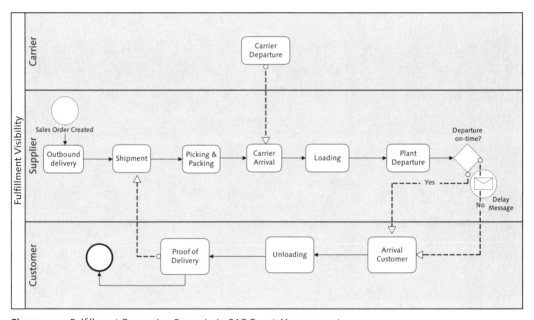

Figure 4.4 Fulfillment Processing Scenario in SAP Event Management

73

Table 4.3 captures the supply chain events for the order fulfillment scenario.

Business Process Event	Type of Event	Event Status	Notification
Picking begin	Expected event		
Picking end	Expected event		
Packing	Expected event		
Arrival carrier	Expected event		
Loading begin	Expected event		
Loading end	Expected event		
Plant departure	Expected event	Transportation status: in transit	
Arrival hub	Expected event		
Departure hub	Expected event		
Arrival customer	Expected event	Transportation status: arrived	
Unloading	Expected event		
Proof of delivery	Expected event		
delay	Unexpected event	Delivery status: delayed	Email to customer

Table 4.3 Order-to-Cash Business Events

The SAP Event Management order-to-cash solution features are:

▶ **Order lifecycle management**
Tracks the status of the order from its inception until delivery. Generates alerts to events that can cause potential delivery disruptions are generated.

▶ **Order promising**
Responds to customer requests in a timely manner with accurate delivery dates.

▸ **Global inventory visibility**

Users are alerted based on inventory positions such as low stock or excess stock.

▸ **Dynamic order sourcing**

Sources parts dynamically from the supply chain in a manner that meets customer needs while minimizing the total delivery cost.

▸ **Transportation mode selection**

Minimizes total delivery costs by making mode selection decisions based on current supply chain status to satisfy customer requests.

▸ **Performance management**

Meets necessary service levels to meet customer expectations.

4.4.2 Business Benefits

The business process benefits to an organization implementing order fulfillment are:

▸ **Improved customer service**

You can respond quickly and efficiently to any deviation in an order delivery plan and meet customer delivery dates as committed.

▸ **Improved perfect order metric**

Coordinating complex orders from the time of their capture through procurement, production, shipping, and delivery to the customer is a key metric in today's business environment. You can maintain the perfect order metric while minimizing total delivery cost.

▸ **Reduced expedited freight costs**

Unpredictable events such as increased demand can cause companies to panic and start expediting freight.

▶ **Reduced charge-backs from customers**
Supply chains today are extended, and order sourcing no longer occurs at a single point, but customer deliveries still must be on time and complete. SAP Event Management allows for synchronization of shipments from multiple origins onto a single order, creating a manageable entity that is equipped to react quickly to issues at any point, thereby maintaining or adjusting customer expectations. Having this ability lessens the number of incomplete or delayed orders, thereby reducing charge-backs from customers.

4.5 Transportation (SCOR - DELIVER)

The transportation business process falls under SCOR - Deliver functional area focusing on the transportation of goods in the supply chain network. The SAP Event Management transportation visibility process covers transportation and custom issues for inbound and outbound processes. SAP Event Management organizes information from all of the trading partners into a single comprehensive system and provides tools to view, respond to, and measure your transportation network.

Transportation planners face the following business challenges:

▶ **International logistics variability**
Huge numbers of products are built in low-cost manufacturing locations across the globe.

▶ **Increased premium freight usage**
To ensure fluidity in supply chains, companies need to ensure that products are at the right place at the right time. For numerous reasons, shipments can be delayed, forcing an organization to use expensive transportation alternatives to keep things flowing.

▸ **Capacity problems during the peak seasons**

Spikes in peak seasons add pressure on transportation resources. Increased fluctuations in end consumer demand force organizations to look for non-contracted carriers to handle increased freight volumes, which increases transportation costs.

▸ **Perfect order metric**

Extended supply chains require organizations to deal with managing a single order from multiple origins moving to a single destination. This causes the creation of multiple shipments that need to be delivered on time at the same time.

4.5.1   Process Overview

This visibility process covers transportation and customs issues for inbound and outbound processes in an international shipment scenario. Because international sea shipments play a large role, the visibility process concentrates mainly on transportation chains for the sea process and on collective shipment roads.

The visibility process encompasses two sub-processes:

▸ International road shipments

▸ International sea shipments

The visibility process combines the two business processes. Whereas the road shipment is based upon a single shipment, the sea shipment is mapped using a transportation chain that consists of a preliminary leg, a main leg, and a subsequent leg.

Figure 4.5 shows collective shipment consisting of multiple inbound or outbound deliveries that are collected from or delivered to various locations. The international sea shipment sub-process describes a transportation chain that consists of three legs: delivery (transportation) to the harbor (via road), main leg of transportation by sea, and subsequent transportation deliveries (via road) to the relevant recipients.

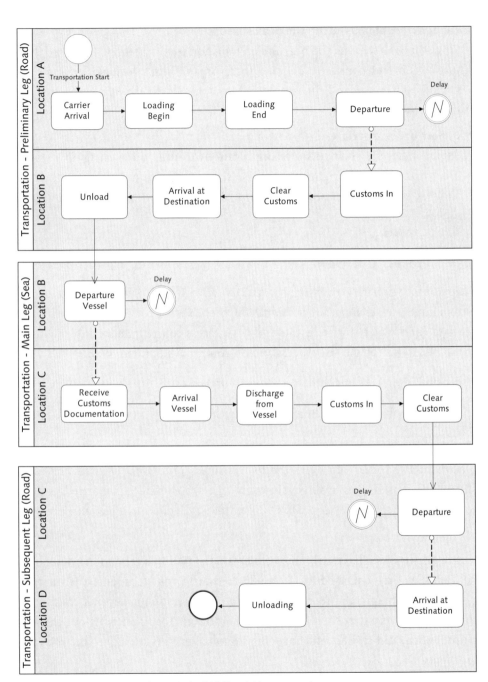

Figure 4.5 Transportation Scenario in SAP Event Management

Table 4.4 captures the supply chain events for the transportation scenario, which is divided into road shipment, sea shipment, and delivery via road shipment.

Road Shipment			
Business Process Event	**Type of Event**	**Event Status**	**Notification**
Carrier arrival	Expected event		
Loading begin	Expected event		
Loading end	Expected event	Transportation status: loaded	
Departure	Expected event	Transportation status: in transit	
Customs in	Expected event	Customs status: customs In	
Clear customs	Expected event	Customs status: customs cleared	
Arrival at destination	Expected event	Transportation status: arrived	
Unload	Expected event	Transportation status: unloaded	
Return empty container	Expected event		
Delay	Unexpected event	Delivery status: delayed	Email to customer
Sea Shipment			
Business Process Event	**Type of Event**	**Event Status**	**Notification**
Departure vessel	Expected event	Transportation status: in transit	
Receive customs documentation	Expected event		
Arrival vessel	Expected event	Transportation status: arrived	

Table 4.4 Transportation Scenario (Road and Sea Shipment) in SAP Event Management

Business Process Event	Type of Event	Event Status	Notification
Discharge from vessel	Expected event		
Customs in	Expected event	Customs status: customs in	
Clear customs	Expected event	Customs status: customs cleared	
Delay	Unexpected event	Delivery status: delayed	Email to customer
Delivery in Road Shipment			
Business Process Event	Type of Event	Event Status	Notification
Departure	Expected event	Transportation status: in transit	
Arrival at destination	Expected event	Transportation status: arrived	
Unloading	Expected event	Transportation status: unloaded	
Delay	Unexpected event	Delivery status: delayed	Email to customer

Table 4.4 Transportation Scenario (Road and Sea Shipment) in SAP Event Management (Cont.)

The SAP Event Management transportation solution features are:

▶ **Shipment visibility**
Tracks the status of the shipment across multiple transportation modes and carriers. Users are notified immediately when shipment disruptions may result in deviations from the delivery plan

▶ **Capacity management**
Alerts are generated when future or current capacity is projected to be greater than current capacity levels.

▶ **Perfect order monitoring**

Synchronizes shipments from multiple origins going to a single destination onto a single order, to ensure that the order is delivered together and completely. Notifications occur when any portion of the order isn't performing to the plan.

▶ **Transportation mode selection**

Minimizes total delivery costs by making mode selection decisions based on current supply chain status to satisfy customer requests,

▶ **Carrier score-carding**

The ability to monitor and measure the performance of carriers against the contracted service levels.

4.5.2 Business Benefits

The business benefits of implementing the transportation visibility process in an organization are:

▶ **Reduction in peak season capacity issues**

Better planning ensures that road and sea shipments are properly planned and booked in advance to allow for peak season shipments.

▶ **Lower overall transportation costs**

The use of the transportation resources allows for close monitoring of lead time and turnaround and helps ensure that transportation costs are minimized.

▶ **Reduce charge-backs from customer**

The fulfillment of customer orders as per delivery dates ensures that customer satisfaction and service levels meet standards.

▶ **Reduce expedited freight cost**

With fewer rush orders and shipments, normal shipments will match the requirement dates, thus reducing the need for expensive freights.

▶ **Improve planner productivity**

The stability of planning allows the transportation planner to manage his resources according to schedule with less operational firefighting.

4.6   Outbound and Inbound Delivery (SCOR - DELIVER)

The outbound and inbound business process falls under SCOR-Deliver functional area supporting the order fulfillment and warehouse activities. The SAP Event Management outbound and inbound visibility process aims to provide visibility across the entire delivery process, from the time an outbound delivery is created until the customer posts proof of delivery for his inbound delivery. Moreover, it does this with varying granularity. It's anticipated that the sales executive (supplier) and the customer is interested in his delivery but that the warehouse manager (supplier or customer) needs more detailed information about the status of the handling units for which he is responsible. Such a closed-loop delivery process is a collaborative process, so it's conceivable that the SAP Event Management system either resides with the supplier or — with some restrictions — in the customer's system landscape.

4.6.1   Process Overview

Outbound processing prepares the goods for shipment to their destination and consists of the following business process steps:

- ▸ Creating outbound deliveries
- ▸ Creating picking orders
- ▸ Picking activity
- ▸ Packing activity
- ▸ Staging and loading
- ▸ Goods issue posting
- ▸ Sending advance shipping notification to business partners

Inbound processing covers the resulting receipt steps:

- ▸ Creating inbound deliveries
- ▸ Unloading
- ▸ Goods receipt posting
- ▸ Sending proof of delivery to the supplier

Figure 4.6 shows the process flow between the customer and supplier, with various business activities supporting the order fulfillment.

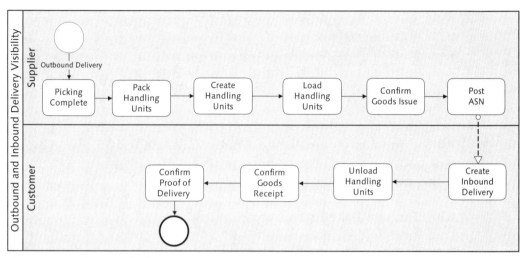

Figure 4.6 Outbound and Inbound Scenario in SAP Event Management

Table 4.5 captures the supply chain events for the outbound and inbound scenarios.

Business Process Event	Type of Event	Event Status	Notification
Picking complete	Expected event	Shipping status: picking complete	
Pack	Expected event	Handling unit outbound status: packed	
Load	Expected event	Handling unit outbound status: loaded	
Goods issue	Expected event	Handling unit outbound + inbound/shipping status: goods Issued	

Table 4.5 Outbound and Inbound Business Events

83

Business Process Event	Type of Event	Event Status	Notification
Unload	Expected event	Handling unit inbound status: unloaded	
Goods receipt	Expected event	Handling unit inbound /shipping status: goods receipt	
Proof of delivery	Expected event	Shipping status: proof of delivery	

Table 4.5 Outbound and Inbound Business Events (Cont.)

4.6.2 Business Benefits

The business benefits for a company implementing outbound and inbound visibility process are:

► **Improved customer service**
Respond quickly and efficiently to any deviation in the order delivery plan.

► **Improved perfect order metric**
Coordinating complex orders from the time of their capture through procurement, production, shipping and delivery to the customer is a key metric in today's environment. Maintain the perfect order metric while minimizing total delivery cost.

► **Stock reduction through greater transparency**
The transparency of goods movement between the supplier and customer help in keeping inventory levels low across customer locations.

► **Warehouse resources planning**
The warehouse manager can plan and optimize the usage of resources properly.

► **Increased internal and collaborative supply chain visibility**
Both internal and external business partners can track order fulfillment and trace the physical location of the goods.

4.7   RFID – Returnable Transport Item (SCOR - RETURN)

The returnable transport items business process falls under SCOR-Return functional area supporting the tracking and tracing company's assets in supply chain network. Returnable transport items (RTIs) include plastic crates, pallets and roll containers, and industry-specific special transport items (equipments) varying in size and value that are reused. These may circulate between specific locations or may be managed by a common RTI pool entity. Moreover, RTIs may move purely within the boundaries of a single physical site or between the locations of a larger individual site, or they may be exchanged or circulated between different locations across business partners or within one business entity. They may also circulate within a larger multi-company supply chain community with an RTI pool owner tracking their assets.

This visibility process aims to enable the tracking of RTI cycles in locations across business partners. With the help of SAP Event Management, customers can monitor a single RTI cycle with its respective statuses and material associations across different business partner locations.

4.7.1   Process Overview

Figure 4.7 shows the returnable transport item process that aims to provide visibility into RTI processing from the time an RTI tag is commissioned until the asset is decommissioned. The business event cycles are:

► Pack (supplier)

► Load (supplier)

► Unload (customer)

► Unpack all or specific child objects (customer)

► Load (customer)

► Unload (supplier)

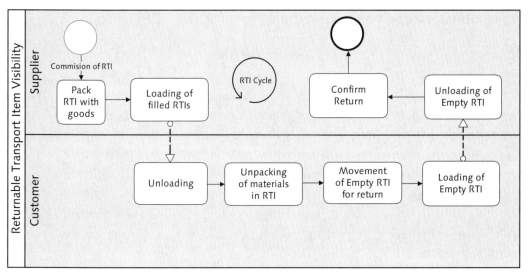

Figure 4.7 Returnable Transport Item Scenario in SAP Event Management

Table 4.6 captures the supply chain events for the returnable transport item scenario.

Business Process Event	Type of Event	Event Status	Notification
Commission of RTI	Expected event	Shipping status: new	
Load	Expected event	Shipping status: in transit	
Unload (at customer)	Expected event	Shipping status: delivered	
Confirm return	Expected event	Shipping status: return confirmed	

Table 4.6 Returnable Transport Items Business Events

4.7.2   Business Benefits

The business benefits of implementing returnable transport item visibility processes in an organization are:

▸ **Reduced shrinkage of returnable transport item stock**
The visibility and monitoring of this asset in the supply chain reduces any shrinkage of stocks.

▸ **Stock reduction through increased supply chain transparency**
The ability to track and trace the current location of equipment helps in faster turnaround and better planning.

▸ **Increased internal and collaborative supply chain visibility**
The ability to view the near real-time status of these equipments collaboratively reduces any effort on either side to create any form of reports.

▸ **Real-time awareness and increased business visibility leading to revenue increases and cost reductions**
In a collaborative environment, the ability to provide near –real-time information increases the customer service level.

4.8   Seasonal Procurement (SCOR - SOURCE)

The seasonal procurement business process falls under the SCOR-Source functional area supporting the company's sourcing strategy. The seasonal procurement visibility process within SAP Event Management covers procurement from the creation of a purchase order for seasonal items to the availability of the articles in the distribution center. The solution also offers tight integration into the procurement controlling workbench, with role-based access for the supplier as part of the retail seasonal procurement add-on.

4.8.1   Process Overview

Figure 4.8 and Table 4.7 show the supply chain events encompassed in this scenario. The seasonal articles should be planned and ordered well in advance to tap the latest order date and reduce storage costs. SAP Event Management helps with tracking and tracing of the merchandise timeline along the supply chain and delivering the merchandise items even with long lead times.

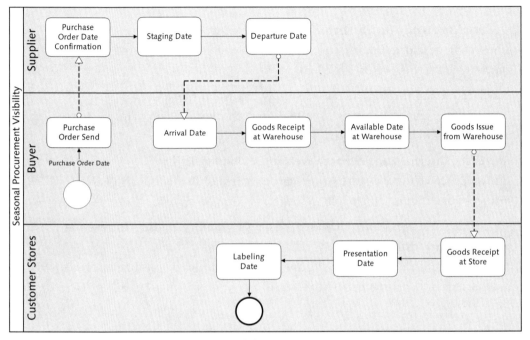

Figure 4.8 Seasonal Procurement Visibility Scenario in SAP Event Management

Business Process Event	Type of Event	Event Status	Notification
Purchase order created	Expected event	Purchase order status: - PO date OK, date early, or date late	
Acknowledgment received	Expected event	Acknowledgment status: acknowledgment on time, too early, or too late	

Table 4.7 Seasonal Procurement Business Events

Business Process Event	Type of Event	Event Status	Notification
Material staging date	Expected event	Purchase order status: material staging date OK, date too Early, or date late	
Departure date	Expected event	Transportation status: merchandise departed on time, departed too late, or departed too early	
Arrival date	Expected event	Transportation status: merchandise arrived on time, arrived too late, or arrived too early	
Rough goods receipt created in SAP ECC	Expected event	Transportation status: tough goods receipt on time, too late, or too early	
Real goods receipt posted in ECC and PO quantity is complete	Expected event	Purchase order status: - PO quantity complete and arrived on time, too early, or too late	
Real goods receipt posted in ECC and PO quantity isn't complete	Unexpected event	Purchase order status: - PO quantity not complete and arrived on time, too early, or too late	

Table 4.7 Seasonal Procurement Business Events (Cont.)

4.8.2   Business Benefits

The business benefits associated with implementing the seasonal procurement visibility process are:

▶ **Monitor processes, stock levels, and different events throughout logistics supply chain**
Monitors from the time a purchase order is placed with an external vendor until the goods arrive in the store and allows you to react promptly to any possible problems.

▶ **Smooth-running procurement processes**
Increases the efficiency and competitiveness of the company and helps in bottom lines.

▶ **Monitoring dates**
Enables the user to quickly obtain information about the current procurement situation and to react to different dates.

▶ **Integration with planning process from strategic to operational levels**
Reduces the storage costs of holding excess inventory.

4.9   Railcar Management (SCOR - DELIVER)

The railcar management business process falls under the SCOR-Deliver functional area supporting the company transportation process using railcars. SAP offers railcar management as part of their custom development offerings. With SAP Event Management, it offers tracking and on-site yard management functionality for railcars. It allows customers to view the location and status of railcars at a plant, warehouse, rail yard, or any other facility. It helps in monitoring crucial events of outbound and return trips, such as switching, loading, unloading, cleaning, weighing, inspecting, and sealing. The events can also be posted using mobile devices.

4.9.1 Process Overview

With railcar management, the client can streamline their railcar operations using railcar tracking, activity monitoring, and cost management functionality. The railcar solution features are:

▶ Railcar extension tracks in-transit railcars assigned to outbound or inbound shipments.

▶ On-site event management allows a company to track the location and status of railcars on site and monitors rail yard activity such as loading and unloading.

▶ Freight cost extension provides enhanced freight routing and billing functionality, including the ability to select the lowest-cost carrier.

▶ The distance-determination service interfaces with third-party providers of road distances to look up actual road miles for shipments.

▶ Tracking of inbound vendor-supplied raw materials to customer plants via rail.

▶ Maintain ability with integrated SAP ERP to track outbound railcars for raw materials and finished goods.

▶ Automated route determination and carrier usage tracking.

▶ Railcar inventory visibility and car tracking at plants.

▶ Ability to track railcar mileage and adjust rapidly to transportation delays.

▶ Integrated supply chain planning processing to improve operational efficiency.

Figure 4.9 shows the business process diagram for the railcar scenario.

4.9.2 Business Benefits

The following business benefits are associated with implementing railcar management visibility process:

▶ Improves responsiveness by reacting quickly to transportation delays and adjusting flexible changes in customer orders or vendor deliveries.

▶ Improves operational efficiency by monitoring and optimizing rail yard operations by reducing manual tracking procedures.

▶ Increases profitability by decreasing shipping costs and charging your customers for the actual transportation expenses incurred.

▶ Maximizes rail fleet utilization and minimizes equipment expenditures.

▶ Reduces detention times and recovers costs of detained railcars.

▶ Schedules preventive maintenance of railcars more accurately and improves customer service.

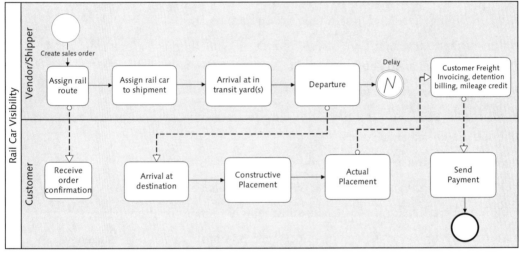

Figure 4.9 Railcar Management Scenario in SAP Event Management

4.10 Summary

This chapter highlighted all of the supply chain visibility processes that SAP delivers. Visibility processes are templates for making the SAP Event Management implementation easier for customers. SAP Event Management visibility processes come with preconfigured business content, a range of functions, and examples for customers to leverage on implementing SAP Event Management for their specific business scenarios.

To summarize the business benefits, companies that deploy supply chain event management systems can expect to achieve operational and economic benefits by delivering high customer satisfaction and reducing the internal supply chain management costs. SAP Event Management provides effective collaboration with business partners to provide visibility of their order fulfillment status. Reduction of supply chain management costs can be achieved by lower inventory levels, lower manufacturing costs, economical transportation costs, and reduced labor costs.

The next chapter looks at the technical architecture and integration aspect of SAP Event Management and the various technical deployment options currently available.

This chapter describes the architectural aspects you should take into account when setting up and integrating an SAP Event Management 5.1 system. It also describes the various SAP Event Management deployment and technical connection options.

5 Architecture in SAP Event Management 5.1

SAP Event Management offers system landscape flexibility by either being used as an add-on based in SAP ERP, as part of SAP SCM, or as an optional add-on with other SAP applications. The objective of this chapter is to give an overview of the technical landscape available for deployment.

The chapter also looks at the basic setup for setting connectivity between applications and the event management and reporting systems and offers insights into various technical connection options.

5.1 System Architecture and Integration

The SAP Event Management architecture is a standard three-tier client-server architecture and is highly scalable. A Web frontend is available as an alternative to the standard SAP GUI presentation client. The operational concepts for SAP Event Management are similar to those of SAP R/3. SAP Event Management is built on the top of the standard SAP Web Application Server (AS) in the SAP NetWeaver AS architecture. The same solution management concepts apply to SAP Event Management as SAP ECC. SAP Event Management can interface with other systems, including other SAP systems and legacy or third-party systems. It can be installed on all database and operating system platforms that support SAP Web AS 6.20.

In the case of high event volume, archiving plays an important role in ensuring optimal database performance.

Below are some key points for integrating and interfacing with SAP Event Management:

▶ SAP Event Management can run as a standalone system and can be integrated with non-SAP systems.

▶ SAP Event Management offers a generic interface to SAP NetWeaver Portal, and all of the dashboards and reports can be designed for integrated view.

▶ SAP Event Management offers Web Dynpro and a web-frontend Web Communication Layer (WCL) that allow the exchange of information with business partners both internally or externally.

▶ SAP Event Management can connect to mobile devices either via a Web frontend or via WebSAPConsole.

▶ SAP Event Management is integrated with SAP Alert Framework available with SAP Web AS with Basis 6.2 to trigger follow-up activities based on the event messages received in the SAP Event Management system.

▶ SAP Event Management can trigger SAP workflow for delivering work items to business partners.

▶ SAP Event Management can integrate with SAP Advanced Planner and Optimizer (APO) Alert Monitor for displaying alerts on event exceptions outside tolerance levels.

Figure 5.1 shows the architectural landscape for SAP Event Management. Various transactions event data are posted from SAP ECC as event messages event handlers in SAP Event Management. Each event message, whether it is a planned or unplanned event, goes through a rule set in SAP Event Management for performing follow-up activities. These activities can be either updating the event status or triggering of workflow or sending email notifications to concerned business partners. The event status is updated in near real time to the web interface to provide wider visibility to internal and external partners in the supply chain. Periodically, the event can be further extracted from SAP NetWeaver Business Warehouse for business process analysis. The report can either capture the trend in the business events or identify supply chain bottlenecks based on the reported or captured reason codes on supply chain events.

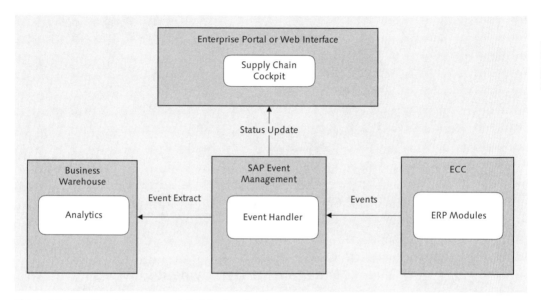

Figure 5.1 SAP Event Management Architecture Landscape

Figure 5.2 captures SAP Event Management with event handlers and Customizing. The web server contains programs in the Java environment that deal with configuration and administrative. The web server can be installed on same machine as SAP Event Management. The web server and SAP Event Management communicate using the Java Connector (JCO) program, which transfers Java to ABAP and vice versa.

Next, let's look at the SAP Event Management deployment options. SAP doesn't recommend installing all components on one host. The distribution can depend on many factors such as sizing, security, available hardware, server load balancing, and so on.

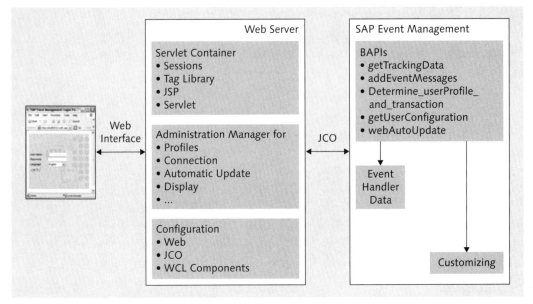

Figure 5.2 SAP Event Management and Web Server Connectivity via Java Connector (JCO)

5.2   SAP Event Management Deployment Options

SAP Event Management is available for deployment in the following system landscapes.

5.2.1   SAP Event Management as an Add-On for SAP ERP

You can deploy SAP Event Management as an add-on for visibility aligned with SAP ERP. This variant is an option for customers who want to use SAP Event Management in combination with the other application, and where no significant data volume is expected. Figure 5.3 shows SAP Event Management installed as a plug-in in the SAP ERP server and able communicate with internal application tables within SAP ECC itself. This option requires volume stress testing for any performance issues when the transactional data volume is large. The event data can be further extracted to SAP NetWeaver BW from SAP ECC for analytics purposes.

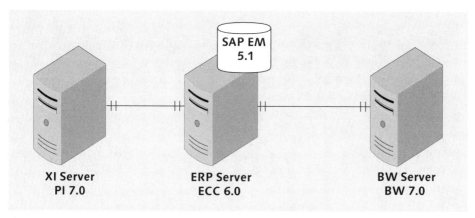

Figure 5.3 SAP Event Management as an Add-On for SAP ERP

5.2.2 SAP Event Management as Part of SAP SCM

This variant is appropriate when enhanced planning functionality from SAP Advanced Planning and Optimization (APO) or other SAP SCM capabilities (e.g., supplier network collaborations [SNCs]) are used or planned in same server. This option has to be used if an existing SAP Event Management customer is upgrading from SAP SCM 4x or SAP SCM 5.0. This variant is also recommended when you expect a high data volume and the stand-alone system is justified. With this option, SAP Event Management isn't seen in the *critical path* on business operations for any performance issues. Figure 5.4 shows the SAP Event Management connectivity options for this scenario showing connectivity with SAP ECC and SAP NetWeaver BW for application and reporting purposes. This is the preferred option for many customers.

5.2.3 SAP Event Management as an Optional Add-On

This option is similar to the SAP ERP add-on where SAP Event Management is used in combination with another application such as the SAP Auto-ID infrastructure, SAP SNC, or SAP TM and no significant data volume is expected. For SAP AII, this variant has to be used when setting up an SAP object event repository in which SAP Event Management is the core component. Figure 5.5 shows a landscape option that is similar to the SAP Event Management as an add-on to SAP ERP option explained earlier.

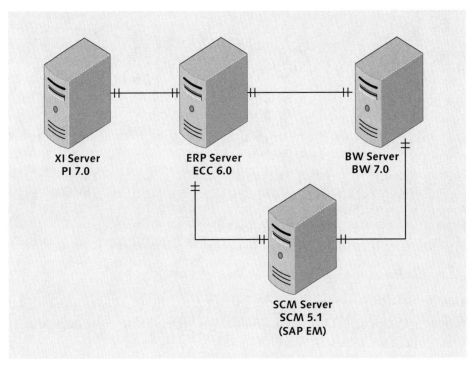

Figure 5.4 SAP Event Management as part of SAP SCM

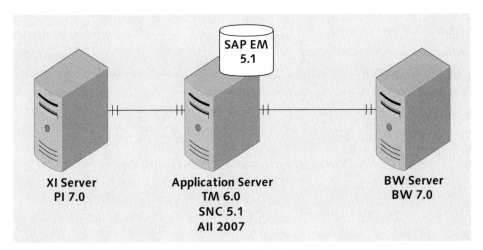

Figure 5.5 SAP Event Management as an Optional Add-On

As discussed above, SAP Event Management can be used as a complimentary application in the SAP Auto-ID infrastructure for product authentication and tracking scenarios. The key objectives of SAP Event Management in this scenario include:

- Tracking products across the supply chain in a multiple-level hierarchy (pallet, case, unique item identifier)
- Traceability of all events related to any object
- Automated authentication to prevent counterfeit
- Alert for unexpected events

Table 5.1 gives a functions overview used across three areas in the SAP Auto-ID infrastructure.

SAP Auto-ID Infrastructure	SAP Event Management	SAP Object Event Repository (OER)
▶ Connect RFID physical world with IT backend systems ▶ Relate RFID data with business processes ▶ Act as middleware between device software (device controller layer/middleware) and SAP ERP systems ▶ Maintain RFID master data (devices, locations, products)	▶ Provide traceability and control over RFID events ▶ Enable notification of events (overdue, expected and unexpected events) ▶ Provide business intelligence over the RFID events	▶ Enable sharing of RFID data across internal and external organizations ▶ Manage local RFID SAP Auto-ID infrastructure centrally ▶ Query RFID data centrally ▶ Enable other business partners to query on RFID data

Table 5.1 SAP Auto-ID Infrastructure Main Functions

5.2.4 Application Component Matrix

Based on the deployment options mentioned in the previous section, this section gives an overview of the visibility business processes and the required application components.

Table 5.2 lists the scenarios where SAP Event Management is an add-on to SAP ECC. SAP Event Management and SAP ECC are seen as mandatory because of events from SAP ECC application tables posting as event messages to SAP Event Management event handlers.

Business Process	SAP Event Management	SAP SCM	SAP ECC	SAP NetWeaver BW
Procurement processing	X		X	(X)
Fulfillment processing	X		X	(X)
Outbound/ inbound delivery	X		X	(X)
Transportation processing	X		X	(X)
Production malfunction processing	X	(X)	X	(X)

Table 5.2 SAP Event Management as an Add-On to SAP ECC. X = mandatory, (X) = optional

Table 5.3 lists the scenarios where SAP Event Management is part of SAP SCM and is connected to SAP ECC.

Business Process	SAP Event Management	SAP SCM	SAP ECC
Procurement processing	X	X	(X)
Fulfillment processing	X	X	(X)
Outbound/inbound delivery	X	X	(X)
Transportation processing	X	X	(X)
Production malfunction processing	X	X	(X)

Table 5.3 SAP Event Management as part of SAP SCM. X = mandatory, (X) = optional

5.3   Setting Up the SAP Event Management System

This section describes how to configure SAP ECC and SAP Event Management for setting up connectivity between SAP ECC, SAP Event Management, and SAP NetWeaver BW applications.

5.3.1   Setting up Communication with SAP Event Management from SAP ECC

You start the communication between the application systems from SAP ECC side:

▶ **Step 1**

Activate SAP Event Management application interface.

We need to activate the plug-in to enable SAP Event Management integration in SAP ECC. If it's not set to active, the business add–ins (BAdIs) and business transaction events (BTEs) are not called. Figure 5.6 shows the maintenance of the entry from Transaction BF11 in the SAP ECC system.

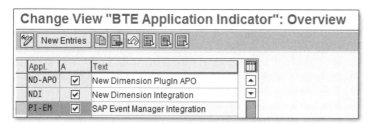

Figure 5.6   Activate SAP Event Management Application Interface

▶ **Step 2**

Define remote function call (RFC) connection to SAP Event Management.

In this step we define the RFC destination for the SAP Event Management server. Figure 5.7 shows Transaction SM59 for the maintenance.

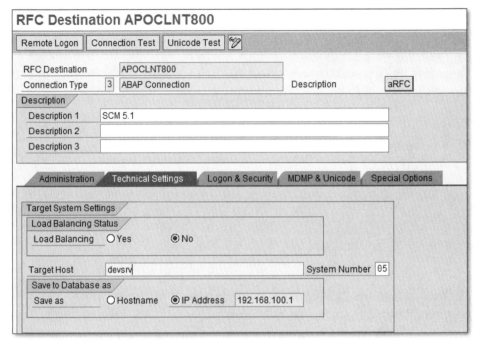

Figure 5.7 Define RFC Connection to SAP Event Management

▶ **Step 3**
Create the logical system for SAP Event Management.

In this step we define the logical system referring to the SAP Event Management system. Figure 5.8 shows Transaction SALE for maintaining the logical system for SAP Event Management.

▶ **Step 4**
Define the SAP Event Management system.

This is the final step on the SAP ECC side, where the event manager is created as a reference entry that will be used in SAP Event Management configurations. Based on this value, SAP ECC knows which logical system and RFC destination to use when communicating with SAP Event Management. Some key points to note:

▶ If you're running SAP Event Management on the same server as the application system, then you also need to reference the logical system defined in SAP Event Management.

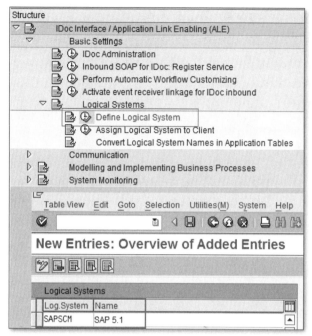

Figure 5.8 Logical System for SAP Event Management

▶ Do not set the local flag when SAP Event Management is running as a stand-alone system on another server. Set it when it's running on the same application system.

▶ RFC connection parameters for the application system and SAP Event Management need to have synchronous communication (Sync) selected in the SAP Production environment for performance reasons. It's fine to set the synchronous in development environment for debugging purposes.

The configuration is made via Transaction /SAPAPO/ASC0TS in SAP ECC (Figure 5.9).

SAP Event Manager Definitions							
Event Manager	EM Log. System	SAP EM	Lo	Dest.		Sync	Descriptn
SAPSCM	SCM	SCM4.0	☐	SCM		☑	SCM 5.1

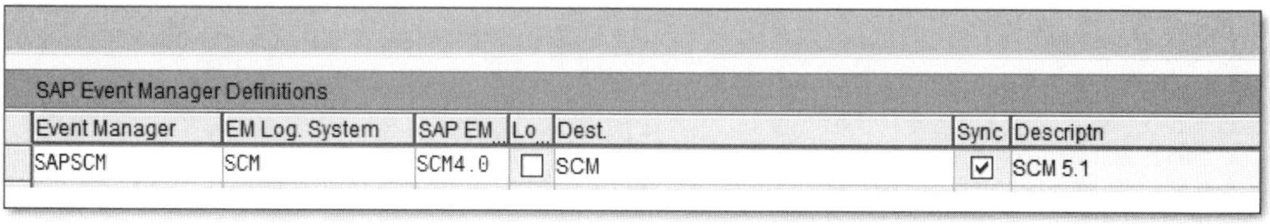

Figure 5.9 Define SAP Event Management system

5.3.2 Setting up Communication with SAP ECC from SAP Event Management

The SAP Event Management communication setup between SAP Event Management and SAP ECC takes three steps:

▶ **Step 1**
Define the RFC connection to SAP ECC.

Define the remote system details of SAP ECC to communicate between the two systems. Figure 5.10 shows the entries made from Transaction SM59 in the SAP SCM environment.

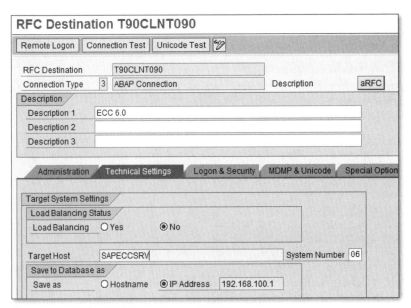

Figure 5.10 Define RFC Connection to SAP ECC

▶ **Step 2**
Create the logical system for SAP ECC.

In this step we define the logical system referring to the application system (SAP ECC). Assign the logical system to the client if the application server is on the same server as SAP Event Management system. Figure 5.11 shows Transaction SALE for maintaining the logical system to SAP ECC shown earlier.

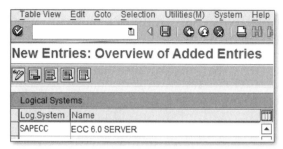

Figure 5.11 Create the Logical System for SAP ECC

▶ **Step 3**

Define the SAP application system.

In this step create the link between the logical name of the application system and its physical destination. In the development environment, we can select SyncCo to enable synchronous communication, but it needs to be unselected when in a quality or production environment for performance reasons. Access Transaction /SAPTRX/TSC0AS to maintain the SAP application system in the SAP SCM environment (Figure 5.12).

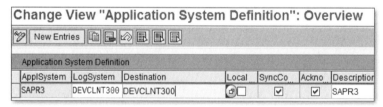

Figure 5.12 Define SAP Application System

5.3.3 Setting up Communication Between SAP Event Management and SAP NetWeaver BW

The communication between SAP Event Management and SAP NetWeaver BW is set up to transfer supply chain event information for analytics and reporting. The communication setup is done in both systems in four steps:

▶ **Step 1**

SAP SCM: Define RFC destination for SAP NetWeaver BW (Figure 5.13).

SAP delivers SAP NetWeaver BW contents for visibility processes. You can easily use this content by copying to active version and activating the objects. Set up the physical connection between SAP Event Management and SAP NetWeaver BW by first defining the RFC connection to SAP NetWeaver BW.

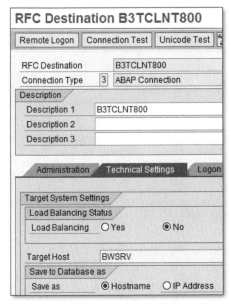

Figure 5.13 RFC Connection to SAP NetWeaver BW from SAP Event Management

► **Step 2**

SAP SCM: Create logical system for SAP NetWeaver BW (Figure 5.14).

Use Transaction SM59 to update the entries for SAP NetWeaver BW.

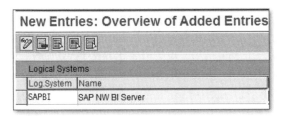

Figure 5.14 Create Logical System for SAP NetWeaver BW

▶ **Step 3**

SAP NetWeaver BW: Define RFC destination for SAP Event Management.

In this step we create a RFC connection to SAP Event Management using Transaction SM59. These are similar steps performed except this is maintained in SAP NetWeaver BW.

▶ **Step 4**

SAP NetWeaver BW: Create logical system for SAP Event Management.

In this final step we define the logical system of SAP Event Management in the SAP NetWeaver BW environment using Transaction SALE. This is similar to the steps performed in SAP SCM and SAP ECC earlier.

5.4   SAP Event Management Technical

SAP Event Management is based on the standardized SAP Business Suite client server architecture. You can opt to install the SAP Event Management application belonging to the SAP SCM solution or an optional add-on to SAP applications, as explained in Section 5.3

5.4.1   Connection of SAP Systems

You can connect SAP Event Management to other SAP systems in two ways:

▶ **Using SAP Basis Plug-In (PI)**

SAP Basis PI is a standardized connection between SAP systems that enables seamless exchange of data between systems. If you've installed SAP R/3 with release 4.0B or higher, the SAP Event Management application interface is automatically available. The SAP Event Management application interface consists of customizing transactions (business process types) for the application and tables in the application systems relevant to SAP Event Management. Figure 5.15 shows the integration of SAP Event Management with R/3 applications and Web Application server.

▶ **Using SAP Exchange Infrastructure (XI)**

See Section 5.4.2 for details.

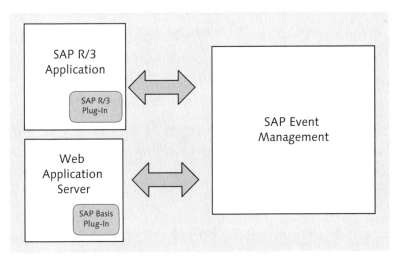

Figure 5.15 SAP Event Management Integration with Basis Plug-In

To process business transaction data from other SAP application systems into SAP Event Management, you should have defined and implemented an interface between the SAP application systems and the SAP Event Management interface. You can use various options to connect business transaction data from other SAP application systems. In all of the options listed below, the information is passed as data containers.

▶ Business adds-ins (BAdIs)

▶ Business transaction events (BTEs)

▶ User exits

▶ Direct calls in the SAP application system

BAdIs are one of the common implementation means for integrating SAP ECC with SAP Event Management. Upon implementation of a standard BAdI, the interface with SAP Event Management via a standard defined application interface and business application programming interface (BAPI) is defined on the SAP Event Management side (Figure 5.16). The application tables to be transferred to SAP Event

Management are entered in function module /SAPAPO/EVENT_MGR_FILL_TABCONT. The application interface out of SAP ECC calls the function module /SAPTRX/EVENT_ MGR_COMMUNICATE for creating either event handler or posting events (expected and unexpected) or event messages on the SAP Event Management side.

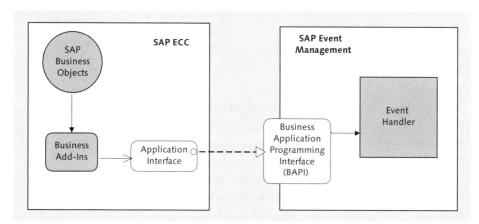

Figure 5.16 SAP Event Management BAdI Implementation

Table 5.4 and Table 5.5 list the SAP pre-delivered R/3 and SAP APO application objects and the corresponding methods to connect to SAP Event Management.

SAP R/3 Business Objects	SAP Event Management Connection Methods
Sales order	Business process type: ESC_SORDER BADI definition: BADI_SD_SALES BADI implementation: /SAPTRX/S_SALESORD Method: SAVE_DOCUMENT
Purchase requisitions	Business process type: ESC_PURREQ BADI definition: ME_REQ_POSTED BADI implementation: /SAPTRX/MM_POREQ Method: POSTED
Purchase orders	Business process type: ESC_PURORD BADI definition: ME_PURCHDOC_POSTED BADI implementation: /SAPTRX/MM_PURCHORD Method: POSTED

Table 5.4 SAP Event Management Connection Methods with SAP R/3

SAP R/3 Business Objects	SAP Event Management Connection Methods
Invoice (sales and distribution)	Business process type: `ESC_SC_INVOICE` BADI definition: `BADI_SD_BILLING` BADI implementation: `/SAPTRX/SD_INVOICE` Method: `INVOICE_DOCUMENT_ADD`
Invoice (material management)	Business process type: `ESC_MM_INVOICE` BADI definition: `INVOICE_UPDATE` BADI implementation: `/SAPTRX/MM_INVOICE` Method: `CHANGE_BEFORE_UPDATE`
Finance clearing document	Business process type: `ESC_FI_CLEARING` BTE 1: `/SAPTRX/PAYMENT_SAVE_BTE_1030` BTE 2: `/SAPTRX/PAYMENT_SAVE_BTE_1040`
Delivery	Business process type: `ESC_DELIV` BADI definition: `LE_SHP_DELIVERY_PROC` BADI implementation: `/SAPTRX/LE_SHIPPING` Method: `SAVE_AND_PUBLISH_DOCUMENT`
Shipment (including handling units)	Business process type: `ESC_SHIPMT` BADI definition: `BADI_LE_SHIPMENT` BADI implementation:`/SAPTRX/LE_SHIPMENT` Method: `BEFORE_UPDATE`
Work orders (for production, process, service, maintenance)	Business process type: `ESC_WRKORC`, `ESC_WRKORD`, `ESC_WOGMVT` BADI definition: `WORKORDER_UPDATE` BADI implementation: `/SAPTRX/PP_WOUPDATE` Method: `BEFORE UPDATE`
Notifications	Business process type: `EPL_NOTIF` Function module coding: `IQSI_POST_NOTIFICATION->` `NFEM_SCEM_INTERFACE_NOTIF`
Inspection lot	Business process type: `EPL_INSPLOT` BADI definition: `INSPECTIONLOT_UPDATE` BADI implementation: `QMEM_SCEM_INTERFACE`

Table 5.4 SAP Event Management Connection Methods with SAP R/3 (Cont.)

SAP R/3 Business Objects	SAP Event Management Connection Methods
Material document	Business process type: ESC_MATDOC BADI definition: MB_DOCUMENT_BADI BADI implementation: /SAPTRX/MM_MATDOC Method: MB_DOCUMENT_BEFORE_UPDATE
Equipment	Business process type: EPL_EQUIPMT BADI definition: EQUI_UPDATE BADI implementation:/SAPTRX/PM_EUIPMT
Handling unit	Business process type: ESC_HAND_UNIT BADI definition: LE_SHIPPING BADI implementation:/SAPTRX/HAND_UNIT

Table 5.4 SAP Event Management Connection Methods with SAP R/3 (Cont.)

SAP APO Business Objects	SAP Event Management Connection Methods
Planned shipment (used for trigger in creating event handler for tendering process when shipments is released from planning)	Business process type: ASC_PLSHIP BADI definition: /SAPPO/VS_CLP1 BADI implementation: /SAPAPO/VS_CLP1 Method: COLLABORATE (called in function module /SAPAPO/VS_X_CLP1)
Planned shipment used for sending events (Web/EDI) when publishing to carrier starts in tendering process	Business Process Type: ASC_PLSHIP BADI Definition: /SAPAPO/VS_CLP2 BADI Implementation: /SAPAPO/VS_CLP2 Method: COLLABORATE (called in function module /SAPAPO/VS_X_CLP2)
Planned shipment (used for sending events (Web/EDI) for carrier response in tendering process	Business process type: ASC_PLSHIP1 BADI definition: /SAPAPO/VS_CLP3 BADI implementation: /SAPAPO/VS_CLP3 Method: COLLABORATE (called in function module /SAPAPO/VS_X_CLP3)

Table 5.5 SAP Event Management Connection Methods with SAP APO

A business application programming interface (BAPI) is a standardized programming interface that provides external access to the SAP systems and data. The following BAPIs are available in SAP Event Management for supporting the various business processes:

▶ `BAPI_EH_POST` for creating event handlers in SAP Event Management

▶ `BAPI_ADDEVENTMSG_02` for sending event messages to SAP Event Management

▶ `BAPI_EH_GET_DATE` for querying information from SAP Event Management

5.4.2 SAP Exchange Infrastructure Integration

Several interfaces are available for connecting SAP Event Management to SAP Exchange Infrastructure (XI). These SAP XI-enabled interfaces allow customers to execute SAP Event Management business processes (including in XML format).

▶ Send event messages to SAP Event Management.

▶ Query SAP Event Management about event handler data.

▶ Create event handlers.

▶ Request tracking service provider profiles (TSP profile request).

▶ Confirm TSP profile requests.

External business partners send the event message in XML format. The SAP XI integration engine receives the event message, processes it, and sends it to SAP Event Management using the RFC (Figure 5.17). We can use interfaces to perform the SAP Event Management activities listed below:

▶ Send event messages.

▶ Get event handler data.

▶ Create or update event handlers.

We can use the available BAPIs of the event handler business object (type /SAPTRX/ EH), or we can use the function modules directly via RFC. We can also send event messages and create or update event handlers using IDocs. However, we can't read event handler data using IDocs.

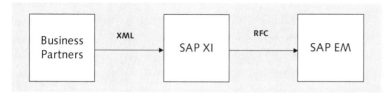

Figure 5.17 SAP XI Integration with SAP Event Management

Table 5.6 describes the various options that we have to send data to and from SAP Event Management.

Description	IDoc Type	RFC	BAPI
Sending event messages	EVMSTA02	/SAPTRX/BAPI_ EHADDEVENTMSG_02	EventHandler. AddEventMessages02
Fetching event handler data	No IDoc available	/SAPTRX/BAPI_EH_GET_ DATA	EventHandler. GetData
Creating or updating event handlers	EHPOST01	/SAPTRX/BAPI_EH_ POST	EventHandler

Table 5.6 BAPI Interfaces with SAP Event Management

5.5   Summary

This chapter touched on the technical aspects related to SAP Event Management. The chapter looked at the technical architecture and integration landscape for SAP Event Management. It discussed the three deployment options and recommendations. You need to consider many factors (e.g., business-critical path, sizing, security, available hardware, server load balancing, etc.) before finalizing the landscape. The chapter also looked briefly at the configuration steps required for setting up the SAP Event Management communication link with SAP ECC and SAP NetWeaver BW. Finally, the chapter looked at the communication methods with various technical options of SAP Basis Plug-In and SAP XI landscapes.

The next chapter describes the detailed customization steps required for setting up the procurement visibility scenario in SAP Event Management.

In today's demand-driven supply network, companies face challenges around market volatility, long lead time, and forecasting error. SAP Event Management respects lean procurement concepts by providing better visibility of inventory management decisions and vendor collaboration.

6 Setting Up a Procure-to-Pay Scenario

As companies improve their sales and operations planning processes, supply chain event management is fast becoming a means of implementing and monitoring those plans. The goal of SAP Event Management is to introduce a proactive control mechanism for managing business events — exceptions in particular — and responding to them dynamically. SAP Event Management allows business rules to be defined in a company's purchasing business process to allow exceptions to be detected and alerts to be routed to the appropriate individual or groups for remediation and resolution.

The chapter starts by introducing the purchasing business scenario and then explains, in detail, the SAP customizations steps required in SAP ECC and SAP SCM environments for setting up the event management purchasing scenario. The chapter ends by highlighting the SAP Event Management capabilities by which the purchasing scenario can be monitored in a business operation environment.

6.1 Business Scenario

The primary objective for a company implementing a purchasing scenario in SAP Event Management is to improve operational efficiency by measuring supplier delivery performance and increase customer satisfaction with stock availability. SAP Event Management offers the opportunity for companies with increased numbers of suppliers and trading partners to view, respond to, and measure the sourcing side of the supply chain.

Below are some of the company's key business drivers for implementing SAP Event Management in a purchasing scenario:

- Visibility of any electronic communications (for example, electronic data exchanges failures)
- Visibility of any potential delays to purchase order delivery dates
- Management by exceptions in a high-transaction-volume environment
- Measurement of supplier delivery performance and supply chain flexibility
- Process efficiency improvement by reduction of transactional data errors
- Automated monitoring of purchase orders for delivery date, quantity, and pricing compliance within tolerance levels
- Alert escalation in terms of purchase order percentage deviation from the delivery date, order quantity, and pricing plan
- Supply chain collaboration and visibility

The SAP Event Management design encompasses the definition of expected events (planned) and unexpected events (exceptions). Expected events are business activities performed as per the transaction lifecycle. Unexpected events are business exceptions that deviate from the expected events of the original plan.

Figure 6.1 shows the various expected and unexpected events identified within the standard purchasing business process. Whereas the expected events are geared toward compliance with purchase order lifecycle milestones, the unexpected events concern management of exceptions deviation outside tolerance levels for delivery date, original quantity request, and order amount.

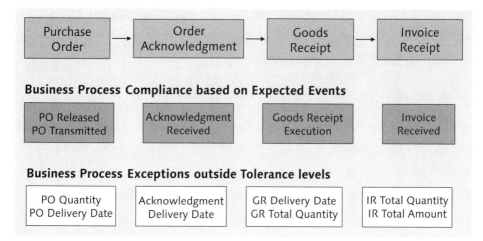

Figure 6.1 Purchasing Business Process

The scenario we're going to model in this chapter is the purchasing workflow between the buyer and supplier as shown in Figure 6.2.

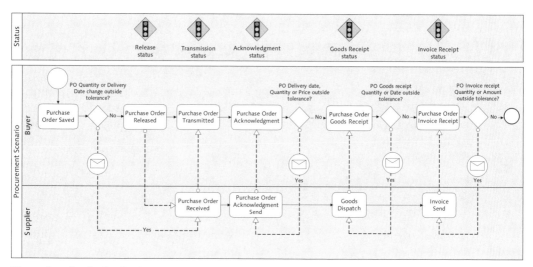

Figure 6.2 Purchasing Business Activities

Table 6.1 lists the event management business activities from the buyer side. Besides monitoring the milestones of the purchase orders, SAP Event Management provides a workflow platform on informing suppliers of the delivery date, quantity, price, or amount differences. Alert notification can also be send to other functional areas based on business priority and issue escalation path.

▶ Informing the order management team of any changes in delivery date and quantities that may affect the stock available to promise (ATP) during the order fulfillment process

▶ Informing supply chain planning of rerunning material requirement planning (MRP) on any changes to goods receipt delivery date and quantities differences

▶ Informing the finance accounts payable team of any invoice quantities and amount differences

Business Process Event	Type of Event	Event Status	Notification
Purchase order (PO) created	Expected	PO created	
Purchase order released	Expected	PO released	
Purchase order quantity or delivery date changed outside the tolerance	Unexpected	PO qty or date difference	Email or report to supplier and order management team
Purchase order transmitted	Expected	PO received	
Order acknowledgment received	Expected	Order acknowledgment received	

Table 6.1 Expected and Unexpected Events

Business Process Event	Type of Event	Event Status	Notification
Order acknowledgment – delivery date, quantity (Qty) or price outside the tolerance	Unexpected	Order acknowledgment – qty or date or price difference	Email or report to Supplier
Purchase order goods receipt (GR)	Expected	GR receipt	
Purchase order goods receipt – total quantity or delivery date outside tolerance	Unexpected	GR with qty or date difference	Email or report to supplier and supply chain planning
Purchase order invoice receipt (IR)	Expected	IR receipt	
Purchase order invoice receipt – total quantity or amount (Amt) outside tolerance	Unexpected	IR with qty or amt difference	Email or report to supplier and accounts payable team

Table 6.1 Expected and Unexpected Events (Cont.)

6.2   SAP ECC Configuration

The SAP ECC configuration involves customization of three objects: business process type, application object type, and event types.

6.2.1   Business Process Type

The purchasing business process type (BPT) involves classification of purchasing business objects or business processes in the application system (SAP ECC) for which we want to manage supply chain events in SAP Event Management. We'll use three SAP-delivered business objects in the purchasing scenario. These are:

▶ ESC_PURORD: purchase orders

▶ ESC_MATDOC: material document

▶ ESC_MM_INVOICE: material management invoice

Start by configuring BPTs as shown in Figure 6.3. In SAP ECC execute Transaction SPRO and follow the menu path INTEGRATION WITH OTHER MYSAP.COM COMPONENTS • EVENT MANAGEMENT INTERFACE • DEFINE APPLICATION INTERFACES • DEFINE BUSINESS PROCESS TYPES.

Dialog Structure	Define Business Process Types			
▽ ◻ Define Business Process Types	BPT	EH Create	EMsg Send	Descriptn
◻ Define Available Application Tables	AII_OBJECT	◻	◻	SAP All Object
	EPL_EQUIPMT	◻	◻	Equipment in SAP R/3 Enterprise
	EPL_INSPLOT	◻	◻	Inspection Lot in SAP R/3 Enterprise
	EPL_NOTIF	◻	◻	Notification in SAP R/3 Enterprise
	ESC_DELIV	◻	◻	Delivery in SAP R/3 Enterprise
	ESC_FI_CLEARING	◻	◻	FI Clearing in SAP R/3 Enterprise
	ESC_MATDOC	◻	☑	Material Document in SAP R/3 Enterprise
	ESC_MM_INVOICE	◻	☑	MM Invoice in SAP R/3 Enterprise
	ESC_PROCPO	◻	◻	Process order (mySAP R/3 Enterprise)
	ESC_PRODOR	◻	◻	Production Order in SAP R/3 Enterprise
	ESC_PURORD	☑	☑	Purchase Order in SAP R/3 Enterprise
	ESC_PURORD_FASHION	◻	◻	Purchase Order (Seasonal Procurement) in SAP R/3 Enterprise 2.0
	ESC_PURREQ	◻	◻	Purchase Requisition in SAP R/3 Enterprise
	ESC_SD_INVOICE	◻	◻	SD Invoice in SAP R/3 Enterprise
	ESC_SHIPMT	◻	◻	Shipment (SAP R/3 Enterprise)
	ESC_SORDER	◻	◻	Sales Order in SAP R/3 Enterprise
	ESC_WOGMVT	◻	◻	Workorder Goods Movements (Production,Service,Maintenance) in SAP R/3 Enterprise
	ESC_WRKORC	◻	◻	Workorder Confirmation (Production, Service, Maintenance) in SAP R/3 Enterprise
	ESC_WRKORD	◻	◻	Workorder (Production, Service, Maintenance) in SAP R/3 Enterprise

Figure 6.3 Business Process Type Tables

In the configuration, EH Create means event handler creation when the business object passes the SAP Event Management relevancy check. EMsg Send means posting of different events for the business process. Note that only one business process type is required to trigger an event handler (EH Create) in SAP Event Management, and only one checkmark is required for the business process types. Because all of the other business process types can post event messages, the checkbox in the EMsg Send column is selected for all of them.

Within the business process types, various standard application tables are embedded (example of purchase order BPT shown in Figure 6.4). The primary tables for purchasing business process types are:

▸ ESC_PURORD: EKKO, EKPO, EKET, EKBES

▸ ESC_MATDOC: MKPF, MSEG

▸ ESC_MM_INVOICE: RBKP, RSEG, RBCO, RBMA

Structure Name	DB Struc. Name	Bus.	Updte Fld Name	No Chg Val	Insert	Updat.	Delete	Key Start	Key Length
CONDITIONS_NEW	KOMV	☐	UPDKZ		I	U	D		
CONDITIONS_OLD	KOMV	☐	UPDKZ		I	U	D		
GEN_INFO_RECORD_NEW	EINA	☐	KZ		I	U	D		
GEN_INFO_RECORD_OLD	EINA	☐							
ORG_INFO_RECORD_NEW	EINE	☐	KZ		I	U	D		
ORG_INFO_RECORD_OLD	EINE	☐							
PARTNER_NEW	EKPA	☐	KZ		I	U	D		
PARTNER_OLD	EKPA	☐	KZ		I	U	D		
PO_ACCOUNT_ASSIGNMENT_NEW	EKKN	☐	KZ		I	U	D		
PO_ACCOUNT_ASSIGNMENT_OLD	EKKN	☐	KZ		I	U	D		
PO_ITEM_NUMBER	EKBES	☐							
PO_SCHED_LINE_ITEM_NEW	EKET	☐	KZ		I	U	D		
PO_SCHED_LINE_ITEM_OLD	EKET	☐	KZ		I	U	D		
PURCHASE_ITEM_NEW	EKPO	☐	KZ		I	U	D		
PURCHASE_ITEM_OLD	EKPO	☐	KZ		I	U	D		
PURCHASE_ORDER_HEADER_NEW	EKKO	☑	KZ		I	U			
PURCHASE_ORDER_HEADER_OLD	EKKO	☐	KZ		I	U			
PURCHASE_REQUISITION	EBAN	☐							
SCHED_AGREEMENT_HEADER_NEW	EKEK	☐	KZ		I	U	D		
SCHED_AGREEMENT_HEADER_OLD	EKEK	☐	KZ		I	U	D		
SCHED_AGREEMENT_RELEASE_NEW	EKEH	☐	UPDKZ		I	U	D		
SCHED_AGREEMENT_RELEASE_OLD	EKEH	☐	UPDKZ		I	U	D		
SHIPPING_DATA	EKPV	☐							
VENDOR_CONFIRMATION_NEW	EKES	☐	KZ		I	U	D		
VENDOR_CONFIRMATION_OLD	EKES	☐	KZ		I	U	D		

Figure 6.4 Application Table for Purchase Order Business Process Types

When a purchase order is saved in the application system, a BAdI identifies the business process type, which is passed to SAP Event Management. It has to match the business process type. The table structures for passing to SAP Event Management are filled in by BAdI. The list of BAdIs supported by SAP Event Management for the purchasing scenario are listed in Chapter 5, Section 5.4.1.

6.2.2 Application Object Type

The application object type determines whether an SAP business object is relevant for SAP Event Management. If the business object is relevant, it determines which data (expected events, attributes, tracking ID) is to be sent to the event handler. It also determines the SAP Event Management system where the purchasing event handler needs to be created.

For the procurement visibility, an application object type is defined for purchase order business process types. When the purchase order is saved, the application object type is the basis with which to extract the data from application system for creating the event handler.

During the purchase order (business object) processing in the application system, the SAP Event Management relevancy is checked, which subsequently triggers the event handler creation in SAP Event Management. Figure 6.5 shows the triggering of the event handler from the application object type via business process type.

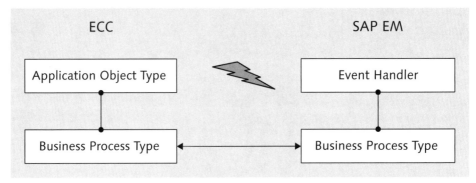

Figure 6.5 Application Object Type Triggers Event Handler Creation in SAP Event Management

Application object type customization involves the definition of control tables, object identification, event management relevancy and parameter setup.

In the General Data tab (shown in Figure 6.6) define the following fields:

▶ **Business Object Extractor**
Used to find the appropriate event handlers for a purchase order (business object) to display the data in the application system. The business object key extractor is defined in transaction /SAPTRX/ASC0TF, where you can use the SAP-delivered function module /SAPTRX/XBO_MM_ITEM_PCM10. Next, assign the function to the application object type in transaction /SAPTRX/ASC0AO.

▶ **Special Fields of an Application Object Type**
You can maintain additional fields for the application object type.

▸ **EM Relevance of Application Object**
Indicates that an application object is relevant for SAP Event Management.

▸ **Application Object Relevant for Queries**
Indicates that the application object is used to retrieve status information from an event handler.

▸ **Stop AO Determination**
Indicates that application object determination does not continue for an application object if one application object type was determined as event management relevant. All other application object types for this application object aren't determined.

▸ **EH Deactivation Ind.**
Indicates that an event handler for an application object is deleted if the application object is no longer relevant.

▸ **Alt. BusProc Type**
Describes the type of business process or object to which an event handler is referenced.

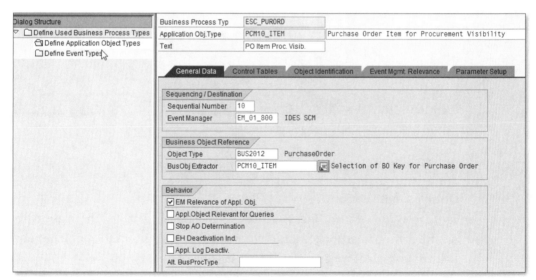

Figure 6.6 Application Object Type – General Tab Definition

In the Control Tables tab (shown in Figure 6.7) define the following fields:

▸ **Main Object and Master Tables**
Two tables are defined: the main table and the master table. The two tables are used to build IDs and parameter data. For the purchasing scenario, the main table represents the application object, which is the purchase order for our scenario. The main table has the data required for creating the purchase order.

▸ The master data contains additional information. The purchasing main object table is Purchase_Item_New, and master table is Purchase_Order_Header_New.

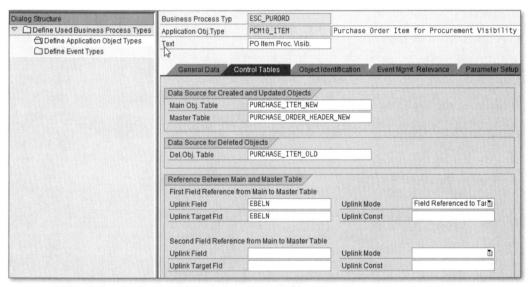

Figure 6.7 Application Object Type – Control Tables

In the Object Identification tab define the following fields:

▸ **Objects Identification**
Two tables are defined: the main table and the master table. The main table describes the actual application object, whereas the master table provides further contextual information for the application object.

In the Event Management Relevance tab define the relevance condition:

▸ **Relevance Condition**

Checks whether a business object is relevant for event handler creation. An event handler will be created of the data defined in the condition for the application object type matches the data in the application object. You can define the relevance condition using either the condition editor or a function. You can access the condition editor (shown in Figure 6.8) via Transaction /SAPTRX/ ASC0TC.

▸ If the relevancy for event handler cannot be determined by a condition statement, then the function can be defined. The function can be written to read SAP Event Management relevance table B025, where condition table data resides.

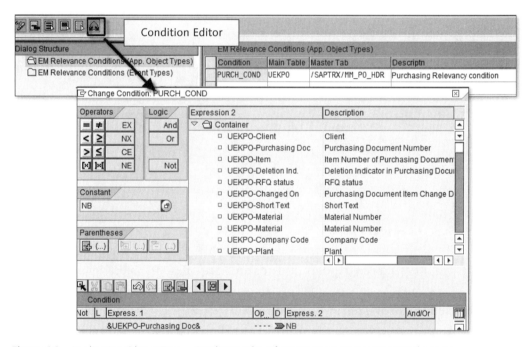

Figure 6.8 Application Object Type – Condition Editor for SAP Event Management Relevancy

▸ Configure the condition table. In SAP ECC execute Transaction SPRO and follow the menu path MATERIAL MANAGEMENT • PURCHASING • MESSAGES • OUTPUT

CONTROL • MESSAGE TYPE • DEFINE MESSAGE TYPE FOR PURCHASE ORDER. In the message type, you can configure different purchasing field combinations. An example of a purchasing scenario is a purchasing organization, plant, and vendor combinations.

In the Parameter Setup tab (shown in Figure 6.9) define the following fields. Set up the extractors in the function using Transaction /SAPTRX/ASC0TF.

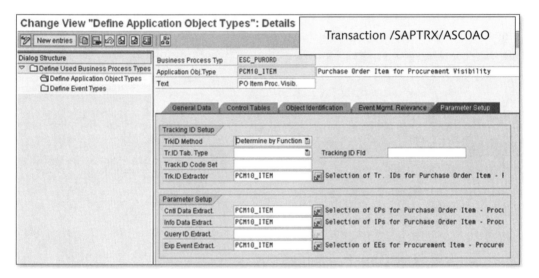

Figure 6.9 Application Object Type – Parameter Setup

▶ **Expected event Extractor**
Used to set up the milestones of the expected events for an application object. The list of expected events depends on the application object type. This allows the user to flexibly create expected events. The expected event list is coded in the function module, which is then attached to the application object type. Figure 6.10 shows the standard SAP expected event extractor and a snapshot of the function module that is embedded in the extractor. In the function module, various purchasing tables are read for identifying the fields to define the purchasing event milestones.

▶ **Control and Info Parameters Extractor**

The parameters are the attributes that are extracted from the business object and published in the event handler. In the application system, two types of parameters are extracted: control and info.

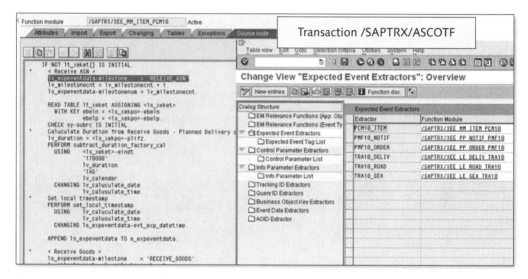

Figure 6.10 Application Object Type – Expected Event Extractor

▶ Control parameters are used to define a condition or control processes in SAP Event Management, for example, an email address send to the alert framework.

▶ Info parameters provide additional information and are displayed and/or used as information for alerts and notification. The data can also be used for query purposes or organization data for transferring to the data warehouse.

▶ Figure 6.11 shows an example of a standard SAP info parameter extractor and function module. As shown, the function module reads the field value from the purchasing tables.

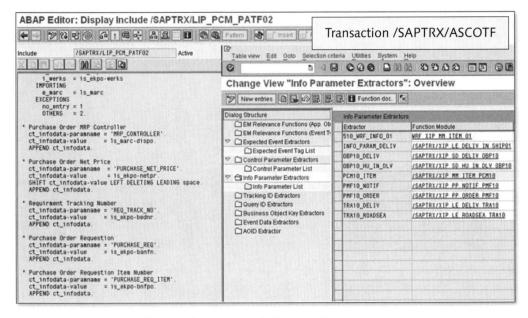

Figure 6.11 Application Object Type – Info Parameter Extractor

▶ **Tracking ID Extractor**

An identification to address an event handler so that an internal or external message can be sent. The tracking ID can be determined from a field or function. If only one tracking ID is necessary, setup of the customizing is sufficient. A function is used if more than one tracking ID is posted to the event handler.

6.2.3 Event Types

The primary function of the event type is posting event messages into an event handler, as identified by a tracking ID. The event type goes through the relevancy check and posts the event message for the particular business transaction. Event types can also be used in determining the information that the application system gives to the event handler in SAP Event Management with the message.

You can use the event type to determine the information that the application system gives to the event handler in SAP Event Management with the message. For the purchasing scenario, you can configure the following event types:

▸ **PO_CHANGE**

Posting of event messages for purchase order delivery date or quantity changes outside defined tolerance levels

▸ **PO_ACKNOWL**

Posting of event messages for order acknowledgment and vendor-confirmed delivery date variance outside defined tolerance levels

▸ **PO_GR**

Posting of event messages for goods receipt and goods receipt delivery date and/or quantity variance outside tolerance levels

▸ **PO_IR**

Posting of event messages for invoice receipt and invoice receipt delivered quantity and/or amount variance outside tolerance levels

Table 6.2 lists the business process types and the corresponding event types and the purpose of each event type. Each event type needs to be defined as per event posting requirements to the corresponding business objects. Whereas the table lists the standard event types that come preconfigured, SAP Event Management offers flexibility in configuring additional event types for posting any additional event messages to SAP Event Management according to your business requirements.

Business Process Type	Event Type	Event Message Reported
ESC_PURORD (purchase order)	PO_CHANGE	Purchase order created Purchase order quantity change Purchase order delivery data change Order acknowledgment received
ESC_PURORD (purchase order)	PO_ACKNOWL	Order acknowledgment received Order acknowledgment delivery date difference Order acknowledgment quantity difference
ESC_MATDOC (material document)	PO_GR	Goods receipt posted Goods receipt quantity difference Goods receipt delivery date difference

Table 6.2 Purchasing Event Types

Business Process Type	Event Type	Event Message Reported
ESC_MM_INVOICE (invoice)	PO_IR	Invoice receipt posted
		Invoice receipt quantity difference
		Invoice receipt amount difference

Table 6.2 Purchasing Event Types (Cont.)

Event type customization involves defining three objects: event management relevancy, control tables, and event data extractor.

▶ **Event management relevancy**

Similar to the application object type, the event type relevancy is the first technical check before the event message code is read. The relevancy can be defined either by the function or by the condition editor. Figure 6.12 shows the two options, with the function being recommended because of performance reasons.

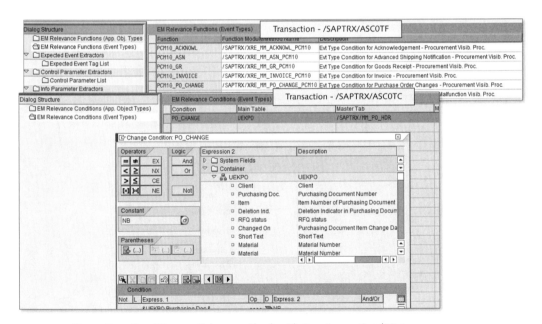

Figure 6.12 Event Types – Relevancy Check with Function or Condition

▶ **Control tables**

The control tables are defined similarly to application object type, as shown in Figure 6.13. The main table has the data required for creating the purchase order, whereas the master data contains additional information.

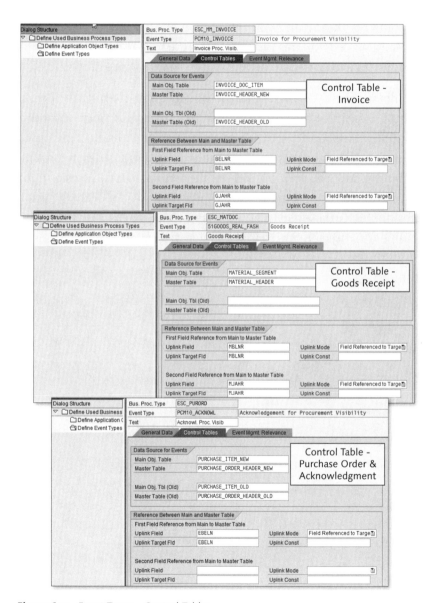

Figure 6.13 Event Types – Control Tables

▶ **Event data extractor**

Extractors of the programming logic are written for event message posting to SAP Event Management. Upon the event type relevancy check, the control tables are read, and then the extractor function logic runs. Figure 6.14 shows an example of the logic written to post purchase order quantity changes outside the tolerance table. During the BAPI call posting of the purchase order event message, the event code (in this case PO_CHANGED_QTY) is carried from the application system and posted in the SAP Event Management event handler.

The key to defining the SAP Event Management events is to establish the proper level of granularity such that the SAP Event Management output yields actionable and value-creating information, but not so granular that the business is inundated with alert messages. One way to manage this is to provide tolerance levels to monitor events and to not notify business users unless the performance falls outside these tolerance ranges. A small SAP custom development is suggested for defining the tolerance tables in SAP ECC. Depending on your business requirement needs, the tolerance values can differ based on purchase order types and supplier combinations.

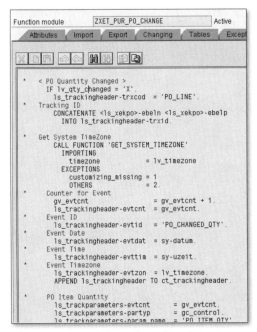

Figure 6.14 Event Type – Event Data Extractor

You can design the tolerance table to be based on the escalation levels, who needs to be informed, and the business process criticality. Depending on the percentage deviation from plan, notifications can be sent to concerned parties in the supply chain. Figure 6.15 shows an example tolerance table definition for purchase order delivery date, quantity delivered, and invoice amount variances based on purchase order type and vendor combinations. The tolerance table can also be defined based on the escalation (high, medium, low) priorities, allowing notification to be based on situation criticality.

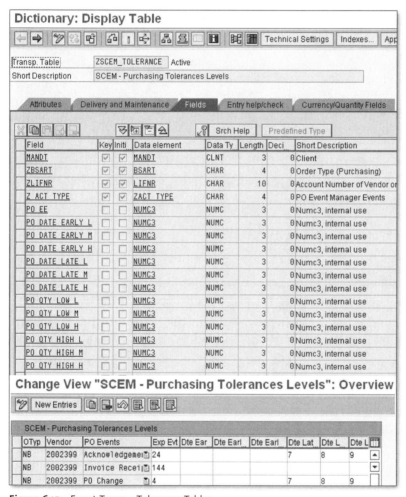

Figure 6.15 Event Types – Tolerance Tables

6.3 Event Posting Techniques

The goal of SAP Event Management is to identify critical situations in the purchasing supply chain by comparing the expected events with the actual events and responding to the event. This requires different parties to communicate event-related information to SAP Event Management.

The event message is used to communicate event-related information from any source to SAP Event Management. SAP provides two interfaces for event message reporting:

▶ BAPI EventHandler.AddEventMessages02 (remote-enabled function module / SAPTRX/BAPI_EH_ADDEVENTMSG_02)

▶ IDoc EVMSTA02

The interfaces of BAPIs and IDocs have the same content, but there are three major differences between the two:

▶ An IDoc has a hierarchical structure, whereas a BAPI has flat one.

▶ A BAPI has a wider available interface and allows files to be sent as attachments.

▶ A BAPI interface has indicators that allow you to control event message processing (for example, synchronous or asynchronous processing).

It's worth mentioning that IDocs aren't automatically generated based on BAPIs. Event messages are derived from the EDI message standards (for example, EDIFACT) and converted into IDoc format. BAPI interfaces have a set of parameters that function as the interfaces of the function module of the underlying BAPI. The BAPI interface consists of a set of input parameters and a set of output tables.

Taking the example of a purchase order release as business process, we'll discuss the input parameters, output tables, and typical code written for posting an event message to SAP Event Management via a BAPI technique.

6.3.1 Input Parameters

Table 6.3 lists the input parameters used during the BAPI processing.

Parameter	Usage
SIMULATE	Flag: Simulation mode (event message is saved in database or not; for test purposes)
BLOCKONERRORIN	Flag: Block processing if syntax error is found (only event messages with valid data are processed)
SKIPCHECK	Flag: Do not carry out syntax error check
SYNCHRONOUS	Synchronous process rather than standard asynchronous mode (mostly used for debugging and test purposes)
BUFFER_MODE	Mode for buffering events messages: Controls the buffering of an event message (event message is saved on the database and isn't processed)
EH_GENERATION_MODE	Mode for generating event handlers: Event messages can be checked for whether they will generate an event handler
EH_GENERATION_FUNCTION	Plug-in function module to generate event handlers
PREPROCESS_MODE	Mode for event message preprocessing: Event messages can be checked if they can be preprocessed
PREPROCESS_FUNCTION	Plug-in function module to preprocess event messages

Table 6.3 Input Parameters Used in BAPI Processing

You can use the simulation mode to step through the event message processing without actually updating the database tables. This is helpful in understanding how the event messages are processed before posting. The synchronous mode is primarily used for test purposes, whereas in a production environment, event messages are always asynchronous for performance reasons.

6.3.2 Output tables

Table 6.4 lists the tables that are passed during the BAPI interface.

BAPI Parameter	Database Structure	Description
TRACKINGHEADER	/SAPTRX/BAPI_EVM_HEADER	Event message header: Contains identification for the event, event handler, sender, recipient, event reasons, date, and time of event occurrence
TRACKLOCATION	/SAPTRX/BAPI_EVM_LOCATIONID	Information about the location where the event occurred
TRACKADDRESS	/SAPTRX/BAPI_EVM_ADDRESS	Address of location and partner
TRACKLOCATIONDESCR	/SAPTRX/BAPI_EVM_LOCDESCR	Description of location
TRACKLOCADDITIONALID	/SAPTRX/BAPI_EVM_LOCADDID	Location additional identifier
TRACKPARTNERID	/SAPTRX/BAPI_EVM_PARTNERID	Partner, header
TRACKPARTNERADDID	/SAPTRX/BAPI_EVM_PARTNERADDID	Partner, additional identifier
TRACKEEMODIFY	/SAPTRX/BAPI_EE_MODIFY	Modification to expected event list
TRACKCONFIRMSTATUS	/SAPTRX/BAPI_EVM_CONFSTAT	Confirmation status
TRACKREFERENCE	/SAPTRX/BAPI_EVM_REFERENCE	Further references
TRACKMEASURESULTS	/SAPTRX/BAPI_EVM_MEASURESULT	Measurement results
TRACKSTATUSATTRIB	/SAPTRX/BAPI_EVM_STATUSATTR	Status attributes

Table 6.4 BAPI Output Table

BAPI Parameter	Database Structure	Description
TRACKPARAMETERS	/SAPTRX/BAPI_EVM_PARAMETER	Parameters
TRACKFILEHEADER	/SAPTRX/BAPI_EVM_FILEHEADER	Attached file: header table
TRACKFILEREF	/SAPTRX/BAPI_EVM_FILEREF	Attached file: reference
TRACKFILEBIN	/SAPTRX/BAPI_EVM_FILEBIN	Attached file: contents (binary)
TRACKFILECHAR	/SAPTRX/BAPI_EVM_FILECHAR	Attached file: contents (file)
TRACKTEXTHEADER	/SAPTRX/BAPI_EVM_TEXTHEADER	Text header
TRACKTEXTLINES	/SAPTRX/BAPI_EVM_TEXTLINES	Text lines
EXTENSIONIN	BAPIPAREX	Standard BAPI extension table
EXTENSIONOUT	BAPIPAREX	Standard BAPI extension table
RETURN		Standard BAPI return table

Table 6.4 BAPI Output Table (Cont.)

Of all of these tables, the table TRACKINGHEADER is the only mandatory parameter of the BAPI. Table 6.5 shows the mandatory fields of the table TRACKINGHEADER.

Field	Usage
EVTCNT	Counter for event (as primary key). One BAPI call can contain any number of event messages — one for event reporting (expected event) and other for event delay (unexpected event). Messages must have this counter because an entry in the header table can correspond to one or more entries in other optional tables.

Table 6.5 BAPI Table for Posting Event Message to SAP Event Management

Field	Usage
EVTCOD	The event is usually identified by two fields: EVTCOD + EVTID. EVTCOD is an external event set that is used to make the external event code unique. Event codes are unique to SAP Event Management (internally), but externally different partners can have their own unique codes. If the internal event code is used in a BAPI interface, the EVTCOD field must be left empty, and only the EVTID field is filled with internal event code.
EVTID	Event code ID: Identification of an event, together with the code set.
TRXCOD	Tracking ID code set
TRXID	Tracking ID code ID: Together with tracking ID code set, identifies an event handler.
EVTDAT	Event date when the event has occurred
EVTTIM	Event time

Table 6.5 BAPI Table for Posting Event Message to SAP Event Management (Cont.)

6.3.3 BAPI Processing

Figure 6.16 shows the technical step performed during the BAPI interface processing. The steps are further described as follows.

▶ **Authorization check**
The system first checks whether the user is authorized to send event messages. The authorization is maintained in Transaction /SAPTRX/TSC0AUTHSND.

▶ **Standard data preprocessing**
The system-created event message GUID (SAP Event Management uses GUID to uniquely identify an event message) converts non sensitive fields to uppercase.

▶ **Fill internal tables with event message database structure**
A set of internal tables, with the structure of event message database tables, are filled based on values contained in the BAPI input table.

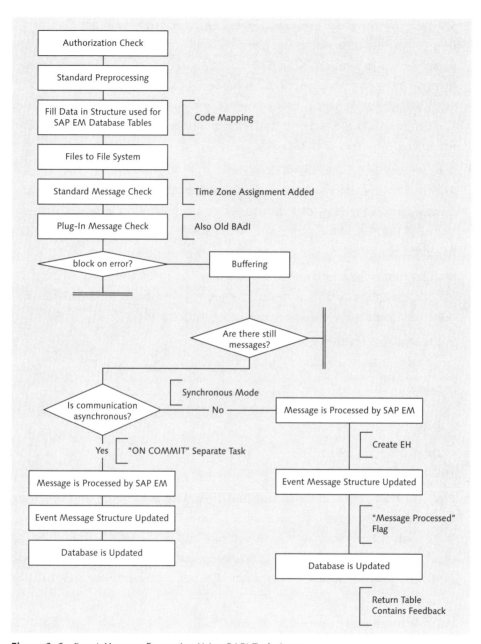

Figure 6.16 Event Message Processing Using BAPI Technique

▶ **Set indicator for event message processing by inactive event handler**
In a typical situation, an event message sent for an inactive event handler (deactivated) isn't processed in SAP Event Management. SAP Event Management offers customization options for processing an event message for an overage, shortage, or damage scenario where the event message is sent much later. You can maintain the three parameters (event code, sender, tracking ID code set) in Transaction /SAPTRX/TSC0MBF.

▶ **Save an attached file to the file system**
SAP Event Management offers options for storing the event message file attachment (digital signatures, digital images etc.) in an application server. Transaction /SAPTRX/TSC0MBF allows you to specify the file path where the files can be stored.

▶ **Standard message check and preprocessing**
Event messages are checked to validate the required fields exist. The check is done for the following entries that exist in event messages:

  ▶ **Event identification**
  Codes that mention what event happened and is being reported

  ▶ **Tracking ID**
  Used to uniquely identify the event handler where the event message needs to be posted

  ▶ **Date and time information**
  When the event occurred

▶ **Plug-in event message check and BAdI interface for adding and updating event messages**
SAP Event Management offers this option for personalized event message checks and a preprocessing plug-in function. Again, you can maintain the three parameters (event code, sender, tracking ID code set) in Transaction /SAPTRX/TSC0MBF.

▶ **Possible block on error**
If the standard or plug-in function module finds a error, and the indicator BLOCKONERRORIN is set to true, the processing of the event message is stopped.

▶ **Buffering**

SAP Event Management offers the option of buffering (saved to database) with the option of being processed later. The parameters that can be buffered are event code, location, sender, and tracking ID code set.

▶ **Set of processing mode**

This occurs after buffering event messages are set to be processed either in synchronous or asynchronous mode.

▶ **Message is processed**

Event message processing includes possible creation of an event handler and additional activities executed by SAP Event Management.

▶ **Database update**

SAP Event Management offers the option of saving the event message in database.

The event messages are saved in a set of internal tables that are different from internal BAPI tables. Event message databases have internal fields like GUID, which link the various tables. Table 6.6 lists the event message tables.

Table	Description
/SAPTRX/EVM_HDR	Header
/SAPTRX/EVM_AFB	Attached file binary contents
/SAPTRX/EVM_AFC	Attached file text contents
/SAPTRX/EVM_AFH	Attached file header
/SAPTRX/EVM_AFR	Attached file reference table
/SAPTRX/EVM_CST	Confirmation details
/SAPTRX/EVM_LAI	Modification to expected event list
/SAPTRX/EVM_LID	Location ID
/SAPTRX/EVM_MER	Measurement result
/SAPTRX/EVM_PAI	Partner additional identifier
/SAPTRX/EVM_PAR	Parameters

Table 6.6 SAP Event Management Event Message Tables

Table	Description
/SAPTRX/EVM_PID	Partners ID
/SAPTRX/EVM_REF	Further reference
/SAPTRX/EVM_STA	Status attributes
/SAPTRX/EVM_THD	Text header
/SAPTRX/EVM_TXL	Text lines

Table 6.6 SAP Event Management Event Message Tables (Cont.)

Table /SAPTRX/EH_EVMSG is always updated with all of the event messages for the event handler. This table belongs to the set of tables for the event handler, not the event message.

6.3.4 BAPI Posting Example – Purchase Order Release

This section gives the sample code for posting an event message for a purchase order release business event. The BAPI posting code is embedded as a user exit in the function module EXIT_SAPMM06E_007. The code is shown in four major sections.

Section 1 is primarily for the definition of event message data, working variables, and BAPI structures.

```
* Event Message data
        ls_trackingheader type /saptrx/bapi_evm_header,
        ls_trackeemodify  type /saptrx/bapi_evm_ee_modify,
        lv_evtcnt type /saptrx/bapi_evm_header-evtcnt,
        lv_modcnt type /saptrx/bapi_evm_header-evtcnt,
* BAPI Structures
        lt_bapi_evm_header type standard table of
/saptrx/bapi_evm_header,
        lt_trackeemodify   type standard table of
/saptrx/bapi_evm_ee_modify,
        lt_bapireturn      type standard table of bapiret2,
```

```
* Working variables
        new_date type sy-datum,
        new_time type sy-uzeit,
* BAPI Calling structures
        v_last_digit,
        v_queue type trfcqout-qname,
        lt_trxserv type standard table of /saptrx/trxserv,
        lw_trxserv type /saptrx/trxserv.
```

Section 2 is for checking the SAP Event Management relevancy and checking whether the event messages need to be posted based on conditions for a tracking ID.

```
DATA:
*    System Timezone
     lv_timezone        TYPE timezone.
field-symbols:
     <fs_ekpo> type  BEKPO.
     check sy-tcode = 'ME28'.

     SELECT SINGLE * FROM b025 WHERE kappl = 'EF'         AND
                             kschl = 'ZEMP'         AND
                             bsart = i_ekko-bsart  AND
                             lifnr = i_ekko-lifnr.
     check sy-subrc = 0.  "Relevant for SAP EM event
     check not I_EKkO is initial.
     check not i_ekko_old is initial.
     check i_ekko-frgke = 'R' and
       i_ekko_old-frgke = 'B' .
       ls_trackingheader-trxcod  = 'PO_NO'.
**   Tracking ID
       ls_trackingheader-trxid = I_EKkO-ebeln.
*    Get System TimeZone
       CALL FUNCTION 'GET_SYSTEM_TIMEZONE'
         IMPORTING
           timezone            = lv_timezone
```

```
        EXCEPTIONS
          customizing_missing = 1
          OTHERS              = 2.
       lv_evtcnt                   = lv_evtcnt + 1.
       ls_trackingheader-evtcnt    = lv_evtcnt.
*      Event ID
       ls_trackingheader-evtid     = 'PO_REL'.
*      Event Date
       ls_trackingheader-evtdat    = sy-datum.
*      Event Time
       ls_trackingheader-evttim    = sy-uzeit.
*      Event Timezone
       ls_trackingheader-evtzon    = lv_timezone.
       APPEND ls_trackingheader TO lt_bapi_evm_header.
**     Mapping table
*      ls_eventid_map-eventid    = ls_events-eventid.
*      ls_eventid_map-evtcnt     = gv_evtcnt.
*       APPEND ls_eventid_map TO c_eventid_map.
*   append ls_trackingheader to lt_bapi_evm_header.
```

Section 3 is for identifying whether the expected event date is new, a deletion, or an update and calling the business process type.

```
**** MODIFY EXPECTED EVENT ENTRY ***
  ls_trackeemodify-evtcnt = lv_evtcnt.
  ls_trackeemodify-evtact = 'I'.
*   "Insert, U=Update, D=Delete                 '
  ls_trackeemodify-language = sy-langu.
*   Set new message and actual Event Date / Time / Timezone
  New_date = sy-datum + 1.
  New_time = sy-uzeit.
  ls_trackeemodify-etxdat = ls_trackeemodify-msgdat = new_date.
  ls_trackeemodify-etxtim = ls_trackeemodify-msgtim = new_time.
  ls_trackeemodify-evtid  = 'PO_REL'.
  lv_modcnt = lv_modcnt + 1.
  ls_trackeemodify-modcnt = lv_modcnt.
```

```
    append ls_trackeemodify to lt_trackeemodify.
call function 'TRFC_SET_QUEUE_NAME'
    exporting
      qname                    = 'EM_ESC_PURORD'
    exceptions
      invalid_queue_name       = 1
      others                   = 2 .
  if sy-subrc <> 0.
    Message i099(b1) with 'Failed to change queue name!'.
    endif.
```

Section 4 is for the actual posting of an event message to SAP Event Management by calling the function /SAPTRX/BAPI_EH_ADDEVENTMSG_02.

```
***** CALL BAPI ***
* Get tracking servers
  select * from /saptrx/trxserv into table lt_trxserv.
  if sy-subrc <> 0.
    message w021(/saptrx/asc).
  endif.
  loop at lt_trxserv into lw_trxserv.

    if not lt_bapi_evm_header is initial.
      call function '/SAPTRX/BAPI_EH_ADDEVENTMSG_02'
        in background task
        destination lw_trxserv-rfcdest
        exporting
          simulate        = space
          synchronous     = space
          eh_generation_mode = 'N'
        tables
          trackingheader    = lt_bapi_evm_header
          trackeemodify     = lt_trackeemodify
          return            = lt_bapireturn.
* Set queue for the Commit as well
      call function 'TRFC_SET_QUEUE_NAME'
```

```
      exporting
        qname                        = 'EM_ESC_PURORD'
      exceptions
        invalid_queue_name           = 1
        others                       = 2 .
  if sy-subrc <> 0.
    Message i099(b1) with 'Failed to change queue name!'.
    endif.


      call function 'BAPI_TRANSACTION_COMMIT'
        in background task
        destination lw_trxserv-rfcdest.
    endif.
ENDLOOP.
    refresh lt_bapi_evm_header.
    refresh lt_trackeemodify.
    refresh lt_bapireturn.
```

6.4   SAP SCM Configuration

The configuration on the SAP SCM side can be divided into five components:

▶ Event handler for monitoring and managing events

▶ Event notification for expected event posting

▶ Reaction to an event for identifying follow-up activities after the event is posted in SAP Event Management

▶ Web communication for displaying the events on the Web

▶ Analytics for extracting the events and measuring supply chain metrics

6.4.1   Event Handler

An event handler lists all of the business process events the business user would like to manage. The core elements of the event handler are expected events and event codes. These define what events you're managing and monitoring in SAP Event Management for the purchasing scenario.

Event Codes

Start the customization by defining event codes. You must configure any expected or unexpected event code for processing in SAP Event Management.

An unexpected event is contained in the list of event codes but not shown in the list of expected events. The unexpected event is only used in the event notifications. Both internal and external event codes are defined. In Transaction SPRO, follow the menu path EVENT MANAGEMENT • EVENT HANDLERS AND EVENT HANDLER DATA • CODES • EVENT CODES.

In the internal event code, you can define reason codes for monitoring the unexpected event's root cause. The reason code can later be analyzed for identifying the improvement opportunities in the procurement process. The external event code is mapped with the event message code, which is passed from the application system. Figure 6.17 shows an example of code definitions.

Expected Event Profile

The next configuration item is the expected event profile. The profile defines what business events you would like to track or monitor and where this information will come from. The profile helps filter only events you want to monitor and manage in SAP Event Management. Figure 6.18 shows how for different group of suppliers (critical versus reliable) we can define different event handlers via expected event profiles. The expected event profile defines:

- List of expected events
- Sequence of expected events (planned)
- Dependencies of events, for example, if an expected event needs to be calculated based on another event
- Expected data and time for the event message
- Check routines for partners (partners sending the event message)
- Check routines for locations (where the event is expected to happen)

149

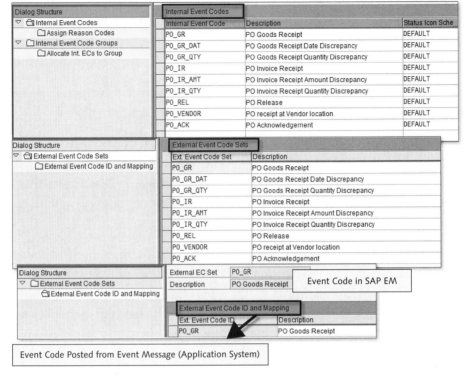

Figure 6.17 Event Codes

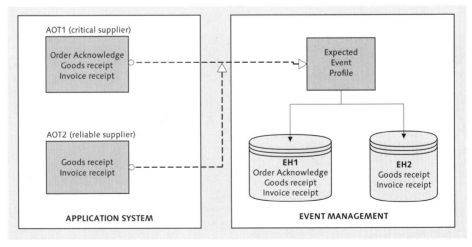

Figure 6.18 Expected Event Profile

Figure 6.19 shows an example of a purchasing scenario.

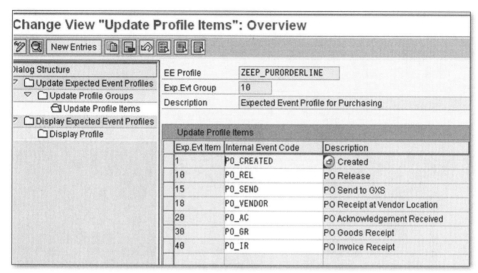

Figure 6.19 Expected Event Profile with Purchasing Expected Event List

Within an expected event profile, we can also configure update activities that control the generate function and the expected event monitor activity.

▶ The generate function identifies the event activity to be used to create the expected events for an event handler. If left blank, the default generate function GENERATE_EVENTS (class /SAPTRX/CL_EXPEV_GENERATOR) is used to generate the expected events.

▶ The expected event (EE) monitor activity is a multitask activity that is performed for an expected event when the expected event monitor program determines that an expected event date has passed without an event message received. Figure 6.20 shows the sample activities for a purchasing scenario attached to the expected event profile. The task activities build a list of proactive tasks (status updates: late or alert notification) for actions if the expected events don't occur as planned.

▶ In a production environment, a routine hourly batch job is scheduled to run program /SAPTRX/EE_MON for any overdue events. Once the event is late, you can send an alert notification to the vendor and buyer, informing them that the event is late.

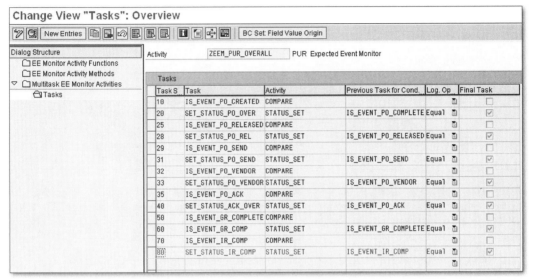

Figure 6.20 Expected Event Activities

Tracking and Query ID

Tracking and query ID helps us identify a specific event handler in SAP Event Management.

▶ Tracking and query ID consists of a tracking code set and tracking code ID, allowing it to be distinguished from different objects with the same IDs. For example, a purchase order can have multiple line items, each creating a unique event handler. The tracking ID can consist of a purchase order number plus a line item for the purchasing scenario.

▶ An event handler can contain more than one tracking ID. These allow multiple parties to report on their event messages as per their records.

▶ When we retrieve information from an event handler, if we need more information, we configure those fields in the query ID. In a majority of cases, the query ID refers to business transaction document reference numbers.

Parameters

Parameters are variables of the objects and processes that are relevant to SAP Event Management. The parameters contain the information from the application system about the application object. The parameters are defined as control, info, and system in SAP Event Management.

▶ You can use control parameters for defining conditions when reacting to a event message. A example of a control parameter is an acknowledgment delivery date from supplier that when compared with the planned delivery date is outside tolerance limits and triggers an alert.

▶ Info parameters provide additional information on business events and can be displayed in the alert message when notifications are send.

▶ System parameters are a special kind of control parameter used to improve performance. These are stored as part of the event handler header (EH header extension). System parameters allow for fast search queries using indexing.

The configuration of SAP Event Management parameters involves four steps:

▶ Control and info parameter definition

▶ System parameter definition

▶ Mapping of parameter using a profile

▶ Assignment of profile to mapping area

The definition of SAP Event Management parameters is similar to how it's done in SAP ECC. There should be data consistency on the data type and the length of the data type. Figure 6.21 shows a purchasing example for a control parameters definition and the mapping profile done between the field values of the SAP ECC application and SAP Event Management.

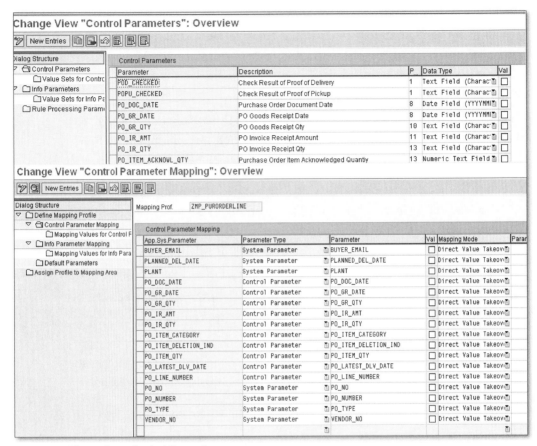

Figure 6.21 Control Parameters

Once the mapping profile is defined, it's assigned with an application object type on the application system (Figure 6.22).

Dialog Structure	Assign Profile to Mapping Area			
	Applic. System	Application Obj.Type	Mapping Profile	Error Mode
▽ ☐ Define Mapping Profile	ECC	PCM10_ITEM	PCM10_ITEM	Map parameter if possible, o
▽ ☐ Control Parameter Mapping				Map parameter if possible, o
☐ Mapping Values for Control Parameters				Map parameter if possible, o
▽ ☐ Info Parameter Mapping				Map parameter if possible, o
☐ Mapping Values for Info Parameters				Map parameter if possible, o
☐ Default Parameters				Map parameter if possible, o
⊟ Assign Profile to Mapping Area				

Figure 6.22 Control Parameter Mapping with the Application Object Type

Status

Status attributes are defined to track the completion of every business process. Status attributes can be broken down into business sub-process as shown below with their respective status icons.

▶ PO Status

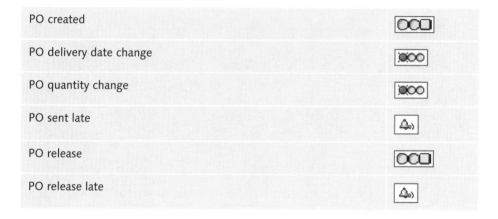

PO created	
PO delivery date change	
PO quantity change	
PO sent late	
PO release	
PO release late	

▶ PO Acknowledgment Status

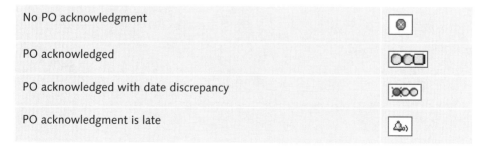

No PO acknowledgment	
PO acknowledged	
PO acknowledged with date discrepancy	
PO acknowledgment is late	

► PO Goods Receipt Status

No PO goods receipt	⊗
PO goods receipt	◯◯◻
PO goods receipt with date discrepancy	▨◯◯
PO goods receipt with qty & date discrepancy	▨◯◯
PO goods receipt with qty discrepancy	▨◯◯
PO goods receipt is late	🔔

► PO Invoice Receipt

No PO invoice receipt	⊗
PO invoice receipt	◯◯◻
Invoice receipt with amount discrepancy	▨◯◯
Invoice receipt with qty discrepancy	▨◯◯
Invoice receipt with qty & amt discrepancy	▨◯◯
Invoice receipt is late	🔔

► The event handler status icons can have the following meanings:

Indicates that the applicable stage of the process has been completed	◯◯◻
Indicates that an exception has occurred that needs attention	▨◯◯
Indicates that the expected event did not occur on expected time and is considered late	🔔

Indicates that the applicable stage of the process has not yet started	⊗
Indicates that an exception has occurred but is informational only	⊙△◇

▶ The Event Message status icons can have the following meanings:

Indicates that the expected event message has been received	⊙⊃⊐
Indicates that the expected event has not been received and is considered overdue	▦○○
Indicates that an unexpected event has occurred	▨

The configuration involves creating status attribute values for processes (in Transaction SPRO, follow the menu path EVENT MANAGEMENT • EVENT HANDLERS • STATUS • DEFINE STATUS ATTRIBUTES) and then attaching them to a status attribute profile (in Transaction SPRO, follow the menu path EVENT MANAGEMENT • EVENT HANDLERS • STATUS • DEFINE STATUS ATTRIBUTE PROFILE).

The default status for a process is attached as the first status in the status attribute profile (example shown in Figure 6.23, where the various invoice status values are checked during the event message posting from SAP ECC). The event status helps business users monitor and identify exceptions on their purchase orders.

Event Handler Type

The event handler type determines:

▶ **Expected event profile**
The list of expected events when you create or change event handlers

▶ **Status attribute profile**
The status when you create or change an event handler

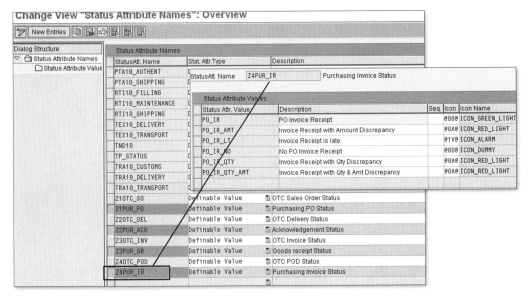

Figure 6.23 Status Attributes in SAP Event Management

▶ **Rule set**

Follow-up activities and notification, which occurs after event notification or if an expected event does not occur

▶ **BW profile**

What event handler data is uploaded to SAP NetWeaver BW

▶ **Authorization profile**

The authorization for displaying event handler data

▶ **Event handler header extension**

What system parameters are contained in the event handler

Each event handler type is assigned to one of the business process types, which are sent from the application system. The event handler type is created based on the condition defined. The condition for the event handler type is usually the application object relevancy check. You maintain the event handler type condition is maintained in Transaction SPRO. Follow the menu path EVENT MANAGEMENT • EVENT HANDLER • EVENT HANDLER TYPE. Figure 6.24 shows the event handler type where different profiles are attached. Also shown is the condition editor where the condition of the event handler creation is defined. The condition is usually the application object type defined in the application system (SAP ECC).

Within the event handler type configuration, we also define the unexpected event codes. The unexpected event code check in the event handler type determines if the event code is checked after the system determines that an event message is reporting an unexpected event. An example of an unexpected event is shown in Figure 6.25.

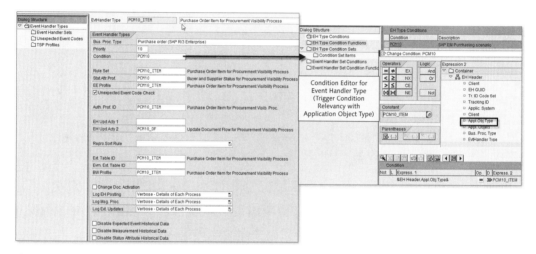

Figure 6.24 Event Handler Type

Event Handler Set

The event handler set:

▶ Groups logical event handlers for representation of an end-to-end business process

▶ Forms relationships between related event handlers

▶ Is displayed to users as a single entity

▶ Can have separate status profiles

▶ Gives a consolidated view of the business process

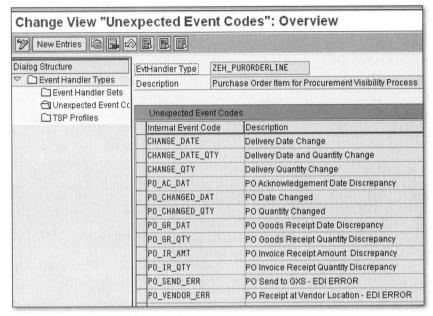

Figure 6.25 Unexpected Event Codes

For purchasing scenarios, if separate event handlers are created for each line item of the purchase order, an event handler set can help consolidate all of the event handlers to give a status overview of the purchase order.

The configuration of an event handler set involves two steps (example shown in Figure 6.26):

▶ **Define the event handler set profile**
In Transaction SPRO, follow the menu path EVENT MANAGEMENT • EVENT HANDLERS • DEFINE EVENT HANDLER SET PROFILES. The event handler set profile is assigned to the event handler type.

▶ **Define the event handler set relations**
In Transaction SPRO, follow the menu path EVENT MANAGEMENT • EVENT HANDLERS • DEFINE EVENT HANDLER SET PROFILES. This specifies the type of relationship the event handlers have in common. Uses control parameters, tracking ID, or query ID code sets.

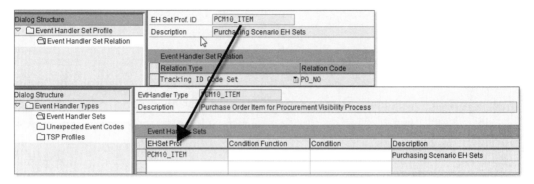

Figure 6.26 Event Handler Set

You can see the result of the event handler set in Transaction /SAPTRX/EH_SET, where the multiple event handlers are grouped (Figure 6.27).

EH Set Browser

Event Handler Set	AppIS	AO Type	Appl. Obj.	Tr. ID CS	Track. ID
▽ ☐ Tracking ID code set PO_NO = 4000079058					
📄 SAPR3 / ZAOT_PUR_STD / 400007905800010	SAPR3	ZAOT_PUR_STD	400007905800010	PO_NO	4000079058
📄 SAPR3 / ZAOT_PUR_STD / 400007905800020	SAPR3	ZAOT_PUR_STD	400007905800020	PO_NO	4000079058
📄 SAPR3 / ZAOT_PUR_STD / 400007905800080	SAPR3	ZAOT_PUR_STD	400007905800080	PO_NO	4000079058
📄 SAPR3 / ZAOT_PUR_STD / 400007905800090	SAPR3	ZAOT_PUR_STD	400007905800090	PO_NO	4000079058
▽ ☐ Tracking ID code set PO_NO = 4000078994					
📄 SAPR3 / ZAOT_PUR_STD / 400007899400010	SAPR3	ZAOT_PUR_STD	400007899400010	PO_NO	4000078994
📄 SAPR3 / ZAOT_PUR_STD / 400007899400020	SAPR3	ZAOT_PUR_STD	400007899400020	PO_NO	4000078994
▷ ☐ Tracking ID code set PO_NO = 4000080207					
▷ ☐ Tracking ID code set PO_NO = 4000025722					
▷ ☐ Tracking ID code set PO_NO = 4000080219					
▷ ☐ Tracking ID code set PO_NO = 4000079059					
▷ ☐ Tracking ID code set PO_NO = 4000080239					

Figure 6.27 Event Handler Set Browser

6.4.2   Event Notification

Event notification is the posting of actual events against planned events. The event message carries a tracking ID and event code. The tracking ID enables SAP Event Management to find the right event handler against which to post the received event message. The event code determines what event has taken place and should be updated in the event handler.

There are various means of posting events in SAP Event Management. The commonly used are:

- **External event code posting**

  In this method, the event code is posted from the application system. Figure 6.28 shows how the mapping is done between the internal codes defined for SAP Event Management with external code interfaced for the application system.

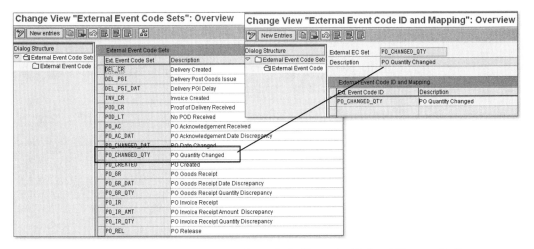

Figure 6.28 SAP Event Management Event Code Mapped with Event Message Posting

- **Manual event posting in SAP Event Management**

  Transaction /SAPTRX/MI02 offers the manual event posting.

- **Remote-enabled function module posting**

  There are two methods: BAPI interface and IDoc. We explained the BAPI interface technique with a code example in Section 6.3, Event Posting Techniques.

- **Web notification**

  The user logs on to SAP Event Management directly with a web interface and posts the event against the tracking ID.

Expected Message Date

You have the option of defining an expected message date in addition to the normal expected event date. This serves as the latest tolerance to the expected event date defined. The expected message date (shown in Figure 6.29) is calculated by the fields for date rule, duration, duration sign, group number, item number, calculation rule, tolerance, and tolerance rule, as explained below:

▶ **Date rule**
Indicates how the date will be set for the expected event message.

▶ **Duration**
A time duration that is added or subtracted from the base date to calculate the expected date.

▶ **Duration sign**
Indicates whether the value in the duration field is to be added or subtracted.

▶ **Group and item number**
Identifies the specific record to use as a basis for calculating the expected event message date.

▶ **Calculation rule**
Indicates which date in the related expected event record is used as the basis for calculating the event message expected date.

▶ **Tolerance**
Contains the duration used for calculating the earliest and latest expected event date.

▶ **Tolerance rule**
Indicates whether the duration in the tolerance field is used to calculate the earliest or latest date or both in the expected event date.

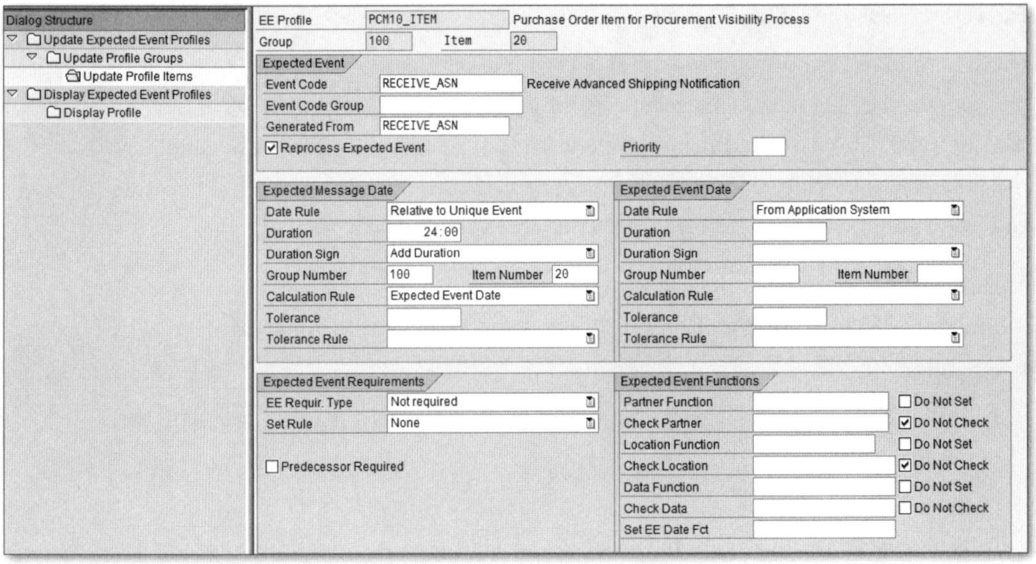

Figure 6.29 Event Message Date

6.4.3 Reaction to Event

Once you've posted the event message code in SAP Event Management, you can define activities for reacting to the particular message. Examples of activities include:

- ► Sending notification via emails
- ► Updating the business process status
- ► Triggering business documents in an application system
- ► Rescheduling all other expected dates in the expected event list
- ► Defining the escalation level

Rule Set

You use rule sets in SAP Event Management to determine what reaction needs to take place for the event message posted. The rule set consists of:

- Customizing, including conditions, rules, and single- or multistep activities
- A plug-in function module to trigger other systems
- Event handler methods

The structure of a rule set (shown in Figure 6.30) consists of single- or multistep activities and function that are:

- Performed when the actual event is posted for the expected event
- Used for triggering activities such as informing business partners, follow-up activities, and uploading data to business warehouse

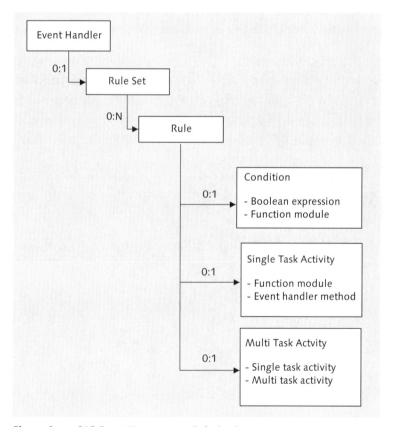

Figure 6.30 SAP Event Management Rule Set Structure

The configuration of a rule set involves three steps:

▶ Set up definitions of rules as per the event code sequence of the business process.

▶ Define rule conditions that fulfill each rule for performing the activity.

▶ Under the activity, you can define the event handler function to perform tasks such as updating statuses and parameters and sending activity IDs to the alert framework.

SAP Event Management uses rule sets to control how event handlers are processed and what automation system steps you need to react to a particular event message posted from the application system (SAP ECC). Examples of automatic responses to events are event status, alert notifications, and parameter updates on event handlers.

Configure the rule set via the menu path EVENT MANAGEMENT • REACTIONS TO EVENT MESSAGES • RULE SET. For better system performance and faster processing, we suggest that you create separate activities for each expected and unexpected event (example shown in Figure 6.31).

Change View "Rules": Overview

Rule Set ZRS_PUR_V2 — Rule Set for Purchasing

Rule Se	Rule	Condition	Activity	True Rule	False Rule
100	PO_CREATED	ZEM_PO_CREATED	ZEM_PO_CREATED	UPDATE_EXPEVENT	
200	PO_RELEASE	ZEM_PUR_REL	ZEM_PO_REL	UPDATE_EXPEVENT	
300	PO_SEND_TO_GXS	ZEM_PUR_SEND	ZEM_PO_SEND	UPDATE_EXPEVENT	
400	PO_ACKNOW_VENDOR	ZEM_PUR_VENDOR	ZEM_PO_VENDOR1	UPDATE_EXPEVENT	
500	PO_ACKNOWL	ZEM_PUR_ACKNOWL	ZEM_PO_AC	UPDATE_EXPEVENT	
600	PO_GR	ZEM_PUR_GR	ZEM_PO_GR	UPDATE_EXPEVENT	
700	PO_IR	ZEM_PUR_IR1	ZEM_PO_IR	UPDATE_EXPEVENT	
800	PO_CHANGED_QTY	ZEM_PUR_CHANGED_QTY	ZEM_PO_CHANGED_QTY	UPDATE_EXPEVENT	
900	PO_CHANGED_DATE	ZEM_PUR_CHANGED_DAT	ZEM_PO_CHANGED_DAT	UPDATE_EXPEVENT	
1000	PO_AC_DATE	ZEM_PUR_ACKNOWL_DATE	ZEM_PO_AC_DAT	UPDATE_EXPEVENT	
1100	PO_GR_DATE	ZEM_PUR_GR_DAT	ZEM_PO_GR_DAT	UPDATE_EXPEVENT	
1200	PO_GR_QTY	ZEM_PUR_GR_QTY1	ZEM_PO_GR_QTY	UPDATE_EXPEVENT	
1300	PO_IR_AMT	ZEM_PUR_IR_AMT	ZEM_PO_IR_AMT	UPDATE_EXPEVENT	
1400	PO_IR_QTY	ZEM_PUR_IR_QTY	ZEM_PO_IR_QTY	UPDATE_EXPEVENT	
1500	PO_SEND_TO_GXS_ERROR	ZEM_PUR_SEND_ERR	ZEM_PO_SEND_ERR	UPDATE_EXPEVENT	
1600	PO_VENDOR_ERROR	ZEM_PUR_VENDOR_ERROR	ZEM_PO_VENDOR_ERR	UPDATE_EXPEVENT	
9100	UPDATE_EXPEVENT		EVM_EE_UPDATE	END_PROCESS	
9900	END_PROCESS		BW_UPLOAD		

Figure 6.31 Rule Set Example for Expected and Unexpected Events

The expected events primarily have steps of updating the status and updating any new parameters posting from the application system. The unexpected events involve steps of notification or sending email alerts to the nominated target group. Figure 6.32 shows an example of a discrepancy posted on the purchase order goods receipt from SAP ECC. The activity steps shown are updating the parameters values, updating the event handler status, and sending alert notification based on escalation levels of high, medium, or low priority fields identified in the event type extractor code.

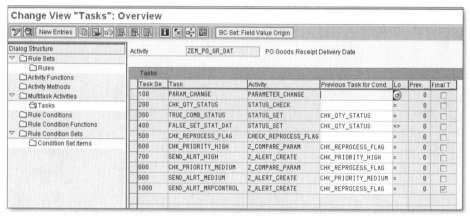

Figure 6.32 Rule Set Activity

Alert Framework

SAP Event Management is integrated into the SAP alert framework functionality. The basic features of the alert framework are:

▸ Simplifies and unifies the alert handling for SAP applications

▸ Is part of SAP's user centric alert solution that includes personalization

▸ Offers one central alert inbox for an enterprise portal

Alert management helps prevent delays in the processing of a critical situation, because it considerably reduces the time it takes for an alert to be detected and processed in critical situations. In SAP Event Management, we use the rule set to set up a connection to the alert framework.

SAP Event Management alert customization involves three steps. The first step is defining the alert category in Transaction ALRTCATDEF. The elements that can be defined in the alert category are:

- ► Alert title, short and long text
- ► Field variables in the form of containers that can be used in the alert title (application data)
- ► Priority
- ► Notification recipients
- ► Escalation procedures
- ► Subsequence activities (in the form of URLs)

Figure 6.33 shows a sample alert category configured to send email notifications based on the acknowledgment delivery date versus the purchase order delivery date variance, with the above-listed alert elements.

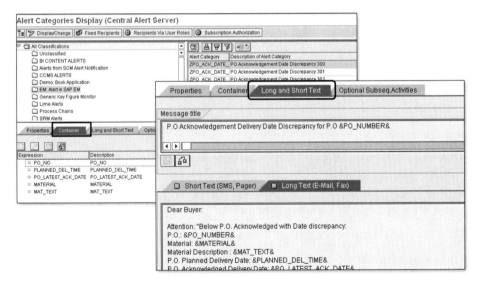

Figure 6.33 Alert Category Definition in SAP Alert Framework

The second step involves mapping the alert variable (container) fields with the SAP Event Management activity ID parameter values. You can configure this by following the SAP SCM IMG menu path EVENT MANAGEMENT • REACTIONS TO EVENT MESSAGES • DEFINE ALERT FRAMEWORK CONNECTION • DEFINE ALERT FRAMEWORK INTEGRATION TO EVENT MANAGEMENT. Figure 6.34 shows in the configuration maps, the alert container elements with SAP Event Management parameter values (system, information, or control).

Dialog Structure	Activity Param.ID	ZPO_ACK_DATE_326
▽ ☐ Assign Alert Categories		
☐ Map Event Managem	Map Event Management Parameters	
	Container Element	EM Attribute ID
	MATERIAL	INFO_MATERIAL
	MAT_TEXT	INFO_MATERIAL_TEXT
	PLANNED_DEL_TIME	CNTR_PO_LATEST_DLV_DATE
	PO_LATEST_ACK_DATE	CNTR_PO_LATEST_ACK_DATE
	PO_NUMBER	SYST_PO_NUMBER

Figure 6.34 Defining Alert Activity Parameter ID in SAP Event Management

The final step involves naming the activity ID step in the rule step by following the menu path SCM IMG • EVENT MANAGEMENT • REACTION TO EVENT MESSAGES • RULE SET • MULTITASK ACTIVITIES. In this step, we input the activity name and activity ID to be triggered as an alert notification. Figure 6.35 shows a sample configuration for sending an alert when a purchase order goods receipt is outside the tolerance level of the committed delivery date from the vendor.

6.4.4 Web Communication

SAP Event Management offers a web interface in two forms: Web Communication Layer (WCL) and Web Dynpro. The web communication serves as either a posting event or a reporting mechanism within SAP Event Management. In the following sections, we'll look at the configuration of Web Dynpro, whereas the following chapter will focus on WCL.

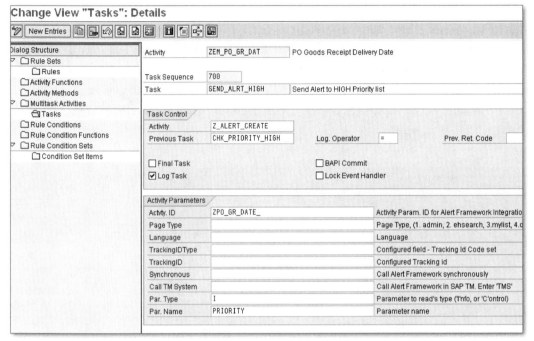

Figure 6.35 Rule Set Triggering Alert in SAP Event Management

The configuration involves defining a tracking scenario and three basic profiles — selection profile, display profile, and user profile. In the profile section, define the fields that the user would like to see as selection criteria fields. The display profile defines the event attributes that the user would like to report on (tracking scenario and display profile field examples shown in Figure 6.36). Do the configuration by following the SCM IMG menu path EVENT MANAGEMENT • WEB INTERFACE.

The user profile is where the display and selection profiles are attached. In the selection profile, we define the way the user inputs the selection fields, as either single or multiple inputs. With the display profile, we configure what details of the event handler we would like to display in the overview and detailed views. Figure 6.37 shows the two profiles in detail and the creation of the user profile.

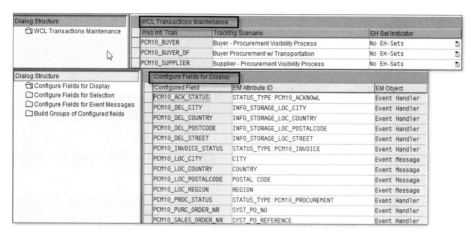

Figure 6.36 Web Interface Tracking Scenario and Field Configuration

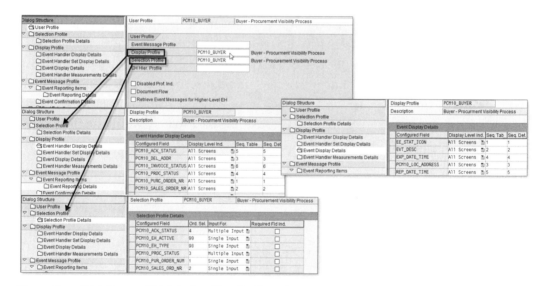

Figure 6.37 Web Dynpro Web Interface User Configuration

The user profile and the tracking scenario are further attached with the specific role or username directly via menu path EVENT MANAGEMENT • WEB INTERFACE OR

EVENT MANAGEMENT • WEB INTERFACE • ASSIGN USER PROFILE AND WCL TRANSACTIONS TO USERS.

6.4.5 Analytics

Event handler data is extracted for SAP NetWeaver Business Warehouse (BW) on the event handler, event, and event group level. This gives companies the opportunity to measure their vendor performance and reliability metrics for use during future contract negotiations. Another metric measurement can be supply chain flexibility on the lead time between the purchase order creation and goods receipt. This helps the company better maintain the purchasing lead time in master data and helps order management schedule the customer sales orders more accurately toward perfect order fulfillment metrics.

The SAP NetWeaver BW setup consists of configuring the BW profile and the extraction setup in SAP Event Management and setting up a process chain (Transaction RSPC) in SAP NetWeaver BW for routine data extraction. Figure 6.38 shows the standard business content flow you can activate for extracting event data from SAP Event Management to SAP NetWeaver BW. SAP Event Management events and parameters are extracted and stored in a data source, which are then transferred to SAP NetWeaver BW data structures.

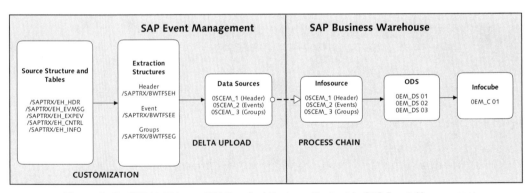

Figure 6.38 SAP NetWeaver BW Standard Business Content in SAP Event Management

BW Profile

The BW profile maps the event handler header and event data, including event groups to extract structures. These extract structures are then copied from SAP Event Management to SAP NetWeaver BW. The header data is used mainly for the selection criteria, whereas the event contains the expected and actual event data. In the group level, a comparison between different events can be captured. For performance reasons, the duration between the two events are calculated in SAP Event Management before loading the data into SAP NetWeaver BW. Customers can enhance an existing append structure for info parameters, control parameters, or event handler header extensions. The parameters need to be appended in the structure /SAPTRX/BWTFSEH.

To configure a BW profile, follow the menu path SCM IMG • EVENT MANAGEMENT • SAP BW INTERFACE • DEFINE SAP BW PROFILE. Three core areas are configured:

- Definition (i.e., parameter values of the event handler)
- Event codes
- Groups (i.e., calculated duration between the events)

In the BW profile definition map, the SAP NetWeaver BW defined parameter with SAP Event Management parameters fields, define the timestamp and header duration calculation.

Next, in BW profile event, simply input all of the event codes and define the event mapping, timestamp, and duration calculation for the event messages.

Lastly, input the duration calculation between the events in the BW profile-groups. Assign the BW profile to the corresponding event handler type. Figure 6.39 shows an example of a BW profile.

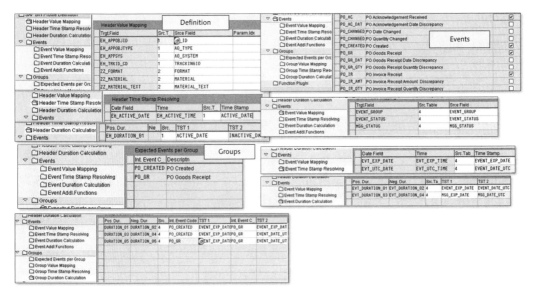

Figure 6.39 BW Profiles in SAP Event Management

BW Extraction

The BW extraction involves four major steps (shown in Figure 6.40):

1. Generate the SAP Event Management data source in Transaction /SAPTRX/ BWGS. The three data sources generated are:

   ▶ 0SCEM_1, containing the parameter values for the event handler

   ▶ 0SCEM_2, containing the event codes and time stamping of the events

   ▶ 0SCEM_3, containing the calculated duration of the events

2. Modify the event handler rule set to include the BWUPLOAD function (menu path IMG • EVENT MANAGEMENT • REACTION TO EVENT MESSAGES • RULE SET). The update type needs to be blank for the first upload. Once the first upload is completed, input the value "X" for the subsequent delta uploads.

3. Initialize the setup tables using Transaction /SAPTRX/BWID.

4. Execute the tnitial data upload to SAP NetWeaver BW using Transaction /SAPTRX/BWIU.

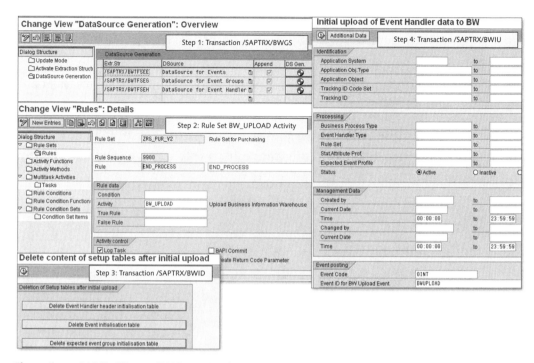

Figure 6.40 SAP NetWeaver BW Extraction Steps in SAP Event Management

6.5 Scenario Monitoring in SAP Event Management 5.1

The key capabilities of SAP Event Management in a supply chain management purchasing context lie in the monitoring, notification, adjustment, and analysis of the supply chain business process, detailed as follows:

▶ Monitoring helps track (e.g., order fulfillment) and trace (location of goods) supply chain process visibility. It provides forewarning to companies so they can react quickly and adjust their supply chain plans.

▶ Notification provides near real-time notification of critical events. It helps you manage by exceptions based on tolerance levels.

▶ Adjustment delivers automatic exception resolution triggers for follow-up activities. This reduces supply chain costs through management of uncertainty in the supply chain.

▶ Analysis provides information for measuring how well your supply chain processes are running.

Figure 6.41 shows the SAP Event Management capabilities that can be modeled for providing supply chain purchasing visibility both within and outside company boundaries.

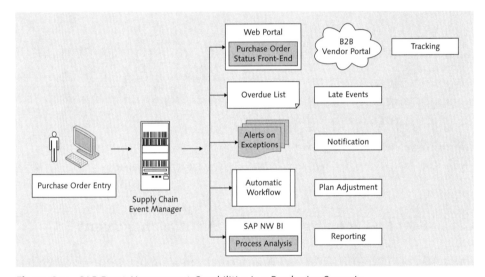

Figure 6.41 SAP Event Management Capabilities in a Purchasing Scenario

6.5.1 Event Handler

Event handlers monitor and manage purchase orders. An event handler lists all of the planned business process events we would like to manage. Each event handler has a unique tracking ID and contains parameters and status information. All of the expected and unexpected event messages from the various sources are posted in the event handler.

Event handlers contain the details listed below (also shown in Figure 6.42):

▶ Expected event planned and actual posting date

▶ Unexpected actual posting date

▶ Parameters: control, system, and info fields to be used for display or selection in reporting events or to be used as criteria in rule set activities conditions

▶ Expected event history for tracking event message posting

▶ Tasks that give the log of rule set activities with the return code

▶ Tracking and query ID

▶ Authorization on the event handler

▶ Current order status

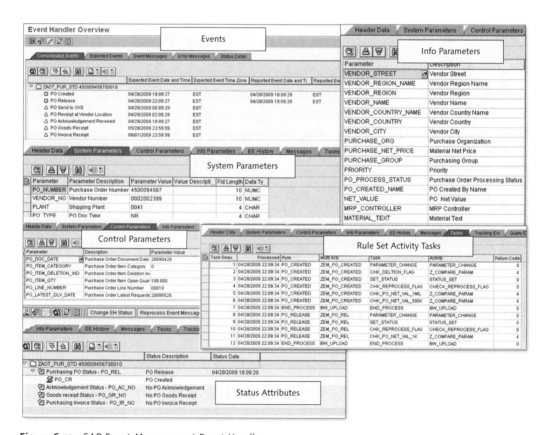

Figure 6.42 SAP Event Management Event Handler

6.5.2   Web Dynpro Reporting

A Web Dynpro report is another interactive means that is used for event reporting and can be made available to internal and external supply chain business partners. The users can identify the list of orders that need business proactive actions and planned event deviations. The report (shown in Figure 6.43) can also serve as a process dashboard to highlight the current business process status.

Create an iView for the Web Dynpro status reporting transaction in SAP NetWeaver to make it interactively available in the SAP enterprise portal.

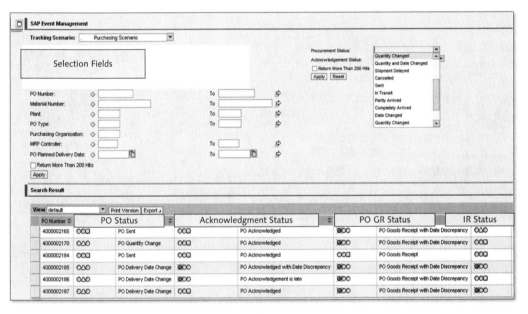

Figure 6.43   SAP Event Management Web Dynpro

6.5.3   Overdue List

One of the most common business requirements we come across is the aging list for the purchase order for which the planned expected events milestones were missed. SAP Event Management offers this functionality in Transaction /SAPTRX/ EE_OVD_LIST (shown in Figure 6.44), the overdue list report that lists all of the events that have missed the planned expected date and time. Users have the flexibility to run the report based on the event code and can do a small custom development to add event handler parameter fields as selection or display fields.

You need to run a routine batch job for program /SAPTRX/EE_MON, which checks the expected event profile and reports the overdue events.

Expected Events Overdue List

Appl System	Appl obj type	Appl obj ID	Track ID Codeset	Tracking ID	Int. EvtCd	MsgExpDate	LtMsgExpDt	Msg Rcvd	Expected Date/Time	Event Date	LatestEvtExpDte
SAPR3	ZAOT_PUR_STD	400000212300010	PO_NO	4000002123	PO_GR				10/20/2008 17:00:00		10/20/2008 17:00:00
SAPR3		400000212400010	PO_NO	4000002124	PO_CREATED				10/13/2008 18:17:21		10/13/2008 18:17:21
SAPR3			PO_NO	4000002124	PO_IR				10/27/2008 17:00:00		10/27/2008 17:00:00
SAPR3			PO_NO	4000002124	PO_GR				10/20/2008 17:00:00		10/20/2008 17:00:00
SAPR3		400000212500010	PO_NO	4000002125	PO_CREATED				10/10/2008 18:29:25		10/10/2008 18:29:25
SAPR3			PO_NO	4000002125	PO_IR				10/27/2008 17:00:00		10/27/2008 17:00:00
SAPR3			PO_NO	4000002125	PO_GR				10/20/2008 17:00:00		10/20/2008 17:00:00
SAPR3			PO_NO	4000002125	PO_AC				10/17/2008 17:00:00		10/17/2008 17:00:00
SAPR3		400000212600010	PO_NO	4000002126	PO_CREATED				10/10/2008 19:39:21		10/10/2008 19:39:21
SAPR3			PO_NO	4000002126	PO_IR				10/27/2008 17:00:00		10/27/2008 17:00:00
SAPR3			PO_NO	4000002126	PO_GR				10/20/2008 17:00:00		10/20/2008 17:00:00
SAPR3		400000212700010	PO_NO	4000002127	PO_CREATED				10/10/2008 19:47:12		10/10/2008 19:47:12
SAPR3			PO_NO	4000002127	PO_IR				10/27/2008 17:00:00		10/27/2008 17:00:00
SAPR3			PO_NO	4000002127	PO_GR				10/20/2008 17:00:00		10/20/2008 17:00:00
SAPR3		400000212700020	PO_NO	4000002127	PO_CREATED				10/10/2008 19:47:12		10/10/2008 19:47:12
SAPR3			PO_NO	4000002127	PO_IR				10/27/2008 17:00:00		10/27/2008 17:00:00
SAPR3			PO_NO	4000002127	PO_GR				10/20/2008 17:00:00		10/20/2008 17:00:00
SAPR3			PO_NO	4000002127	PO_AC				10/17/2008 17:00:00		10/17/2008 17:00:00

Figure 6.44 SAP Event Management Overdue List

6.5.4 Alert Inbox

The SAP alert framework (Figure 6.45) offers the alert inbox feature for consolidating all of the SAP Event Management alerts in one place. Instead of getting notification via emails, business users can opt to use the alert inbox for SAP Event Management alerts and perform any required follow-up business activity.

The alert inbox can be either part of the enterprise portal universal list or can be triggered manually by executing Transaction code ALRTINBOX in SAP Event Management.

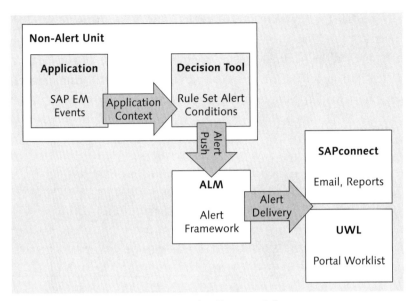

Figure 6.45 SAP Event Management Alert Framework flow

6.6 Summary

This chapter provided detailed customization steps for setting up an SAP Event Management environment for a purchasing scenario. SAP Event Management capabilities are based on monitoring purchase order fulfillment and providing forewarning to business managers if the supplier supports any exceptions about the delay of delivery date or reported variance on quantities or amounts. Notifications provide near real-time information about critical events and help to manage exceptions by setting realistic tolerance levels. SAP Event Management provides the notification capability on purchase orders and plans automatic adjustment or business workflow triggers for any required follow-up activities. Purchasing analytics provide the means to measure supplier performance and trend analysis to negotiate contracts with suppliers. All of these capabilities help reduce a company's supply chain costs through proactive management of uncertainty in supply chains with up-to-date transparent information about the location, status, and quantity of orders.

The next chapter looks at the manufacturing visibility processes delivered by SAP Event Management. The chapter highlights how to achieve integration between planning, manufacturing, and plant maintenance with effective communication and collaboration using SAP Event Management functionality.

This chapter describes in detail the business scenario and customization steps required to set up a manufacturing order and malfunction notification handling scenario in SAP Event Management 5.1 and reporting features for monitoring the process.

7 Setting Up a Manufacturing Scenario

A production line breakdown usually causes disruptions to the execution of manufacturing planning. If a breakdown cannot be repaired easily, many manufacturing orders could possibly be affected. SAP Event Management offers increased visibility across various manufacturing departments to manage these exceptions. SAP pre-delivers standard content (visibility processes) that supports the production order malfunction scenario.

This chapter starts by highlighting the business scenario and then details the customization requirements in SAP ECC and SAP SCM for setting up the manufacturing monitoring scenario. This chapter also gives insight into how the authorization model can be set up in SAP Event Management.

7.1 Business Scenario

The production malfunction visibility process covers machine breakdowns within the production process. The scenario fills the gap that exists between the supply chain planning and execution systems by providing near real-time visibility of the events occurring on the shop floor. The production malfunction visibility process covers up following functions:

► Triggering follow-up activities

► Monitoring and controlling the production process, including possible disruptions caused by machine breakdowns

▶ Establishing a close link between planning and execution departments by creating alerts if any problems arise

▶ Extracting the data to SAP NetWeaver BW for analyzing the business process

The production process commences once the site scheduler releases the orders from the planning team. The production execution commences on the shop floor as planned. A notification is sent to the plant maintenance team when a machine (resource) breakdown occurs for fixing the machine. Also, an alert is sent to the planning team for rescheduling the production orders because there will be a delay in completion. The production commences once the machine is fixed. Subsequent production events are completed and goods receipt to inventory is also monitored in this scenario (Figure 7.1).

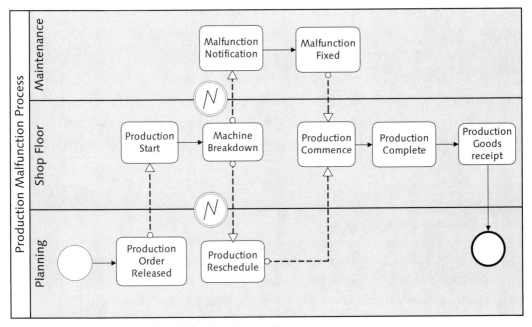

Figure 7.1 Production Malfunction Business Process

Table 7.1 lists the supply chain events that occur in this business process.

Business Process Event	Type of Event	Event Status	Notification
Release manufacturing order	Expected	Order status: released	
Start manufacturing order	Expected	Order status: started	
Machine breakdown	Unexpected	Order status: affected by breakdown	SAP APO Production Planning and Detailed Scheduling alert to production planner
Rescheduling manufacturing order	Unexpected	Order status: rescheduled	
Malfunction in process	Expected	Notification status: in process	
Release malfunction task	Expected		
Complete malfunction task	Expected		
Complete malfunction	Expected	Notification status: completed	
Finish manufacturing order	Expected	Order status: finished	
Deliver manufacturing order	Expected	Order status: delivered	

Table 7.1 Scenario of Expected and Unexpected Events

Because the production malfunction visibility process aims to bring together information from different functional areas, it consists of monitoring two areas:

▶ **Manufacturing order completion**
Tracks the release, completion, and goods receipt of production orders.

▶ **Malfunction notification completion**
Tracks the unplanned notification completion for machine (resource) rectification.

All of the events are reported from SAP ECC, and the subsequent event message posting into SAP Event Management triggers follow-up activities (via rule set). The follow-up activities can be sent as alert notifications to business partners, updates of the order status, or event data information to SAP NetWeaver Business Warehouse for analytics.

7.2   SAP ECC Configuration

The following details the SAP ECC configuration customization of three objects: business process type, application object type, and event type.

7.2.1   Business Process Type

The scenario is managed by the creation of two event handlers in SAP Event Management. One event handler monitors the manufacturing order progress from release to goods receipt, whereas other is for malfunction notification directed toward plant maintenance. We'll use two SAP-delivered business process types (BPTs) for the scenario:

▶ **ESC_WRKORD**
Work order (production, service, maintenance) in SAP R/3

▶ **EPL_NOTIF**
Notification in SAP R/3

Both the BPTs are used in creating the event handler and sending event messages in SAP Event Management. The configuration fields EH Create and EMsg Send are selected in the configuration (see Figure 7.2). In SAP ECC Transaction SPRO, follow the menu path INTEGRATION WITH OTHER MYSAP.COM COMPONENTS • EVENT MANAGEMENT INTERFACE • DEFINE APPLICATION INTERFACES • DEFINE BUSINESS PROCESS TYPES).

Change View "Define Business Process Types": Overview

New Entries

Dialog Structure	Define Business Process Types			
▽ Define Business Proces	BPT	EH Create	EMsg Send	Descriptn
Define Available Appl	EPL_EQUIPMT	☐	☐	Equipment in SAP R/3 Enterprise
	EPL_INSPLOT	☐	☐	Inspection Lot in SAP R/3 Enterprise
	EPL_NOTIF	☑	☑	Notification in SAP R/3 Enterprise
	ESC_DELIV	☐	☐	Delivery in SAP R/3 Enterprise
	ESC_FI_CLEARING	☐	☐	FI Clearing in SAP R/3 Enterprise
	ESC_MATDOC	☐	☐	Material Document in SAP R/3 Enterprise
	ESC_MM_INVOICE	☐	☐	MM Invoice in SAP R/3 Enterprise
	ESC_PURORD	☐	☐	Purchase Order in SAP R/3 Enterprise
	ESC_PURREQ	☐	☐	Purchase Requisition in SAP R/3 Enterprise
	ESC_SD_INVOICE	☐	☐	SD Invoice in SAP R/3 Enterprise
	ESC_SORDER	☐	☐	Sales Order in SAP R/3 Enterprise
	ESC_WOGMVT	☐	☐	Workorder Goods Movements (Production,Service,Maintenance) in SAP R/3 Enterpr
	ESC_WRKORC	☐	☐	Workorder Confirmation (Production, Service, Maintenance) in SAP R/3 Enterprise
	ESC_WRKORD	☑	☑	Workorder (Production, Service, Maintenance) in SAP R/3 Enterprise

Figure 7.2 Manufacturing Scenario Business Process Types

Various standard application tables are embedded within the business process types. The primary tables for the manufacturing business process types (see Figure 7.3 for manufacturing and Figure 7.4 for plant maintenance) are:

▶ **ESC_WRKORD**
RESB, CAUFV, AFPO, MLST, AFVC, AFVU, AFVV, AFFT, AFFV, PLAF, IHPA, AFFH, NPTX, AFAB, AFFL, JEST

▶ **ESC_NOTIF**
WQMMA, WQMUR, WQFE, VIQMEL, IHPAVB, WQMSM

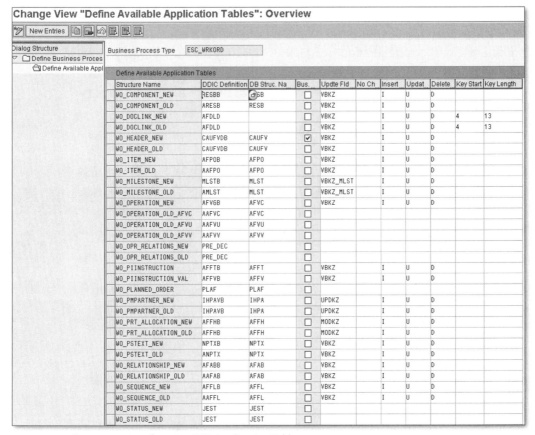

Figure 7.3 Manufacturing BPT Application Table

The BPTs are made active (Figure 7.5) in Transaction /SAPTRX/ASC0AO. In SAP ECC Transaction SPRO, follow the menu path INTEGRATION WITH OTHER MYSAP.COM COMPONENTS • EVENT MANAGEMENT INTERFACE • DEFINE APPLICATION INTERFACES • DEFINE USED BUS. PROCESS. TYPES, APPL. OBJ TYPES AND EVENT TYPES. The update mode Update Task indicates that processing of SAP Event Management code and communications related to these BPTs will occur in an update task using an update process.

Change View "Define Available Application Tables": Overview

New Entries

Dialog Structure
▽ ☐ Define Business Proces
  ☐ Define Available Appl

Business Process Type   EPL_NOTIF

Define Available Application Tables

Structure Name	DDIC Definition	DB Struc. Name	Bus.	Updte Fld	No Ch	Insert	Updat	Delete	Key Start	Key Length
ACTIVITIES_NEW	WQMMA	WQMMA	☐	AEKNZ		I	U	D		
ACTIVITIES_OLD	WQMMA	WQMMA	☐	AEKNZ		I	U	D		
CAUSES_NEW	WQMUR	WQMUR	☐	AEKNZ		I	U	D		
CAUSES_OLD	WQMUR	WQMUR	☐	AEKNZ		I	U	D		
CHANGE_MODE	PLM_NOTIF_CHANGE	PLM_NOTIF_CHANGE	☐	AEKNZ		I	U	D		
DEFECTS_NEW	WQMFE	WQMFE	☐	AEKNZ		I	U	D		
DEFECTS_OLD	WQMFE	WQMFE	☐	AEKNZ		I	U	D		
NOTIFICATION_HEADER_NEW	VIQMEL	VIQMEL	☑							
NOTIFICATION_HEADER_OLD	VIQMEL	VIQMEL	☐							
PARTNER_NEW	IHPAVB	IHPAVB	☐	UPDKZ		I	U	D		
PARTNER_OLD	IHPAVB	IHPAVB	☐	UPDKZ		I	U	D		
STATUS_NEW	PLM_OBJECT_STATUS	PLM_OBJECT_STATUS	☐							
STATUS_OLD	PLM_OBJECT_STATUS	PLM_OBJECT_STATUS	☐							
TASKS_NEW	WQMSM	WQMSM	☐	AEKNZ		I	U	D		
TASKS_OLD	WQMSM	WQMSM	☐	AEKNZ		I	U	D		
TASK_STATUS_NEW	PLM_OBJECT_STATUS	PLM_OBJECT_STATUS	☐							
TASK_STATUS_OLD	PLM_OBJECT_STATUS	PLM_OBJECT_STATUS	☐							

Figure 7.4 Plant Maintenance BPT Application Table

Change View "Define Used Business Process Types": Overview

New Entries

Dialog Structure
▽ ☐ Define Used Business F
  ☐ Define Application Ol
  ☐ Define Event Types

Define Used Business Process Types

Bus. Proc. Type	Update Mode	BPT Process Mode	Description
EPL_NOTIF	Update Task	Active	Notification in SAP R/3 Enterprise
ESC_DELIV	Update Task	D Inactive	Delivery in SAP R/3 Enterprise
ESC_FI_CLEARING	Update Task	D Inactive	FI Clearing in SAP R/3 Enterprise
ESC_MM_INVOICE	Update Task	D Inactive	MM Invoice in SAP R/3 Enterprise
ESC_PURORD	Update Task	D Inactive	Purchase Order in SAP R/3 Enterprise
ESC_SHIPMT	Update Task	D Inactive	
ESC_WRKORD	Update Task	Active	Workorder (Production, Service, Maintenance) in SAP R/3 Enterprise

Figure 7.5 Business Process Type Activation

7.2.2   Application Object Type

You can use application object types (AOTs) to determine whether a business object is relevant for SAP Event Management toward the creation of an event handler. It's also responsible for the data to be extracted for:

▶ Expected events

▶ Parameters (information and control)

▶ Tracking IDs

▶ Query IDs

Several AOTs can be assigned to one BPT. These are then processed according to their priority and transferred to SAP Event Management.

Application Object Type – Work Order

From Transaction /SAPTRX/ASC0AO select the business process type esc_wrkord. Select Define Application Object Type and then PMF10_ORDER. The tabs that need maintenance are General data and Event Management Relevance.

► In the General Data tab (Figure 7.6):

　► Select the SAP Event Management logical system in the Event Manager field.

　► Select the Object Type BUS2048 for Manufacturing Order.

　► Select Bus. Object Extractor PMF10_ORDER.

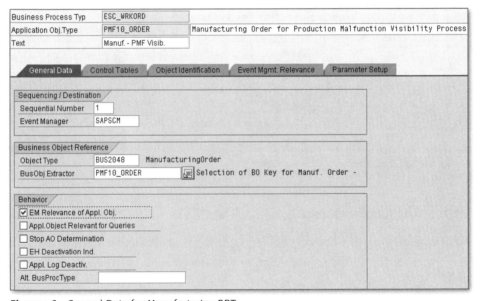

Figure 7.6 General Data for Manufacturing BPT

- In the Control Tables tab:
  - Define the main table WO_HEADER_NEW.
- In the Object Identification tab:
  - Select the AO ID field as order number– AUFNR.
- In the Event Management Relevance tab:
  - Check the code behind the relevance function module `PMF10_ORDER` by clicking on the local ABAP icon. The code comes with a default check of order type 10 (production order) or 40 (process order). In addition the code, also check if the order has been released (Figure 7.7).

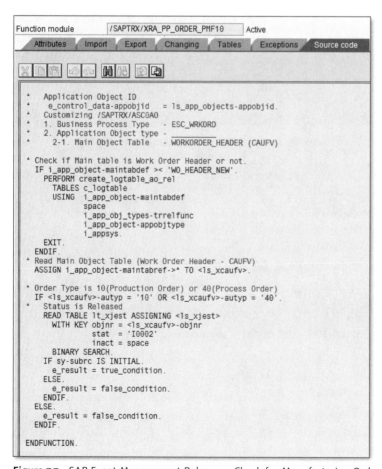

Figure 7.7 SAP Event Management Relevancy Check for Manufacturing Order

▶ In the Parameter Setup tab (Figure 7.8):

  ▶ Select the tracking object as manufacturing order number.

  ▶ Select PMF10_ORDER for the info, control, query, and expected events.

  ▶ In the expected event function module, the defined expected events are release, start, and finish, whereas the deliver (goods receipt) event is calculated in SAP Event Management.

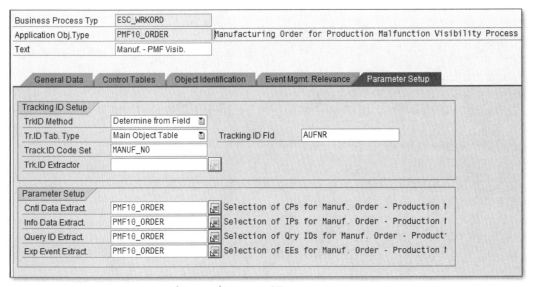

Business Process Typ	ESC_WRKORD	
Application Obj.Type	PMF10_ORDER	Manufacturing Order for Production Malfunction Visibility Process
Text	Manuf. - PMF Visib.	

General Data | Control Tables | Object Identification | Event Mgmt. Relevance | **Parameter Setup**

Tracking ID Setup

TrkID Method	Determine from Field		
Tr.ID Tab. Type	Main Object Table	Tracking ID Fld	AUFNR
Track.ID Code Set	MANUF_NO		
Trk.ID Extractor			

Parameter Setup

Cntl Data Extract.	PMF10_ORDER	Selection of CPs for Manuf. Order - Production
Info Data Extract.	PMF10_ORDER	Selection of IPs for Manuf. Order - Production
Query ID Extract.	PMF10_ORDER	Selection of Qry IDs for Manuf. Order - Product
Exp Event Extract.	PMF10_ORDER	Selection of EEs for Manuf. Order - Production

Figure 7.8 Parameters for Manufacturing AOT

Application Object Type – Notification

From Transaction /SAPTRX/ASC0AO select the business process type epl_notif. Select Define Application Object Type and then PMF10_NOTIF. The tabs that need maintenance are General Data and Event Management Relevance.

► In the General Data tab (Figure 7.9):

  ► Select the SAP Event Management logical system in the Event Manager field.

► In the Control Tables tab:

  ► Define the Main table NOTIFICATION_HEADER_NEW.

► In the Object Identification tab:

  ► Select the AO ID field as Notification number –QMNUM.

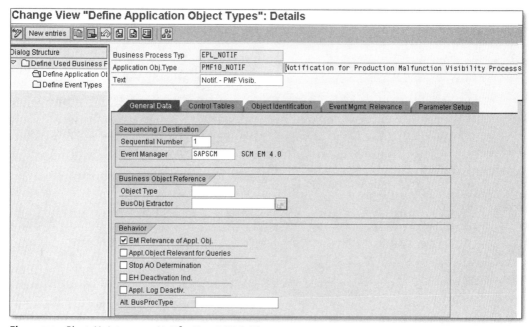

Figure 7.9 Plant Maintenance Notification AOT Settings

► In the Event Management Relevance tab (Figure 7.10):

  ► You can check the SAP Event Management relevancy either by using a function module condition or via the condition editor. For this scenario, define the condition values that are applicable for your company scenario.

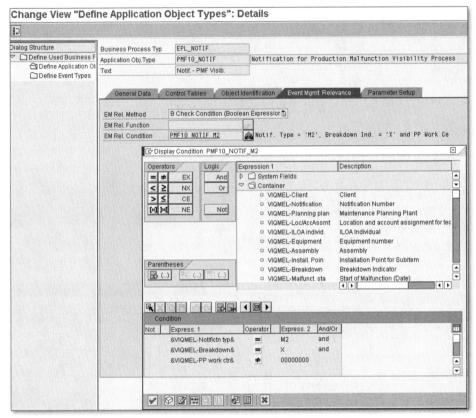

Figure 7.10 Condition Editor for Notification Relevancy for SAP Event Management

7.2.3 Event Types

Event types determine whether a change to a business object is relevant to SAP Event Management toward creation and posting of event message in SAP Event Management. Several event types can be assigned to one BPT. These are then processed according to their priority and transferred to SAP Event Management.

Event Type – Work Order

From Transaction /SAPTRX/ASC0AO select the business process type esc_wrkord. Select Define Event Types and then PMF10_ORDER. The tabs that need maintenance are General data and Event Management Relevance.

▸ In the General Data tab:

▸ In the Event Data Extractor field enter PMF10_ORDER. This function module commences once the event type passes the SAP Event Management relevancy check similar to application object type. The function module reports the business events (Table 7.2) based on the tracking ID of manufacturing number. Figure 7.11 shows a sample code of the manufacturing order finish written on the function module.

Business Process Type	Event Type	Event Messages
ESC_WRKORD (manufacturing order)	PMF10_ORDER	Manufacturing order release: REL_MANUF_ORD
		Manufacturing order start: START_MANUF_ORD
		Manufacturing order finish: FINISH_MANUF_ORD
		Manufacturing order deliver: DELIV_MANUF_ORD
		Manufacturing order reschedule: RESCHED_MANUF_ORD

Table 7.2 Event Message Reported from Manufacturing Event Type

▸ In the Event Management Relevance tab:

▸ Check the code behind the relevance function module `PMF10_ORDER` by clicking the local ABAP icon. The code comes with a default check of order type 10 (production order) or 40 (process order). In addition to the code, also check if the order has been released (Figure 7.7).

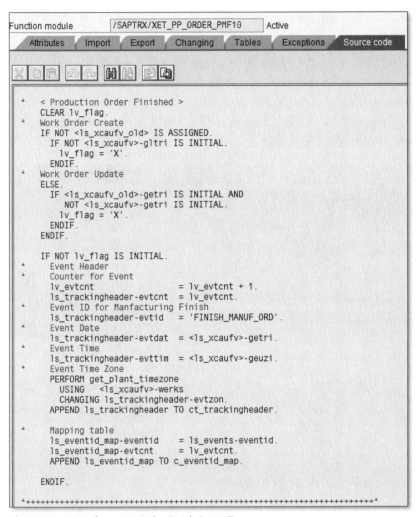

```
Function module        /SAPTRX/XET_PP_ORDER_PMF10      Active

   Attributes     Import     Export     Changing     Tables     Exceptions     Source code


*    < Production Order Finished >
     CLEAR lv_flag.
*    Work Order Create
     IF NOT <ls_xcaufv_old> IS ASSIGNED.
       IF NOT <ls_xcaufv>-gltri IS INITIAL.
         lv_flag = 'X'.
       ENDIF.
*    Work Order Update
     ELSE.
       IF <ls_xcaufv_old>-getri IS INITIAL AND
          NOT <ls_xcaufv>-getri IS INITIAL.
         lv_flag = 'X'.
       ENDIF.
     ENDIF.

     IF NOT lv_flag IS INITIAL.
*      Event Header
*      Counter for Event
       lv_evtcnt                  = lv_evtcnt + 1.
       ls_trackingheader-evtcnt   = lv_evtcnt.
*      Event ID for Manfacturing Finish
       ls_trackingheader-evtid    = 'FINISH_MANUF_ORD'.
*      Event Date
       ls_trackingheader-evtdat   = <ls_xcaufv>-getri.
*      Event Time
       ls_trackingheader-evttim   = <ls_xcaufv>-geuzi.
*      Event Time Zone
       PERFORM get_plant_timezone
         USING    <ls_xcaufv>-werks
         CHANGING ls_trackingheader-evtzon.
       APPEND ls_trackingheader TO ct_trackingheader.

*      Mapping table
       ls_eventid_map-eventid     = ls_events-eventid.
       ls_eventid_map-evtcnt      = lv_evtcnt.
       APPEND ls_eventid_map TO c_eventid_map.

     ENDIF.

*+++++++++++++++++++++++++++++++++++++++++++++++++++++++++++++++++++++++++*
```

Figure 7.11 *Manufacturing Order Finish Event Type*

Event Type – Notification

From Transaction /SAPTRX/ASC0AO select the business process type epl_notif. Select Define Event Types and then PMF10_NOTIF. The tabs that need maintenance are General Data and Event Management Relevance.

▶ In the General Data tab:

▶ In the Event Data Extractor field enter PMF10_NOTIF. This function module commences once the event type passes the SAP Event Management relevancy check similar to application object type. The function module reports the business events (Table 7.3) based on tracking ID of notification number. The code reads the notification status from table listed in Transaction code BS23 as:

▶ I0068 OSNO Outstanding Notification

▶ I0070 NOPR Notification In Process

▶ I0072 NOCO Notification Completed

▶ I0154 TSOS Task Outstanding

▶ I0155 TSRL Task Released

▶ I0156 TSCO Task Completed

Business Process Type	Event Type	Event Messages
EPL_NOTIF (notification number)	PMF10_NOTIF	Machine breakdown: MACH_BREAK
		Notification in process: MALF_NOTIF_IN_PROC
		Release malfunction task: REL_MALF_TASK
		Complete malfunction task: COMPL_MALF_TASK
		Complete notification: COMPL_MALF_NOTIF

Table 7.3 Event Message Reported from Plant Maintenance Event Type

▶ In the Event Management Relevance tab (Figure 7.10):

▶ You can check the SAP Event Management relevancy either by using a function module condition or via the condition editor. For this scenario, define the condition values that are applicable for your company scenario.

7.3   SAP SCM Configuration

The configuration in SAP SCM can be divided into four components:

▶ **Event handler**
Monitoring of events in both manufacturing and plant maintenance

▶ **Reaction to event**
Identifying follow-up activities after event message posting in SAP Event Management

▶ **Web communication with authorization model:**
Displaying events on the Web

▶ **Analytics**
Measuring metrics

7.3.1   Event Handler

For our scenario, we have two independent event handlers created in SAP Event Management: one for monitoring and management of manufacturing orders and the other for monitoring the malfunction notification completion by the plant maintenance team. The unexpected event machine breakdown during the manufacturing process triggers the creation of a second event handler. The configuration of the event handler involves objects described below.

Event Codes

List all of the expected and unexpected event codes that will be reported from the application system. For our scenario, the expected events are listed in Table 7.4. In Transaction SPRO follow the menu path EVENT MANAGEMENT • EVENT HANDLERS AND EVENT HANDLER DATA • CODES • EVENT CODES.

Expected Event Profile

The profile defines which expected events you want to track according to the planned milestone in sequence. The profile also helps in developing dependencies across events. For example, deliver manufacturing order is calculated based on finish manufacturing order.

Event Handler	Event Codes
PMF10_ORDER	Manufacturing order release: REL_MANUF_ORD
	Manufacturing order start: START_MANUF_ORD
	Manufacturing order finish: FINISH_MANUF_ORD
	Manufacturing order deliver: DELIV_MANUF_ORD
	Manufacturing order reschedule:- RESCHED_MANUF_ORD
PMF10_NOTIF	Machine breakdown: MACH_BREAK
	Notification in process: MALF_NOTIF_IN_PROC
	Release malfunction task: REL_MALF_TASK
	Complete malfunction task: COMPL_MALF_TASK
	Complete notification: COMPL_MALF_NOTIF

Table 7.4 Event Codes for Manufacturing Malfunction Scenario

Figure 7.12 shows the two expected event profiles created for the scenario.

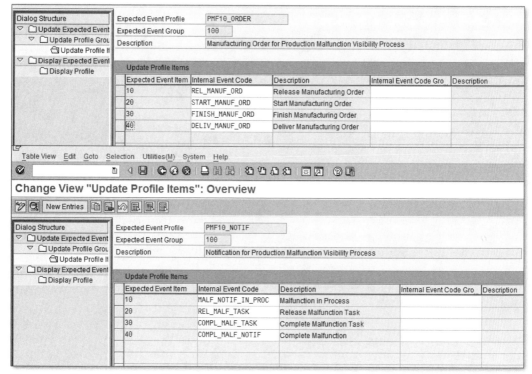

Figure 7.12 Expected Event Profiles

In the profile, there is an option for defining an expected message date in addition to the normal expected event date. This serves as the latest tolerance to the expected event date. The expected event date can be posted from the application system or can be calculated based on another event. Tolerances can also be set for calculating the earliest and latest expected event dates. Figure 7.13 shows the example of mapping the SAP Event Management event code FINISH_MANUF_ORD with the FINISH_WRKORD event message code posted from the application system with a tolerance of two hours. Figure 7.14 shows the example of internal event code calculation within SAP Event Management from a relative event. The expected event code DELIV_MANUF_ORD is calculated from the previous event FINISH_WRKORD in SAP Event Management.

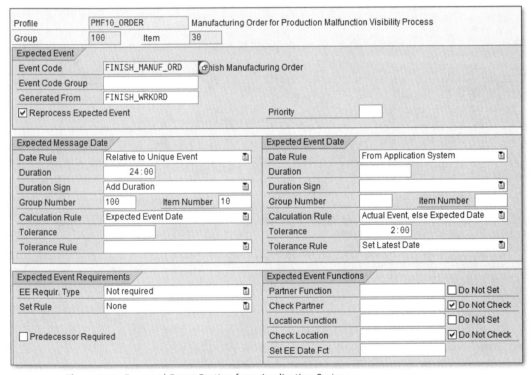

Figure 7.13 Expected Event Posting from Application System

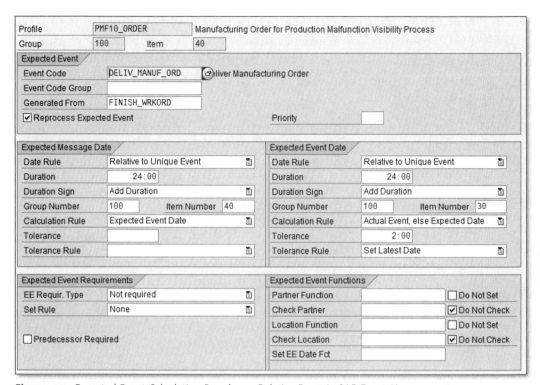

| Profile | PMF10_ORDER | Manufacturing Order for Production Malfunction Visibility Process |
| Group | 100 | Item | 40 |

Expected Event

Event Code	DELIV_MANUF_ORD	Deliver Manufacturing Order
Event Code Group		
Generated From	FINISH_WRKORD	
☑ Reprocess Expected Event		Priority	

Expected Message Date

Date Rule	Relative to Unique Event
Duration	24:00
Duration Sign	Add Duration
Group Number	100	Item Number	40
Calculation Rule	Expected Event Date
Tolerance	
Tolerance Rule	

Expected Event Date

Date Rule	Relative to Unique Event
Duration	24:00
Duration Sign	Add Duration
Group Number	100	Item Number	30
Calculation Rule	Actual Event, else Expected Date
Tolerance	2:00
Tolerance Rule	Set Latest Date

Expected Event Requirements

EE Requir. Type	Not required
Set Rule	None
☐ Predecessor Required	

Expected Event Functions

Partner Function		☐ Do Not Set
Check Partner		☑ Do Not Check
Location Function		☐ Do Not Set
Check Location		☑ Do Not Check
Set EE Date Fct		

Figure 7.14 Expected Event Calculation Based on a Relative Event in SAP Event Management

Within the expected event profile, we can also configure expected event monitor activity, which monitors the expected event getting completed according to the defined milestones. The overdue events can be pulled from the overdue list report in SAP Event Management (Transaction code /SAPTRX/EE_OVD_LIST).

Parameter Mapping

By assigning the parameter mapping area, we can define how the parameter information coming from the application system can be mapped with parameters defined in SAP Event Management. The configuration is done with Transaction /SAPTRX/TSCOPDM. In Transaction SPRO, follow the menu path EVENT

MANAGEMENT • EVENT HANDLERS AND EVENT HANDLER DATA • PARAMETERS • DEFINE PARAMETER MAPPING. To assign the mapping profile to the application system, copy the existing entries for AO type PMF10_ORDER and PMF10_NOTIF and enter the application system (Figure 7.15).

Change View "Assign Profile to Mapping Area": Overview of Selected Set

Dialog Structure	Assign Profile to Mapping Area			
▽ ☐ Define Mapping Profile	ApplSystem	AO Type	MapProfile	Error Mode
▽ ☐ Control Parameter M	SAPECC	PMF10_NOTIF	PMF10_NOTIF	Map parameter if possible, otherwise assign input parameter▣
☐ Mapping Values f	SAPECC	PMF10_ORDER	PMF10_ORDER	Map parameter if possible, otherwise assign input parameter▣
▽ ☐ Info Parameter Mapp				
☐ Mapping Values f				▣
☐ Default Parameters				▣
☐ Assign Profile to Mappin|				▣

Figure 7.15 Parameter Mapping Between Application System and SAP Event Management

Status

Status attributes help in defining the different statuses for the event handler. Three status attributes (Figure 7.16) are defined for our scenario:

▶ Manufacturing order status

▶ Manufacturing breakdown status

▶ Notification status

The status attribute is then attached with two status profiles. The first profile is for the Production Planner role where the manufacturing order status and manufacturing breakdown status attributes are attached, whereas the Production Supervisor role is associated with the malfunction notification status attribute.

Event Handler

Two event handler types are defined for the scenario. Each event hander (Figure 7.17) is assigned to one business process type that is sent from the application system. The condition applies where the event handler checks the relevancy on the

SAP Event Management side. Various profiles (i.e., expected event profile, status attribute, rule set, BW profile, authorization profile) are attached within the event handler and the unexpected event code. The unexpected event code (Table 7.5) checks if the event message reported from the application system is unexpected.

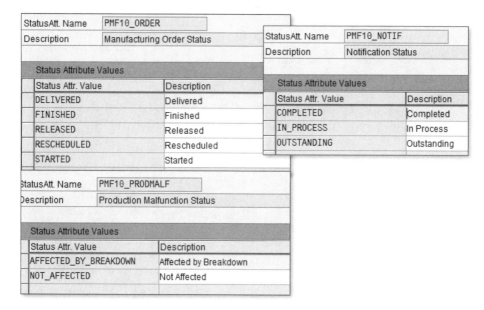

Figure 7.16 Status Attribute Values

Event Handler	Unexpected Event Codes
PMF10_ORDER	Machine breakdown: MACH_BREAK Reschedule manufacturing order: RESCHED_MANUF_ORD BW upload: BWUPLOAD
PMF10_NOTIF	Machine breakdown: MACH_BREAK BW upload: BWUPLOAD

Table 7.5 Unexpected Event Codes

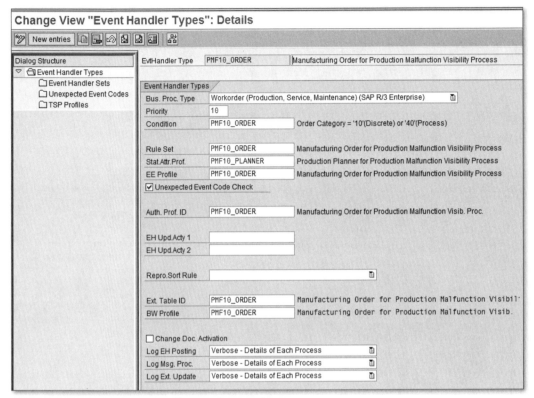

Figure 7.17 Event Handler Type for Manufacturing

Event Handler Set

The event handler set (Figure 7.18) is configured to give visibility across the two event handlers. The set helps in grouping logical events to give complete visibility of end-to-end business process flow. The two-step configuration involves:

▶ Defining event handler set relations, which are assigned to the event handler set profile. In Transaction SPRO, follow the menu path EVENT MANAGEMENT • EVENT HANDLERS • DEFINE EVENT HANDLER SET PROFILES.

▶ Defining the event handler set profile, which is assigned to the event handler type. Both the manufacturing and notification event handler is defined with common event handler set relation. In Transaction SPRO, follow the menu path EVENT MANAGEMENT • EVENT HANDLERS • DEFINE EVENT HANDLER SET PROFILES.

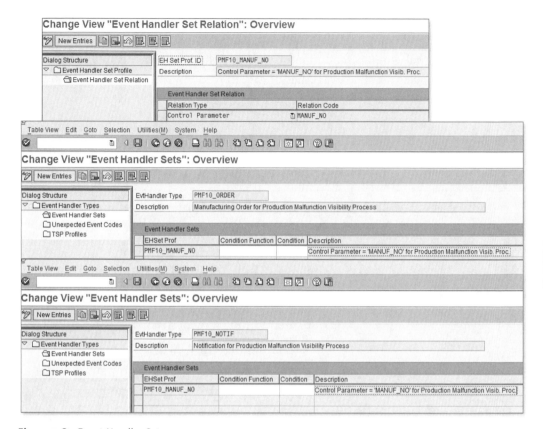

Figure 7.18 Event Handler Set

7.3.2 Reaction to Event

Rules are executed via a rule set when the event messages are reported from the application system. When an event message arrives, the type of the event handler is determined. The relevant rule is embedded in the event handler type, and the condition can be defined for the rule. The condition can determine to execute the rule or not.

You perform the configuration in Transaction /SAPTRX/TSC0TR by selecting the rule sets PMF10_ORDER and PMF10_NOTIF. Figure 7.19 shows rule sets maintained for manufacturing and plant maintenance. Maintain the relevant rule conditions and activities. It's highly recommended that you efficiently code the sequence of activities within the rule set because they can become performance hogs. The use of true or false in the condition for each rule eliminates the need to run through all of the rules when an event message is received from application systems. Table 7.6 lists the rule activities and the tasks associated with each activity.

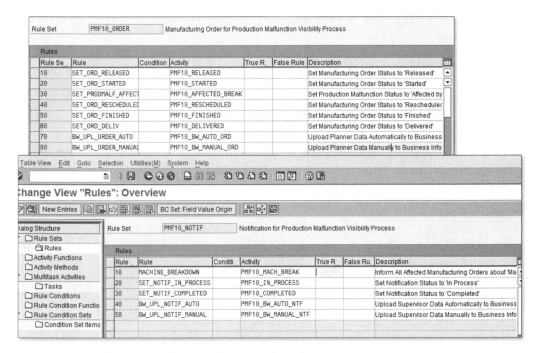

Figure 7.19 Rule Set for Manufacturing and Notification Event Messages

Rule Activity	Tasks
PMF10_RELEASED	Event code check: EVENT_CODE_CHECK
PMF10_STARTED	Status update: STATUS_CHECK
PMF10_AFFECTED_BREAK	
PMF10_RESCHEDULED	
PMF10_FINISHED	
PMF10_DELIVERED	

Table 7.6 Rule Activity and Tasks

Rule Activity	Tasks
PMF10_BW_AUTO_ORD	Event code check: EVENT_CODE_CHECK BW upload: BW_UPLOAD BW upload error log: ERROR_MESSAGE_LOG
PMF10_BW_MANUAL_ORD	Event code check: EVENT_CODE_CHECK Status update: STATUS_CHECK BW upload: BW_UPLOAD BW upload error log: ERROR_MESSAGE_LOG
PMF10_MACH_BREAK	Event code check: EVENT_CODE_CHECK Event reporting: IS_EVENT_REPORTED APO create alert: SEND_PPDS_APO_ALERT
PMF10_IN_PROCESS	Event code check: EVENT_CODE_CHECK EH status update: STATUS_CHECK EH set status update: EHSET_STATUS_CHECK
PMF10_COMPLETED	Event code check: EVENT_CODE_CHECK EH status update: STATUS_CHECK APO delete alert: SEND_PPDS_APO_ALERT
PMF10_BW_AUTO_NTF	Event code check: EVENT_CODE_CHECK BW upload: BW_UPLOAD BW upload error log: ERROR_MESSAGE_LOG
PMF10_BW_MANUAL_NTF	Event code check: EVENT_CODE_CHECK Status update: STATUS_CHECK BW upload: BW_UPLOAD BW upload error log: ERROR_MESSAGE_LOG

Table 7.6 Rule Activity and Tasks (Cont.)

The activity task EVENT_CODE_CHECK is an SAP-delivered activity that takes the parameter internal event code and returns a zero value if the internal code is the same, or else returns nonzero. Similarly, activity task STATUS_SET takes two parameters as inputs — the status attribute name and the value, which are pre-configured in the status profile. SEND_PPDS_APO_ALERT creates and deletes SAP APO alerts for monitoring in alert monitor. BW_UPLOAD extracts and loads the data into SAP NetWeaver BW.

7.3.3 Web Communication Layer (WCL) with Authorization Model

The Web Communication Layer (WCL) enables a web platform for business partners to communicate directly using SAP Event Management. You can use the WCL can be used for both business process status retrieval and event reporting. The WCL offered as a separate software package communicates to SAP Event Management using Java Server Page (JSP) technology. The SAP-delivered and SAP designed WCL screen sequence (Figure 7.20) is fixed, but more screens can be designed using Java coding.

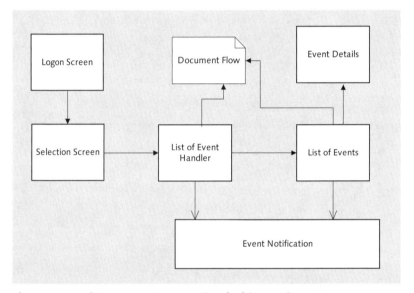

Figure 7.20 Web Communication Layer Standard Screens Sequence

Authorization

Next, let's look at the settings for event reporting and status retrieval in the WCL. We can use Authorization Profile to customize the contents that are displayed and the options for confirming events, for example, if a partner is only allowed to see the manufacturing orders. Also, we can use Filter Profile to customize the contents that are displayed and options for confirming events, for example, which event handler field information can be seen by business partners.

The available roles in SAP Event Management (Transaction PFCG) are:

▶ **/SAPTRX/SAP_EM_USER** – The user of this activity group can:

  ▶ Run reports for displaying event handler data

  ▶ Enter and send event messages

  ▶ Update event handler data by reporting events

▶ **/SAPTRX/SAP_EM_ADMIN** – The user of his activity group can perform following event handler activities:

  ▶ Configure the settings for creating event handlers

  ▶ Run reports for displaying or changing event handler data

  ▶ Run reports for monitoring event handlers

  ▶ Send event messages to SAP Event Management

The available authorization objects are:

▶ X_EM_EH (display event handler)

▶ X_EM_EH_CH (change event handler data)

▶ X_EM_EVM (send event messages)

The production planner role has mrp_area, mrp_controller, plant, and production scheduler as parameters built for authorization, whereas the production supervisor role has plant and work_center as authorization parameters (Figure 7.21).

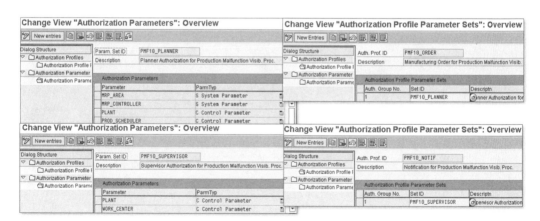

Figure 7.21 Authorization Profile in SAP Event Management

Two filter profiles are available for this visibility scenario — pmf10_planner for the production planner and pmf10_supervisor for the production supervisor. The filter profile can be assigned to the user role or to the user directly to ensure that only the appropriate event handler components are displayed to the user.

Users can only log on to the web interface if they have been assigned to a user profile. For each WCL transaction, assign the user profile of choice and give it in order of display (Figure 7.22). Assign the relevant web interface transactions and user profiles to the users. If changes are made to the profiles and layouts in customizing, the profiles needs to be reloaded in the web interface. The profile can be manually reloaded on the web interface admin page (Figure 7.22).

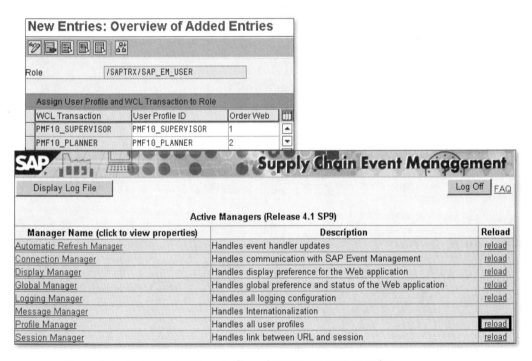

Figure 7.22 Assignment of User Profile and WCL Transaction to Roles

7.3.4   Analytics

The initial setup for BW extraction is similar to the steps outlined in Section 6.4.5 in Chapter 6. In this section, we'll focus on the BW initial and delta upload activities for analytics.

There are two options for the upload: manual upload or upload via process chain. In both the cases, we have to specify the following selection criteria for all three info packages to restrict the upload related to the scenario: eh_type = pmf10_notif and eh_type = pmf10_order.

▶ **Manual upload**

Schedule the InfoPackage for Delta Initialization for all three InfoSources (0SCEM_1, 0SCEM_2, and 0SCEM_3).

  ▶ The data will be transferred to the respective Operational Data Store (ODS) objects. To transfer the data to the InfoCubes, you have to perform the following steps:

  ▶ Wait until all three ODS (0EM_DS01, 0EM_DS02, and 0EM_DS03) are active.

  ▶ Transfer the data for the two ODS (0EM_DS02 and 0EM_DS03) manually to the corresponding InfoCube (0EM_C03).

▶ **Upload via process chain**

To simplify the manual upload steps listed above, a predefined process chain is delivered. This process chain triggers the automatic data upload from SAP Event Management to SAP NetWeaver BW (directly from the setup tables in SAP Event Management to the InfoCube 0EM_C02 in SAP NetWeaver BW).

  ▶ Select Edit Process Chains (CTRL + SHIFT + F7). In the left-hand frame, navigate to:

  ▶ SCEM folder: Grouping, SCEM: Process Chain for Delta Initialization. Select EXECUTE (F8).

The data from the setup tables in SAP Event Management is uploaded to SAP NetWeaver BW and is transferred all the way to the InfoCube. After the initial upload has been completed, the setup tables should be initialized again to free the obsolete database space.

7.4 Scenario Monitoring in SAP Event Management 5.1

The production supervisor, together with his team, is responsible for ensuring that the plan created by the production planner is carried out. Their area of responsibility extends across a production area or one or more production lines. They check the availability of resources (production lines and machines, materials, and personnel), distribute the tasks and work packages, release them for execution, and monitor their execution and their confirmation. The supervisor initiates the correction of malfunctions and deviations, documents them, and makes usage decisions for in-process quality inspections. The production supervisor has personnel responsibility and sometimes also cost center responsibility for his area. Using various forms of analysis, the supervisor checks whether the following goals are being met in his area:

▶ Optimal use of resources (production lines and machines, materials, and personnel)

▶ Provision of the required quantities of a product at the correct time

▶ Maintenance of the required product quality

As required, the production supervisor initiates or coordinates the necessary improvements, for example, maintenance tasks.

As this visibility process brings together information from different areas, it consists of two independent tracks: Manufacturing order handling status provides information about the progression of the production process, whereas the notification status provides information about the malfunction handling. The status values change when particular events are reported from the application system.

For this scenario, the following evaluations are available in SAP NetWeaver BW:

► Number of manufacturing orders affected by a machine breakdown

  ► The report contains the relevant key figures describing how many manufacturing orders were endangered by a machine breakdown.

  ► The information is collected in the notification event handler. The report provides information about the number of manufacturing orders that were affected by a machine breakdown. The number varies depending on the release time chosen and the absolute number and duration of the manufacturing orders. It does, however, indicate the extent to which the production planner had to intervene.

► Number of machine breakdowns that affected a manufacturing order

  ► The report responds to how many machine breakdowns have affected a manufacturing order.

  ► The report provides information about the number of machine breakdowns that affected a manufacturing order. The number varies depending on the release time chosen and the duration of the manufacturing orders. It does, however, allow you to draw conclusions about possible weak spots in the production process.

► Frequency of rescheduling of manufacturing orders

  ► By evaluating the number of times a released manufacturing order has been rescheduled, you can draw conclusions about the quality of planning and, in connection with the number of machine breakdowns, find both weak spots and possible potential for improvements to the machine infrastructure.

The document program in the SAP ERP system can make a remote function call (RFC) to provide the visibility of the event handler in the document that is concerned with this particular set of events (Figure 7.23).

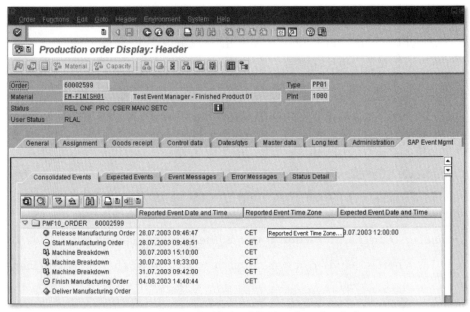

Figure 7.23 SAP Event Management Embedded in R/3 Manufacturing Order

The planner can also log on to the WCL (Figure 7.24) to view the status of his manufacturing orders.

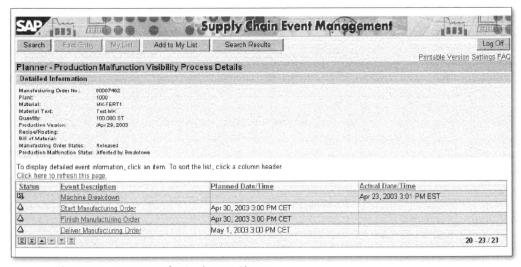

Figure 7.24 WCL View for Production Planner

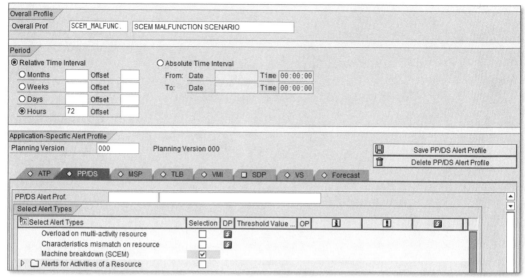

Figure 7.25 SAP APO Alert for Machine Breakdown in Alert Profile

In the exceptional situation of a machine breakdown, SAP APO PP/DS alert (Figure 7.25) available on the SAP APO alert monitor, which is updated as a follow-up activity from the rule set. The alert is generated via activity function SEND_PPDS_APO_ALERT in the rule set.

7.5   Summary

The production malfunction visibility process covers machine breakdowns within the production process and aims to fill the gaps between planning and execution systems. This chapter provided an overview of the customization steps necessary to set up the monitoring and handling scenario with follow-up activities and BW analytics.

The next chapter focuses on the order-to-cash business process setup in SAP Event Management for better customer service and satisfaction during the order fulfillment business process.

SAP Event Management offers increased visibility of real-time status of orders, deliveries, billing, and proof of delivery information with the overall goal of reducing cycle time from order placement till collection of cash. This chapter describes in detail the customization steps and monitoring capabilities for the scenario in SAP Event Management 5.1.

8 Setting Up an Order-to-Cash Scenario

Cash is king. It's also the lifeblood of any company, and it flows through an order-to-cash cycle. The order-to-cash business process is at the heart of any company's supply chain. Industry research has indicated that improving the performance of the order fulfillment process translates to better business performance and competitive industry advantage. Ensuring the smooth flow of order-to-cash business processes (receiving the order, fulfilling the order, billing, and getting paid) is vitally important, yet companies face significant challenges in controlling orders as they progress through the entire fulfillment process. In the current business environment, users lack near real-time visibility of the steps involved in this end-to-end process. Business users are constantly challenged by an inability to sense upstream and downstream changes, and the relevant data is not easily linked back to the order-to-cash process.

SAP Event Management offers the end-to-end business process visibility for monitoring of sales orders, deliveries, invoices, and proof of deliveries. Exception management and other functional area integration provides full transparency among business partners of the sales documents' status. The objective of this chapter is to walk through the configurations required for setting up the SAP Event Management monitoring functionality for the order-to-cash business process.

8.1 Business Scenario

Whereas every company has a unique order-to-cash business model, most companies face similar kinds of challenges related to inventory accuracy, on-time delivery, freight costs, and labor productivity. The business process requires tight integration of the order management team with transportation, logistics, and finance for delivering orders as promised. There are many key challenges for which companies are looking for a supply chain visibility tool:

▶ Order information is inaccurate, making it impossible to assign a correct delivery date due to poor planning.

▶ Insufficient lead time and multiple-line-item handling process.

▶ Sales orders material availability check issues with inventory shortages.

▶ Freight consolidation issues by not loading the transportation vehicles efficiently for specific transportation routes.

▶ Orders are processed manually instead of automatically in background.

▶ Orders are changed multiple times during the sales orders, deliveries, shipment, goods issue, or invoice stages.

The order-to-cash visibility process (Figure 8.1) aims to provide visibility into order management processing, from the time sales orders are received in the SAP system for processing into the outbound processing at the warehouse until the time when the customers post the proof of delivery and are invoiced.

The process requires all of the sub-processes be executed with a high percentage of reliability to maintain the commitment given to customers on delivery dates. This aligns with the corporate strategy of *perfect order* fulfillment, which is defined as the percentage of orders that are delivered in full and on time to the initial request and/or commit date and match the customer documentation (invoice, purchase order, receipt).

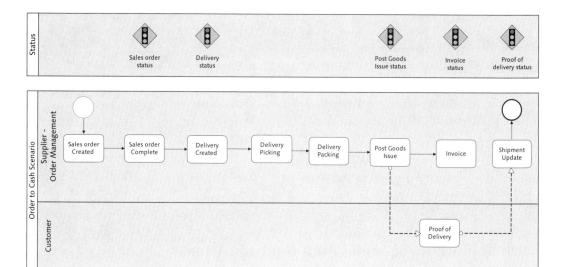

Figure 8.1 Order-to-Cash Business Scenario

The goal of SAP Event Management in order-to-cash business operations is to:

▶ Reduce supply chain costs (expedite shipments) by resolving disruptions and discrepancies more effectively and identifying the root cause.

▶ Minimize customer impact and reduce lost sales due to cancelled or disputed orders by being alert to problems well in advance.

▶ Focus on automation toward exception by management and ensuring that all the sales orders and deliveries are processed in a timely manner.

Table 8.1 lists the business events that are planned in the order-to-cash scenario. Depending on the business priority, the user may opt to monitor only a few critical events from the list.

Business Process Event	Type of Event	Event Status	Notification
Sales order created	Expected	Sales order created	
Sales order block	Unexpected	Sales order block	Email to order management

Table 8.1 Expected and Unexpected Events Related to the Scenario

Business Process Event	Type of Event	Event Status	Notification
Delivery date late (outside tolerance)	Unexpected	Delivery date late	Email to order management
Sales order complete	Expected	Sales order complete	
Delivery created	Expected	Delivery create	
Delivery delay	Unexpected	Delivery delay	Email to order management
Delivery picking	Expected	Delivery pick	
Delivery packing	Expected	Delivery pack	
Post goods issue	Expected	Delivery goods issue	
Shipment created	Expected	Shipment created	
Invoice created	Expected	Invoice created	
Proof of delivery (POD) received	Expected	POD received	

Table 8.1 Expected and Unexpected Events Related to the Scenario (Cont.)

8.2 SAP ECC Configuration

The SAP ECC configuration involves customization of three objects: business process type, application object type, and event type.

8.2.1 Business Process Type

In this scenario, one event handler is created for each sales order (or sales order schedule line item). The SAP-delivered business process types you can be used for the scenario are:

- ESC_SORDER: sales order
- ESC_DELIV: delivery
- ESC_SHIPMT: shipment
- ESC_SD_INVOICE: SD invoice

The event handler is created during the sales order save, so EH Create is selected only for ESC_SORDER, whereas EMsg Send is selected for all of the BPTs. All the business process types (sales orders, delivery, shipment, invoice) sends the event message to SAP Event Management (Figure 8.2). In SAP ECC Transaction SPRO, follow the menu path INTEGRATION WITH OTHER MYSAP.COM COMPONENTS • EVENT MANAGEMENT INTERFACE • DEFINE APPLICATION INTERFACES • DEFINE BUSINESS PROCESS TYPES.

Change View "Define Business Process Types": Overview

New Entries

Dialog Structure
▽ Define Business Proces
  Define Available Appl

Define Business Process Types

BPT	EH Create	EMsg Send	Descriptn
EPL_EQUIPMT	☐	☐	Equipment in SAP R/3 Enterprise
EPL_INSPLOT	☐	☐	Inspection Lot in SAP R/3 Enterprise
EPL_NOTIF	☐	☐	Notification in SAP R/3 Enterprise
ESC_DELIV	☐	☑	Delivery in SAP R/3 Enterprise
ESC_FI_CLEARING	☐	☐	FI Clearing in SAP R/3 Enterprise
ESC_HAND_UNIT	☐	☐	Handling unit
ESC_MATDOC	☐	☐	Material Document in SAP R/3 Enterprise
ESC_MM_INVOICE	☐	☐	MM Invoice in SAP R/3 Enterprise
ESC_PURORD	☐	☐	Purchase Order in SAP R/3 Enterprise
ESC_PURORD_FASHION	☐	☐	Purchase Order (Seasonal Procurement) in SAP R/3 Enterprise 2.0
ESC_PURREQ	☐	☐	Purchase Requisition in SAP R/3 Enterprise
ESC_SD_INVOICE	☐	☑	SD Invoice in SAP R/3 Enterprise
ESC_SHIPMT	☐	☑	Shipment (SAP R/3 Enterprise)
ESC_SORDER	☑	☑	Sales Order in SAP R/3 Enterprise
ESC_WOGMVT	☐	☐	Workorder Goods Movements (Production,Service,Maintenance) in SAP R/3 Enterp
ESC_WRKORC	☐	☐	Workorder Confirmation (Production, Service, Maintenance) in SAP R/3 Enterprise
ESC_WRKORD	☐	☐	Workorder (Production, Service, Maintenance) in SAP R/3 Enterprise

Figure 8.2 Business Process Types for Order-to-Cash Scenario

Within the BPTs, the sample application tables that are used are:

- **ESC_SORDER**
  VBAP, VBAK, VBPA, VBUP, VBFA, KOMV,VBEP, VBUK

- **ESC_DELIV**
  VBUK,LIKP, LIPS, VBFA, VEKP, VEPO, VBPA

▶ **ESC_SHIPMT**

VTTP, VTTS, VTSP, VTTK, VBPA, VEKP, VEPO, LIPS, LIKP, SADR

▶ **ESC_SD_INVOICE**

VBRK, VBRP, VBPA, KONV

SAP offers various processing models for the BPT to help you understand the application interface (Figure 8.3). The possible options are:

▶ **Active**

The application objects of the BPT are processed, and communication to SAP Event Management is established to control the event handlers.

▶ **Inactive**

The application objects of this BPT are not processed. This mode can be used to generally switch off the connection to SAP Event Management for the BPT.

▶ **Maintenance**

The application objects of the BPT are processed, but no data is sent to SAP Event Management. Instead, the extracted control and info parameters and the expected event milestone tags are inserted into the parameter definitions of the corresponding plug-in functions.

Define Used Business Process Types			
Bus. Proc. Type	Update Mode	BPT Process Mode	Description
AII_OBJECT	Update Task (\	Active	SAP All Object
EPL_NOTIF	Update Task (\	Active	Notification in SAP R/3 Enterprise
ESC_DELIV	Update Task (\	Active	Delivery in SAP R/3 Enterprise
ESC_FI_CLEARING	Update Task (\	Active	FI Clearing in SAP R/3 Enterprise
ESC_MATDOC	Update Task (\	Active	Material Document in SAP R/3 Enterprise
ESC_MM_INVOICE	Update Task (\	Active	MM Invoice in SAP R/3 Enterprise
ESC_PRODOR	Update Task (\	Active	Production Order in SAP R/3 Enterprise
ESC_PURORD	Update Task (\	Active	Purchase Order in SAP R/3 Enterprise
ESC_PURORD_FASHION	Update Task (\	Active	Purchase Order (Seasonal Procurement) in SAP R/3 Enterprise 2.0
ESC_SHIPMT	Update Task (\	Active	Shipment (SAP R/3 Enterprise)
ESC_SORDER	Update Task (\	Simulation	Sales Order in SAP R/3 Enterprise
ESC_WRKORD	Update Task (\	Active	Workorder (Production, Service, Maintenance) in SAP R/3 Enterprise
		Inactive	
		Maintenance	
		Simulation	

Figure 8.3 Business Process Type Processing Modes

▶ **Simulation**

The application objects of the BPT are processed, and communication to SAP Event Management is established to control the event handlers. The steps of the application object handling are processed separately, and intermediate results are displayed onscreen to allow inspection of the data and communication setup. Event manager data is not stored when the simulation is done.

8.2.2 Application Object Type

The application system checks the event management relevance condition or function for an application object type following the order of the sequential numbers. The application object type is used to determine the supply chain event management relevance (SCEM relevance) of objects or processes in the application system. You determine the SCEM relevance by using a condition that you define in the application system and that you assign to an application object type. SAP Event Management processes the incoming event messages only for objects or processes that fulfill this condition.

You use the application object type (AOT) to determine the tracking IDs that identify objects. In this way, either you or a system can send internal or external messages to this object, and SAP Event Management can execute the SCEM process.

You can use the application object type to determine the control, info, and system parameters. SAP Event Management needs these for information and query purposes and to check the SCEM process.

The application system writes the application object type and the application object ID into a status table. Together with the name of the application system, they provide a unique reference between the application object and event handler. The system uses this reference to refer to the business object and its business process type. An *n*-to-one relationship exists with the business process types in the application system. To configure the order-to-cash AOT (Figure 8.4), in SAP ECC Transaction SPRO, follow the menu path INTEGRATION WITH OTHER MYSAP.COM COMPONENTS • EVENT MANAGEMENT INTERFACE • DEFINE APPLICATION INTERFACES • DEFINE USED APPL. OBJ. TYPE.

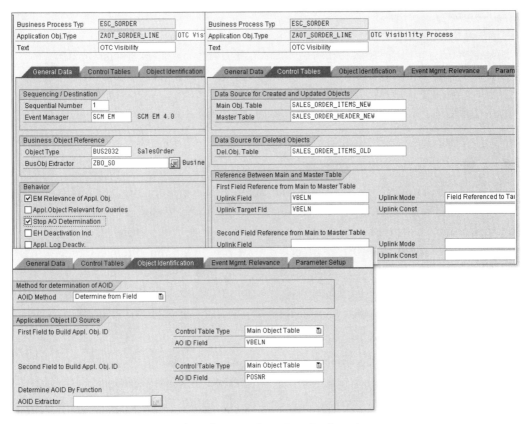

Figure 8.4 Order-to-Cash Application Object Type Configuration

In addition to the normal configuration, various ABAP functions need to be coded for the business object extractor, the SAP Event Management relevance function, and parameter (info, control) extractor functions.

Business Object Extractor

Begin by configuring the extractor ZBO_SALESORDER. In SAP ECC Transaction SPRO, follow the menu path INTEGRATION WITH OTHER MYSAP.COM COMPONENTS • EVENT MANAGEMENT INTERFACE • DEFINE APPLICATION INTERFACES • DEFINE SAP EM INTERFACE FUNCTIONS. You can create the function module ZSAPTRX_XBO_SALESOR- DER by copying from function module template /SAPTRX/BUSOBJKEY_TEMPLATE. A modified sample code may look like the following.

```
FUNCTION ZSAPTRX_XBO_SALESORDER.

*"----------------------------------------------------------
*"*"Local Interface:
*"  IMPORTING
*"     REFERENCE(AO_TYPE_DEFINITION) LIKE  /SAPTRX/AOTYPES STRUCTURE
*"         /SAPTRX/AOTYPES
*"     REFERENCE(TABLE_CONTAINER) TYPE  TRXAS_TABCONTAINER
*"     REFERENCE(AO_TYPE_DYN_DATA) TYPE  TRXAS_APPTYPE_TABS_WA
*"     REFERENCE(AO_DYN_DATA) TYPE  TRXAS_APPOBJ_CTAB_WA
*"     REFERENCE(MAIN_TABLE_STRUCT) TYPE  /SAPTRX/STRUCDATADEF
*"     REFERENCE(MAIN_TABLE_REF) TYPE REF TO  DATA
*"     REFERENCE(MASTER_TABLE_STRUCT) TYPE  /SAPTRX/STRUCDATADEF
*"     REFERENCE(MASTER_TABLE_REF) TYPE REF TO  DATA
*"  EXPORTING
*"     REFERENCE(BUSOBJ_KEY) TYPE  /SAPTRX/BUSOBJKEY
*"  TABLES
*"      TABLE_DEFINITIONS STRUCTURE  /SAPTRX/AOALLTAB
*"      BUSOBJ_KEYFIELDS STRUCTURE  SWOTDV
*"      BUSOBJ_KEYS STRUCTURE  /SAPTRX/BUSOBJ_KEY
*"      LOGTABLE STRUCTURE  BAPIRET2 OPTIONAL
*"  EXCEPTIONS
*"      DATA_MODEL_ERROR
*"      STOP_PROCESSING
*"----------------------------------------------------------
*** Generic Definitions
  DATA: ls_current_table TYPE trxas_tabcontainer_wa.
  FIELD-SYMBOLS:
        <main_table_record>.
*** Sales Order Related Definitions
  TYPES: ltyt_vbak TYPE STANDARD TABLE OF /saptrx/sd_sds_hdr.
  DATA:  ls_vbak_wa TYPE /saptrx/sd_sds_hdr.
  FIELD-SYMBOLS: <vbak_record> TYPE ltyt_vbak,
                 <vbeln> like uvbap-vbeln.
* in general, BO may consist of several key fields so a loop is used.
```

```
In this case however, there is only one.
  clear busobj_key.
  LOOP AT busobj_keys.
    READ TABLE table_definitions WITH KEY
         trk_obj_type = ao_dyn_data-trkobjtype
         dbtab = busobj_keys-tablename
         act_botab_ind = 'X'.
    IF sy-subrc <> 0.
      RAISE data_model_error.
    ENDIF.
* Get appropriate tables / records out of appl. tabl container
    ASSIGN main_table_ref->* TO <main_table_record>.
    READ TABLE table_container INTO ls_current_table
             WITH KEY tabledef = ao_type_dyn_data-maintabdef
             BINARY SEARCH.
* BO Key is Sales Order Number (VBELN)
    IF busobj_keys-tablename = 'VBAK' AND
       busobj_keys-fieldname = 'VBELN'.
* switch between several main tables
      CASE ao_type_dyn_data-maindbtabdef.
* case 1: main table = Sales Order Header
        WHEN 'VBAK'.
          ASSIGN COMPONENT 'VBELN' OF
                 STRUCTURE <main_table_record> TO <vbeln>.
          ASSIGN ls_current_table-tableref->* TO <vbak_record>.
          READ TABLE <vbak_record> INTO ls_vbak_wa
            WITH KEY vbeln = <vbeln>.
          CONCATENATE busobj_key ls_vbak_wa-vbeln
              INTO busobj_key.
      ENDCASE.
    ENDIF.
* loop over all BO key fields
  ENDLOOP.
ENDFUNCTION.
```

Application Object Type Relevance

Configure the extractor ZRA_SALESORDER. You can create the function module ZSAP-TRX_XRA_SALESORDER by copying from function module template /SAPTRX/EVMGMT_RELEV_TEMPLATE. A modified sample code may look like the following.

```
FUNCTION ZSAPTRX_XRA_SALESORDER.
*"----------------------------------------------------------------
*"*"Local Interface:
*"  IMPORTING
*"     REFERENCE(I_APPSYS) TYPE  /SAPTRX/APPLSYSTEM
*"     REFERENCE(I_APP_OBJ_TYPES) TYPE  /SAPTRX/AOTYPES
*"     REFERENCE(I_ALL_APPL_TABLES) TYPE  TRXAS_TABCONTAINER
*"     REFERENCE(I_APPTYPE_TAB) TYPE  TRXAS_APPTYPE_TABS_WA
*"     REFERENCE(I_APP_OBJECT) TYPE  TRXAS_APPOBJ_CTAB_WA
*"  EXPORTING
*"     VALUE(E_RESULT) LIKE  SY-BINPT
*"  TABLES
*"      C_LOGTABLE STRUCTURE  BAPIRET2 OPTIONAL
*"  EXCEPTIONS
*"      PARAMETER_ERROR
*"      RELEVANCE_DETERM_ERROR
*"      STOP_PROCESSING
*"----------------------------------------------------------------*
*** EVENT HANDLER RELEVANCE
  FIELD-SYMBOLS:
*   Work Structure for Sales Order Header New
    <ls_xvbak>     TYPE /saptrx/sd_sds_hdr.
* Check if Master table is Sales Order Header or not.
  IF i_app_object-mastertabdef >< 'SALES_ORDER_HEADER_NEW'.
    PERFORM create_logtable_ao_rel
      TABLES c_logtable
      USING  space
           i_app_object-mastertabdef
           i_app_obj_types-trrelfunc
```

227

```
                     i_app_object-appobjtype
                     i_appsys.
       EXIT.
     ENDIF.
* Read Master Object Table (Sales Order Header - VBAK)
     ASSIGN i_app_object-mastertabref->* TO <ls_xvbak>.
     e_result = false_condition.
     IF <ls_xvbak>-auart = 'OR'.
       e_result = true_condition.
     ENDIF.
ENDFUNCTION.
*&---------------------------------------------------------------------*
*&      Form  create_logtable_ao_rel
*&---------------------------------------------------------------------*
*       Create Log table for Tr-cd: /SAPTRX/ASAPLOG
*---------------------------------------------------------------------*
*       <-> CT_LOGTABLE        Logging table
*       --> IV_MAINTABDEF      Main table
*       --> IV_MASTERTABDEF    Master table
*       --> IV_EXTRACTOR       Extractor
*       --> IV_APPOBJTYPE      Application Object type
*       --> IV_APPSYS          Application system
*---------------------------------------------------------------------*
FORM create_logtable_ao_rel
   TABLES    ct_logtable       STRUCTURE bapiret2
   USING     iv_maintabdef     TYPE /saptrx/strucdatadef
             iv_mastertabdef   TYPE /saptrx/strucdatadef
             iv_extractor      TYPE /saptrx/trrelfunc
             iv_appobjtype     TYPE /saptrx/aotype
             iv_appsys         TYPE /saptrx/applsystem.
   DATA: ls_bapiret LIKE bapiret2.
   IF NOT iv_maintabdef IS INITIAL.
     MESSAGE ID '/SAPTRX/ASC' TYPE 'E' NUMBER 087
       WITH iv_maintabdef
```

```
            iv_extractor
            'AOT'
            iv_appobjtype
      INTO ls_bapiret-message.
    ls_bapiret-type       = 'E'.
    ls_bapiret-id         = '/SAPTRX/ASC'.
    ls_bapiret-number     = 087.
    ls_bapiret-message_v1 = iv_maintabdef.
    ls_bapiret-message_v2 = iv_extractor.
    ls_bapiret-message_v3 = 'AOT'.
    ls_bapiret-message_v4 = iv_appobjtype.
    ls_bapiret-system     = iv_appsys.
    APPEND ls_bapiret TO ct_logtable.
  ENDIF.
  IF NOT iv_mastertabdef IS INITIAL.
    MESSAGE ID '/SAPTRX/ASC' TYPE 'E' NUMBER 088
      WITH iv_mastertabdef
            iv_extractor
            'AOT'
            iv_appobjtype
      INTO ls_bapiret-message.
    ls_bapiret-type       = 'E'.
    ls_bapiret-id         = '/SAPTRX/ASC'.
    ls_bapiret-number     = 088.
    ls_bapiret-message_v1 = iv_mastertabdef.
    ls_bapiret-message_v2 = iv_extractor.
    ls_bapiret-message_v3 = 'AOT'.
    ls_bapiret-message_v4 = iv_appobjtype.
    ls_bapiret-system     = iv_appsys.
    APPEND ls_bapiret TO ct_logtable.
  ENDIF.
ENDFORM.                        " create_logtable_ao_rel
```

Control and Info Parameter Extractor

Configure the extractor ZCP_SALESORDER & ZIP_SALESORDER. You can create the function module ZSAPTRX_XCP_SALESORDER & ZSAPTRX_XIP_SALESORDER by copying from function module template /SAPTRX/CONTROL_PARAM_TEMPLATE & /SAPTRX/INFO_PARAM_TEMPLATE. A modified sample code may look like the following.

```
FUNCTION ZSAPTRX_XCP_SALESORDERLINE.
*"----------------------------------------------------------------
*"*"Local Interface:
*"  IMPORTING
*"     REFERENCE(I_APPSYS) TYPE   /SAPTRX/APPLSYSTEM
*"     REFERENCE(I_APP_OBJ_TYPES) TYPE   /SAPTRX/AOTYPES
*"     REFERENCE(I_ALL_APPL_TABLES) TYPE   TRXAS_TABCONTAINER
*"     REFERENCE(I_APP_TYPE_CNTL_TABS) TYPE   TRXAS_APPTYPE_TABS
*"     REFERENCE(I_APP_OBJECTS) TYPE   TRXAS_APPOBJ_CTABS
*"  TABLES
*"     E_CONTROL_DATA STRUCTURE   /SAPTRX/CONTROL_DATA
*"     E_LOGTABLE STRUCTURE   BAPIRET2 OPTIONAL
*"  EXCEPTIONS
*"     PARAMETER_ERROR
*"     CDATA_DETERMINATION_ERROR
*"     TABLE_DETERMINATION_ERROR
*"     STOP_PROCESSING
*"----------------------------------------------------------------
  DATA:
*   Container with references
    ls_one_app_tables   TYPE trxas_tabcontainer_wa,
*   Definition of all application objects
    ls_app_objects      TYPE trxas_appobj_ctab_wa,
*   Sales Order Header
    lt_vbak             TYPE SORTED TABLE OF /saptrx/sd_sds_hdr
                             WITH UNIQUE KEY vbeln,
*   Bapi Logging Table
    ls_bapiret          LIKE bapiret2.
```

```
      FIELD-SYMBOLS:
*     Sales Order Header
      <lt_vbak> TYPE STANDARD TABLE,
*     Work Structure for Sales Order Header
      <ls_vbak> TYPE /saptrx/sd_sds_hdr,
*     Sales Order Line
      <lt_vbap> TYPE STANDARD TABLE,
*     Work Structure for Sales Order Line
      <ls_vbap> TYPE vbapvb.
* <1> Read necessary application tables from table reference
* <1-1> Shipment Header (VTTK)
*   READ TABLE i_all_appl_tables INTO ls_one_app_tables
*     WITH KEY tabledef = 'SHIPMENT_HEADER_NEW'
*     BINARY SEARCH.
*   IF NOT sy-subrc IS INITIAL.
*     RAISE cdata_determination_error.
*   ELSE.
*     ASSIGN ls_one_app_tables-tableref->* TO <lt_xvttk>.
*     lt_xvttk[] = <lt_xvttk>[].
*   ENDIF.
*
* <2> Fill general data for all control data records
* Logical System ID of an application system
  e_control_data-appsys     = i_appsys.
* Application Object type
  e_control_data-appobjtype = i_app_obj_types-aotype.
* Login Language
  e_control_data-language   = sy-langu.
* <3> Loop at application objects for getting Sales Order item data
  LOOP AT i_app_objects INTO ls_app_objects.
*
*     Application Object ID
      e_control_data-appobjid   = ls_app_objects-appobjid.
*     Read Main Object Table (Sales Order)
```

```
        ASSIGN ls_app_objects-maintabref->* TO <ls_vbap>.
*   Check if Main table is Sales Order item or not.
    IF NOT <ls_vbap> IS ASSIGNED.
      MESSAGE ID '/SAPTRX/ASC' TYPE 'E' NUMBER 087
        WITH ls_app_objects-maintabdef
             i_app_obj_types-controldatafunc
             'AOT'
             ls_app_objects-appobjtype
          INTO ls_bapiret-message.
      ls_bapiret-type       = 'E'.
      ls_bapiret-id         = '/SAPTRX/ASC'.
      ls_bapiret-number     = 087.
      ls_bapiret-message_v1 = ls_app_objects-maintabdef.
      ls_bapiret-message_v2 = i_app_obj_types-controldatafunc.
      ls_bapiret-message_v3 = 'AOT'.
      ls_bapiret-message_v4 = ls_app_objects-appobjtype.
      ls_bapiret-system     = i_appsys.
      APPEND ls_bapiret TO e_logtable.
      EXIT.
    ELSE.
*   Read Sales Order Line Info
*     Item Category
      e_control_data-paramname = 'ITEM_CAT'.
      e_control_data-value     = <ls_vbap>-pstyv.
      APPEND e_control_data.
    ENDIF.
*   Read Master Object Table (Sales Order Header)
    ASSIGN ls_app_objects-mastertabref->* TO <ls_vbak>.
*   Check if Master table is Sales Order header or not.
    IF NOT <ls_vbak> IS ASSIGNED.
      MESSAGE ID '/SAPTRX/ASC' TYPE 'E' NUMBER 087
        WITH ls_app_objects-mastertabdef
             i_app_obj_types-controldatafunc
             'AOT'
```

```
            ls_app_objects-appobjtype
          INTO ls_bapiret-message.
        ls_bapiret-type       = 'E'.
        ls_bapiret-id         = '/SAPTRX/ASC'.
        ls_bapiret-number     = 087.
        ls_bapiret-message_v1 = ls_app_objects-mastertabdef.
        ls_bapiret-message_v2 = i_app_obj_types-controldatafunc.
        ls_bapiret-message_v3 = 'AOT'.
        ls_bapiret-message_v4 = ls_app_objects-appobjtype.
        ls_bapiret-system     = i_appsys.
        APPEND ls_bapiret TO e_logtable.
        EXIT.
      ELSE.
*     Read Sales Order Header info using Sales Order Number
*        Customer Number
        e_control_data-paramname = 'CUSTOMER_AG'.
        e_control_data-value     = <ls_vbak>-kunnr.
        APPEND e_control_data.
*        Sales Org
        e_control_data-paramname = 'SALES_ORG'.
        e_control_data-value     = <ls_vbak>-vkorg.
        APPEND e_control_data.
*        Creation Date
        e_control_data-paramname = 'CREATE_DATE'.
        e_control_data-value     = <ls_vbak>-erdat.
        APPEND e_control_data.
*        Creation Time
        e_control_data-paramname = 'CREATE_TIME'.
        e_control_data-value     = <ls_vbak>-erzet.
        APPEND e_control_data.
      ENDIF.
*     Index
      e_control_data-paramindex = <ls_vbap>-objnr.
    ENDLOOP.
ENDFUNCTION.
```

After the code, also maintain the parameter fields (Figure 8.5) in the configuration. In ECC Transaction SPRO, follow the menu path INTEGRATION WITH OTHER MYSAP. COM COMPONENTS • EVENT MANAGEMENT INTERFACE • DEFINE APPLICATION INTERFACES • DEFINE SAP EM INTERFACE FUNCTIONS.

Dialog Structure	Extractor	ZCP_SALESORDERLINE		Sales Order Line Control Parameter

Control Parameter List

Parameter	Description	Pa	Data Type
CREATE_DATE	Sales Order Creation Date	8	D Date Field (YYYYMMDD)
CREATE_TIME	Sales Order Creation Time	6	T Time Field (HHMMSS)
CUSTOMER_AG	Sold to customer	10	C Text Field (Character Strir
ITEM_CAT	Item Category	4	C Text Field (Character Strir
SALES_ORG	Sales Organization	4	C Text Field (Character Strir

Extractor	ZIP_SALESORDERLINE		Sales Order Line Info Parameters

Info Parameter List

Parameter	Description	Pa	Data Type
CREATE_USER	Sales Order Created By User	10	C Text Field (Character Strir
MATERIAL	Material Number	18	C Text Field (Character Strir
NET_PRICE	Net Price for order line	11	C Text Field (Character Strir
SOLD_TO_NAME	Sold To Name	35	C Text Field (Character Strir

Figure 8.5 Control and Info Parameter List Maintenance in Configuration

Query ID Extractor

Configure the extractor ZQI_SALESORDER. You can create the function module ZSAP-TRX_XQI_SALESORDER by copying from function module template /SAPTRX/QUERY_ID_TEMPLATE. The template code may be modified for doing the relevancy check and looking at the example Query ID: Customer Purchase Order.

Expected event Extractor

Configure the extractor ZEE_SALESORDER. You can create the function module ZSAP-TRX_XEE_SALESORDER by copying from function module template /SAPTRX/EXP_EVENT_TEMPLATE. The template code may be modified for doing the relevancy check and inputting the expected event list. The code may look like the following.

```
FUNCTION ZSAPTRX_XEE_SALESORDER.
*"----------------------------------------------------------------
*"*"Local Interface:
*"  IMPORTING
*"     REFERENCE(I_APPSYS) TYPE  /SAPTRX/APPLSYSTEM
*"     REFERENCE(I_APP_OBJ_TYPES) TYPE  /SAPTRX/AOTYPES
*"     REFERENCE(I_ALL_APPL_TABLES) TYPE  TRXAS_TABCONTAINER
*"     REFERENCE(I_APP_TYPE_CNTL_TABS) TYPE  TRXAS_APPTYPE_TABS
*"     REFERENCE(I_APP_OBJECTS) TYPE  TRXAS_APPOBJ_CTABS
*"  TABLES
*"      E_EXPEVENTDATA STRUCTURE  /SAPTRX/EXP_EVENTS
*"      E_MEASRMNTDATA STRUCTURE  /SAPTRX/MEASR_DATA OPTIONAL
*"      E_INFODATA STRUCTURE  /SAPTRX/INFO_DATA OPTIONAL
*"      E_LOGTABLE STRUCTURE  BAPIRET2 OPTIONAL
*"  EXCEPTIONS
*"      PARAMETER_ERROR
*"      EXP_EVENT_DETERM_ERROR
*"      TABLE_DETERMINATION_ERROR
*"      STOP_PROCESSING
*"----------------------------------------------------------------
DATA:
*   Container with references
    ls_one_app_tables    TYPE trxas_tabcontainer_wa,
*   Definition of all application objects
    ls_app_objects       TYPE trxas_appobj_ctab_wa,
*   Milestone Counter
    lv_milestonecnt      TYPE /saptrx/seq_num VALUE 0,
*   Event expected date/time
    lv_tsmp              TYPE /saptrx/event_exp_datetime,
*   Time Zone
    lv_timezone          TYPE tznzone,
*   Item Identification
    ls_itemidentfields   TYPE /saptrx/itemidentfields,
*   Bapi Logging Table
```

```
        ls_bapiret          LIKE bapiret2,
        lt_vbep             TYPE STANDARD TABLE OF vbepvb,
        wa_vbep             TYPE vbepvb,
        lv_date             LIKE sy-datum,
        lv_time             LIKE sy-uzeit,
        lv_timestamp        TYPE timestamp,
        lv_result_timestamp TYPE timestamp,
        lv_duration         TYPE i.
    FIELD-SYMBOLS:
*    Sales Order Item
     <lt_vbap> TYPE STANDARD TABLE,
*    Work Structure for Sales Order Header
     <ls_vbak>       TYPE /saptrx/sd_sds_hdr,
*    Sales Order Line
     <ls_vbap> TYPE vbapvb,
*    Sales Order Schedule Line
     <ls_vbep> TYPE vbepvb.
* <1> Read necessary application tables from table reference
** <1-1> Schedule Line (VBEP)
*   READ TABLE i_all_appl_tables INTO ls_one_app_tables
*     WITH KEY tabledef = 'SCHEDULE_LINE_ITEMS_NEW'
*     BINARY SEARCH.
*   IF NOT sy-subrc IS INITIAL.
*     RAISE table_determination_error.
*   ELSE.
*     ASSIGN ls_one_app_tables-tableref->* TO <lt_vbep>.
*     lt_vbep[] = <lt_vbep>[].
*   ENDIF.
* <2> Fill general data for all control data records
* Logical System ID of an application system
  e_expeventdata-appsys     = i_appsys.
* Application Object type
  e_expeventdata-appobjtype = i_app_obj_types-aotype.
* Login Language
```

```
      e_expeventdata-language    = sy-langu.
*    Get System TimeZone
     CALL FUNCTION 'GET_SYSTEM_TIMEZONE'
       IMPORTING
         timezone                = lv_timezone
       EXCEPTIONS
         customizing_missing = 1
         OTHERS              = 2.
* <3> Loop at application objects for getting Sales Order item data
     LOOP AT i_app_objects INTO ls_app_objects.
*    Application Object ID
     e_expeventdata-appobjid = ls_app_objects-appobjid.
     ASSIGN ls_app_objects-maintabref->* TO <ls_vbap>.
*    Check if Main table is Sales Order item or not.
     IF NOT <ls_vbap> IS ASSIGNED.
       MESSAGE ID '/SAPTRX/ASC' TYPE 'E' NUMBER 087
         WITH ls_app_objects-maintabdef
              i_app_obj_types-controldatafunc
              'AOT'
              ls_app_objects-appobjtype
         INTO ls_bapiret-message.
       ls_bapiret-type       = 'E'.
       ls_bapiret-id         = '/SAPTRX/ASC'.
       ls_bapiret-number     = 087.
       ls_bapiret-message_v1 = ls_app_objects-maintabdef.
       ls_bapiret-message_v2 = i_app_obj_types-controldatafunc.
       ls_bapiret-message_v3 = 'AOT'.
       ls_bapiret-message_v4 = ls_app_objects-appobjtype.
       ls_bapiret-system     = i_appsys.
       APPEND ls_bapiret TO e_logtable.
       EXIT.
     ENDIF.
     ASSIGN ls_app_objects-mastertabref->* TO <ls_vbak>.
*    Check if Master table is Sales Order Header or not.
```

```
IF NOT <ls_vbak> IS ASSIGNED.
  MESSAGE ID '/SAPTRX/ASC' TYPE 'E' NUMBER 087
    WITH ls_app_objects-mastertabdef
         i_app_obj_types-controldatafunc
         'AOT'
         ls_app_objects-appobjtype
    INTO ls_bapiret-message.
  ls_bapiret-type       = 'E'.
  ls_bapiret-id         = '/SAPTRX/ASC'.
  ls_bapiret-number     = 087.
  ls_bapiret-message_v1 = ls_app_objects-mastertabdef.
  ls_bapiret-message_v2 = i_app_obj_types-controldatafunc.
  ls_bapiret-message_v3 = 'AOT'.
  ls_bapiret-message_v4 = ls_app_objects-appobjtype.
  ls_bapiret-system     = i_appsys.
  APPEND ls_bapiret TO e_logtable.
  EXIT.
ENDIF.
CLEAR lv_milestonecnt.
**    Local time zone
*     CALL FUNCTION 'TZON_LOCATION_TIMEZONE'
*       EXPORTING
*         if_country        = <ls_xvtts>-land1a
*         if_region         = <ls_xvtts>-regioa
*         if_zipcode        = <ls_xvtts>-pstlza
*       IMPORTING
*         ef_timezone       = lv_timezone
*       EXCEPTIONS
*         no_timezone_found = 1
*         OTHERS            = 2.
  e_expeventdata-evt_exp_tzone = lv_timezone.
*   Sales Order Created
  e_expeventdata-milestone    = gc_event_socreated.
  lv_milestonecnt             = lv_milestonecnt + 1.
```

```
    e_expeventdata-milestonenum = lv_milestonecnt.
    CONCATENATE sy-datum sy-uzeit INTO lv_tsmp.
    IF sy-subrc IS INITIAL.
      e_expeventdata-evt_exp_datetime = lv_tsmp.
    ELSE.
      CLEAR e_expeventdata-evt_exp_datetime.
    ENDIF.
    APPEND e_expeventdata.
*    Sales Order Complete
    e_expeventdata-milestone     = gc_event_socomplete.
    lv_milestonecnt              = lv_milestonecnt + 1.
    e_expeventdata-milestonenum = lv_milestonecnt.
    lv_duration = 240.
    lv_timestamp = lv_tsmp.
    CALL FUNCTION 'TIMECALC_MOVE'
      EXPORTING
        timestamp = lv_timestamp
        duration  = lv_duration
        timezone  = lv_timezone
        direction = '+'
      IMPORTING
        RESULT    = lv_result_timestamp.
    lv_tsmp = lv_result_timestamp.
    IF sy-subrc IS INITIAL.
      e_expeventdata-evt_exp_datetime = lv_tsmp.
    ELSE.
      CLEAR e_expeventdata-evt_exp_datetime.
    ENDIF.
    APPEND e_expeventdata.
*** Delivery Processing
* Get the schedule delivery details.
    PERFORM read_appl_tables_sched_det
      TABLES lt_vbep
      USING  i_all_appl_tables.
```

```
* Delivery Created
    e_expeventdata-milestone      = gc_event_delcreated.
    lv_milestonecnt               = lv_milestonecnt + 1.
    e_expeventdata-milestonenum   = lv_milestonecnt.
    LOOP AT lt_vbep INTO  wa_vbep
      WHERE vbeln = <ls_vbap>-vbeln
        AND posnr = <ls_vbap>-posnr.
      lv_date = wa_vbep-mbdat.
      lv_time = wa_vbep-mbuhr.
      IF wa_vbep-bmeng > 0.
        EXIT.
      ENDIF.
    ENDLOOP.
    CONCATENATE lv_date lv_time INTO lv_tsmp.
    e_expeventdata-evt_exp_datetime = lv_tsmp.
    APPEND e_expeventdata.
* Delivery Picked
    e_expeventdata-milestone      = gc_event_delpicked.
    lv_milestonecnt               = lv_milestonecnt + 1.
    e_expeventdata-milestonenum   = lv_milestonecnt.
    LOOP AT lt_vbep INTO  wa_vbep
      WHERE vbeln = <ls_vbap>-vbeln
        AND posnr = <ls_vbap>-posnr.
      lv_date = wa_vbep-lddat.
      lv_time = wa_vbep-lduhr.
      IF wa_vbep-bmeng > 0.
        EXIT.
      ENDIF.
    ENDLOOP.
    CONCATENATE lv_date lv_time INTO lv_tsmp.
    e_expeventdata-evt_exp_datetime = lv_tsmp.
    APPEND e_expeventdata.
* Delivery Packed
    e_expeventdata-milestone      = gc_event_delpicked.
```

```
        lv_milestonecnt              = lv_milestonecnt + 1.
        e_expeventdata-milestonenum  = lv_milestonecnt.
        LOOP AT lt_vbep INTO  wa_vbep
          WHERE vbeln = <ls_vbap>-vbeln
            AND posnr = <ls_vbap>-posnr.
          lv_date = wa_vbep-lddat.
          lv_time = wa_vbep-lduhr + 3600.    "1 hour after picking
          IF wa_vbep-bmeng > 0.
            EXIT.
          ENDIF.
        ENDLOOP.
        CONCATENATE lv_date lv_time INTO lv_tsmp.
        e_expeventdata-evt_exp_datetime = lv_tsmp.
        APPEND e_expeventdata.
* Delivery Post Goods Issue
        e_expeventdata-milestone     = gc_event_delpgi.
        lv_milestonecnt              = lv_milestonecnt + 1.
        e_expeventdata-milestonenum  = lv_milestonecnt.
        LOOP AT lt_vbep INTO  wa_vbep
          WHERE vbeln = <ls_vbap>-vbeln
            AND posnr = <ls_vbap>-posnr.
          lv_date = wa_vbep-wadat.
          lv_time = wa_vbep-wauhr.
          IF wa_vbep-bmeng > 0.
            EXIT.
          ENDIF.
        ENDLOOP.
        CONCATENATE lv_date lv_time INTO lv_tsmp.
        e_expeventdata-evt_exp_datetime = lv_tsmp.
        APPEND e_expeventdata.
*** Invoice Processing
*    Invoice Created
        e_expeventdata-milestone     = gc_event_invcreated.
        lv_milestonecnt              = lv_milestonecnt + 1.
```

```
    e_expeventdata-milestonenum = lv_milestonecnt.
    lv_duration = 2880.
    lv_timestamp = lv_tsmp.
    CALL FUNCTION 'TIMECALC_MOVE'
      EXPORTING
        timestamp = lv_timestamp
        duration  = lv_duration
        timezone  = lv_timezone
        direction = '+'
      IMPORTING
        RESULT    = lv_result_timestamp.
    lv_tsmp = lv_result_timestamp.
    IF sy-subrc IS INITIAL.
      e_expeventdata-evt_exp_datetime = lv_tsmp.
    ELSE.
      CLEAR e_expeventdata-evt_exp_datetime.
    ENDIF.
    APPEND e_expeventdata.
*** POD Processing
*    POD Received
    e_expeventdata-milestone    = gc_event_podcreated.
    lv_milestonecnt             = lv_milestonecnt + 1.
    e_expeventdata-milestonenum = lv_milestonecnt.
    lv_duration = 720.
    lv_timestamp = lv_tsmp.
    CALL FUNCTION 'TIMECALC_MOVE'
      EXPORTING
        timestamp = lv_timestamp
        duration  = lv_duration
        timezone  = lv_timezone
        direction = '+'
      IMPORTING
        RESULT    = lv_result_timestamp.
    lv_tsmp = lv_result_timestamp.
    IF sy-subrc IS INITIAL.
```

```
        e_expeventdata-evt_exp_datetime = lv_tsmp.
    ELSE.
      CLEAR e_expeventdata-evt_exp_datetime.
    ENDIF.
    APPEND e_expeventdata.
    CALL FUNCTION 'TIMECALC_MOVE'
      EXPORTING
        timestamp = lv_timestamp
        duration  = lv_duration
        timezone  = lv_timezone
        direction = '+'
      IMPORTING
        RESULT    = lv_result_timestamp.
    lv_tsmp = lv_result_timestamp.
    IF sy-subrc IS INITIAL.
      e_expeventdata-evt_exp_datetime = lv_tsmp.
    ELSE.
      CLEAR e_expeventdata-evt_exp_datetime.
    ENDIF.
    APPEND e_expeventdata.
**  Check in
*   e_expeventdata-milestone    = 'CHECK_IN'.
*   lv_milestonecnt             = lv_milestonecnt + 1.
*   e_expeventdata-milestonenum = lv_milestonecnt.
*
*   CONCATENATE <ls_xvttk>-dpreg <ls_xvttk>-upreg INTO lv_tsmp.
*
*   IF sy-subrc IS INITIAL.
*     e_expeventdata-evt_exp_datetime = lv_tsmp.
*   ELSE.
*     CLEAR e_expeventdata-evt_exp_datetime.
*   ENDIF.
*
**  Create Item Ident
*   ls_itemidentfields-docno = <ls_xvttk>-tknum.
```

```
*     ls_itemidentfields-posnr = space.
*     ls_itemidentfields-etenr = space.
*     ls_itemidentfields-tbnam = 'VTTK'.
*     ls_itemidentfields-dfnam = 'DAREG'.
*     ls_itemidentfields-tfnam = 'UAREG'.
*
*     CALL FUNCTION '/SAPTRX/ITEMIDENT_GET_GUID'
*       EXPORTING
*         is_itemidentfields = ls_itemidentfields
*       IMPORTING
*         ev_itemidentifier  = e_expeventdata-itemident.
*
*     APPEND e_expeventdata.
   ENDLOOP.
ENDFUNCTION.
```

Complete the configuration by inputting the expected event list coded on the function (Figure 8.6).

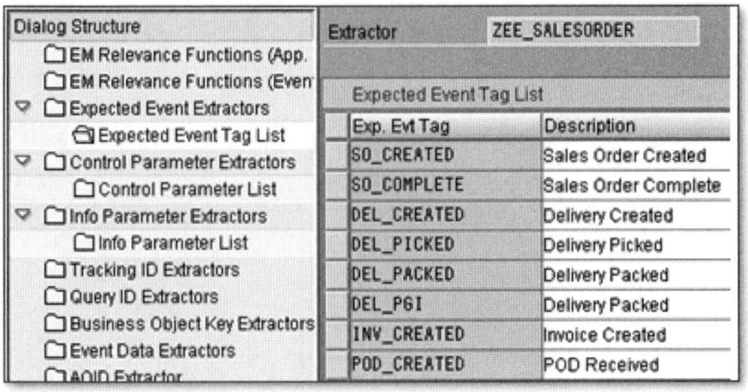

Figure 8.6 Expected Event List

8.2.3 Event Types

Event types help with event notification from the application system. The events reported can either be planned or unplanned events requiring follow-up actions.

The event type for an order-to-cash scenario is broken into four sections by business process type (BPT):

- Sales order BPT (ESC_SORDER)
- Delivery BPT (ESC_DELIV)
- Invoice BPT (ESC_SD_INVOICE)
- Shipment BPT (ESC_SHIPMT)

Sales Order Event Type

Two event types — sales order created and sales order complete —fall under this category. The trigger of the event type requires the sales order document BAdI (BADI_SD_SALES) implementation (Figure 8.7), which is triggered during the sales order document save.

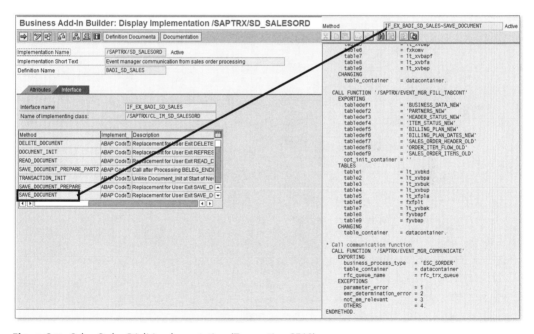

Figure 8.7 Sales Order BAdI Implementation (Transaction SE19)

The event type requires the creation of function module codes for the event data extractors. For the relevancy, you can use the same check that was used in the application object (Figure 8.8). The sales order created event type is created for each sales order line item that also creates an event handler in SAP Event Management. The sales order complete event type looks at the completion of sales order processing in SAP table VBUP. The event type uses a unique tracking ID for sending the event code (message) to SAP Event Management once the conditions are fulfilled. You can create the function module ZSAPTRX_XET_SO_COMPLETE by copying from function module template /SAPTRX/EVENT_TYPE_TEMPLATE. The function module primarily consists of two section definitions — header and mapping table. The sample code for the sales order complete event may look like the following.

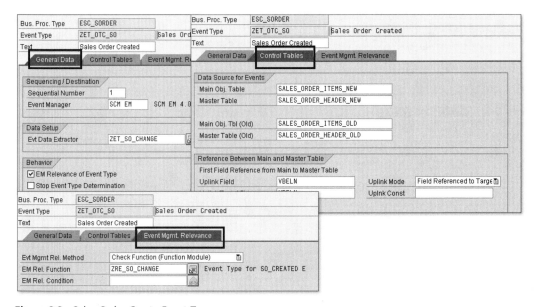

Figure 8.8 Sales Order Create Event Type

```
FUNCTION ZXET_SO_CO.
*"----------------------------------------------------------------
--
*"*"Local Interface:
*"  IMPORTING
*"     REFERENCE(I_APPSYS) TYPE  /SAPTRX/APPLSYSTEM
*"     REFERENCE(I_EVENT_TYPE) TYPE  /SAPTRX/EVTYPES
```

```
*"      REFERENCE(I_ALL_APPL_TABLES) TYPE  TRXAS_TABCONTAINER
*"      REFERENCE(I_EVENT_TYPE_CNTL_TABS) TYPE  TRXAS_EVENTTYPE_TABS
*"      REFERENCE(I_EVENTS) TYPE  TRXAS_EVT_CTABS
*"  TABLES
*"      CT_TRACKINGHEADER STRUCTURE  /SAPTRX/BAPI_EVM_HEADER
*"      CT_TRACKLOCATION STRUCTURE  /SAPTRX/BAPI_EVM_LOCATIONID
*"        OPTIONAL
*"      CT_TRACKADDRESS STRUCTURE  /SAPTRX/BAPI_EVM_ADDRESS OPTIONAL
*"      CT_TRACKLOCATIONDESCR STRUCTURE  /SAPTRX/BAPI_EVM_LOCDESCR
*"        OPTIONAL
*"      CT_TRACKLOCADDITIONALID STRUCTURE  /SAPTRX/BAPI_EVM_LOCADDID
*"        OPTIONAL
*"      CT_TRACKPARTNERID STRUCTURE  /SAPTRX/BAPI_EVM_PARTNERID
*"        OPTIONAL
*"      CT_TRACKPARTNERADDID STRUCTURE  /SAPTRX/BAPI_EVM_PARTNERADDID
*"        OPTIONAL
*"      CT_TRACKESTIMDEADLINE STRUCTURE  /SAPTRX/BAPI_EVM_ESTIMDEADL
*"        OPTIONAL
*"      CT_TRACKCONFIRMSTATUS STRUCTURE  /SAPTRX/BAPI_EVM_CONFSTAT
*"        OPTIONAL
*"      CT_TRACKNEXTEVENT STRUCTURE  /SAPTRX/BAPI_EVM_NEXTEVENT
*"        OPTIONAL
*"      CT_TRACKNEXTEVDEADLINES STRUCTURE  /SAPTRX/BAPI_EVM_NEXTEVDEADL
*"        OPTIONAL
*"      CT_TRACKREFERENCES STRUCTURE  /SAPTRX/BAPI_EVM_REFERENCE
*"        OPTIONAL
*"      CT_TRACKMEASURESULTS STRUCTURE  /SAPTRX/BAPI_EVM_MEASRESULT
*"        OPTIONAL
*"      CT_TRACKSTATUSATTRIB STRUCTURE  /SAPTRX/BAPI_EVM_STATUSATTR
*"        OPTIONAL
*"      CT_TRACKPARAMETERS STRUCTURE  /SAPTRX/BAPI_EVM_PARAMETERS
*"        OPTIONAL
*"      CT_TRACKFILEHEADER STRUCTURE  /SAPTRX/BAPI_EVM_FILEHEADER
*"        OPTIONAL
```

```
*"      CT_TRACKFILEREF STRUCTURE   /SAPTRX/BAPI_EVM_FILEREF OPTIONAL
*"      CT_TRACKFILEBIN STRUCTURE   /SAPTRX/BAPI_EVM_FILEBIN OPTIONAL
*"      CT_TRACKFILECHAR STRUCTURE   /SAPTRX/BAPI_EVM_FILECHAR OPTIONAL
*"      CT_TRACKTEXTHEADER STRUCTURE   /SAPTRX/BAPI_EVM_TEXTHEADER
*"       OPTIONAL
*"      CT_TRACKTEXTLINES STRUCTURE   /SAPTRX/BAPI_EVM_TEXTLINES
*"       OPTIONAL
*"      CT_TRACKEEMODIFY STRUCTURE   /SAPTRX/BAPI_EVM_EE_MODIFY OPTIONAL
*"      CT_EXTENSIONIN STRUCTURE   BAPIPAREX OPTIONAL
*"      CT_EXTENSIONOUT STRUCTURE   BAPIPAREX OPTIONAL
*"      CT_LOGTABLE STRUCTURE   BAPIRET2 OPTIONAL
*"   CHANGING
*"     REFERENCE(C_EVENTID_MAP) TYPE   TRXAS_EVTID_EVTCNT_MAP
*"   EXCEPTIONS
*"     PARAMETER_ERROR
*"     EVENT_DATA_ERROR
*"     STOP_PROCESSING
*"-------------------------------------------------------------------
--

Top Include
* TYPE-POOLS:trxas.
*-------------------------------------------------------------------
-*
  DATA:
*   Container with references
    ls_one_app_tables  TYPE trxas_tabcontainer_wa,
*   Definition of all event types
    ls_events          TYPE trxas_evt_ctab_wa,
*   Bapi for message input: message Header
    ls_trackingheader  TYPE /saptrx/bapi_evm_header,
*   Bapi for parameters
    ls_trackparameters TYPE /saptrx/bapi_evm_parameters,
*   Event Mapping
    ls_eventid_map     TYPE trxas_evtid_evtcnt_map_wa,
```

```
*    ITEM STATUS Line New
     lt_xvbup           TYPE STANDARD TABLE OF vbupvb,
*    ITEM STATUS Line OLD
     lt_xvbup_old       TYPE STANDARD TABLE OF vbupvb,
*    System Timezone
     lv_timezone        TYPE timezone,
      lv_trxid              TYPE /saptrx/trxid,
*    System Timezone
       lv_time TYPE sytime,
       lv_date TYPE sydatum,
       lv_time_local TYPE sytime,
       lv_date_local TYPE sydatum.
   FIELD-SYMBOLS:
*    Work Structure for Sales Order Line New
     <ls_xvbap_old>       TYPE vbapvb,
     <ls_xvbap>        TYPE vbapvb,
     <fs_xvbup>           TYPE vbupvb,
     <fs_xvbup_old>          TYPE vbupvb.


** <1> Read necessary application tables from table reference
*  PERFORM read_appl_tables_po_change
*    TABLES lt_xeket
*          lt_xeket_old
*    USING  i_all_appl_tables.


* <2> Fill general data for all control data records
* Login Language
  ls_trackingheader-language   = sy-langu.
* <3> Loop at event objects for getting purchase order item data

  LOOP AT i_events INTO ls_events.
    UNASSIGN: <ls_xvbap_old>, <ls_xvbap>.


* Check if Main Old table is Sales Order Line or not.
```

```
    IF ls_events-maintabdef >< 'SALES_ORDER_ITEMS_NEW'.
      PERFORM create_logtable_et_rel
        TABLES ct_logtable
        USING  ls_events-maintabdef
               space
               i_event_type-trrelfunc
               ls_events-eventtype
               i_appsys.
      EXIT.
    ENDIF.
    ASSIGN ls_events-maintabref->* TO <ls_xvbap>.


* Check if Main Old table is Sales Order Line or not.
    IF ls_events-mainoldtabdef >< 'SALES_ORDER_ITEMS_OLD'.
      PERFORM create_logtable_et_rel
        TABLES ct_logtable
        USING  ls_events-mainoldtabdef
               space
               i_event_type-trrelfunc
               ls_events-eventtype
               i_appsys.
      EXIT.
    ENDIF.
    ASSIGN ls_events-mainoldtabref->* TO <ls_xvbap_old>.
*     CHECK <ls_xvbap_old> IS ASSIGNED.


* <1> Read necessary application tables
* <1-1> From table reference
    PERFORM read_appl_tables_item_status
      TABLES  lt_xvbup
              lt_xvbup_old
      USING  i_all_appl_tables.


    READ TABLE lt_xvbup_old ASSIGNING <fs_xvbup_old>
```

```
      WITH KEY vbeln = <ls_xvbap>-vbeln
               posnr = <ls_xvbap>-posnr.
   IF <fs_xvbup_old> IS ASSIGNED.
     CHECK not ( <fs_xvbup_old>-uvall = 'C' and
                 <fs_xvbup_old>-besta = 'C' ).
    endif.
   READ TABLE lt_xvbup ASSIGNING <fs_xvbup>
    WITH KEY vbeln = <ls_xvbap>-vbeln
             posnr = <ls_xvbap>-posnr.
   CHECK sy-subrc = 0.
   CHECK <fs_xvbup> IS ASSIGNED.
   CHECK ( <fs_xvbup>-uvall = 'C' AND
           <fs_xvbup>-besta = 'C' ).


   ls_trackingheader-trxcod  = 'SO_LINE'.
*   Tracking ID
   CONCATENATE <ls_xvbap>-vbeln <ls_xvbap>-posnr
     INTO ls_trackingheader-trxid.
*   Get System TimeZone
   CALL FUNCTION 'GET_SYSTEM_TIMEZONE'
     IMPORTING
       timezone            = lv_timezone
     EXCEPTIONS
       customizing_missing = 1
       OTHERS              = 2.
   gv_evtcnt                 = gv_evtcnt + 1.
   ls_trackingheader-evtcnt  = gv_evtcnt.
*     Event ID
   ls_trackingheader-evtid   = 'SO_COMPLETE'.
*     Event Date
   ls_trackingheader-evtdat  = sy-datum.
*     Event Time
   ls_trackingheader-evttim  = sy-uzeit.
*     Event Timezone
```

```
            ls_trackingheader-evtzon   = lv_timezone.
            APPEND ls_trackingheader TO ct_trackingheader.


*      Mapping table
            ls_eventid_map-eventid     = ls_events-eventid.
            ls_eventid_map-evtcnt      = gv_evtcnt.
            APPEND ls_eventid_map TO c_eventid_map.
         ENDLOOP.
      ENDFUNCTION.
```

Delivery Event Type

The delivery event type sends the delivery created, delivery picked, delivery packed, delivery post goods issue information to SAP Event Management. The event types require BAdI (LE_SHP_DELIVERY_PROC) implementation with the save and publish document method. Figure 8.9 shows the configuration for the event type.

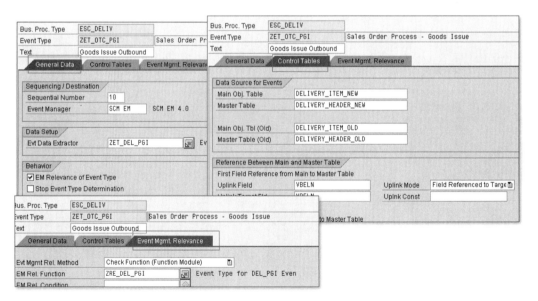

Figure 8.9 Delivery Event Type

The sample code for delivery post goods issue may look like the following.

```
FUNCTION ZXRE_DEL_PGI.
*"----------------------------------------------------------------
--
*"*"Local Interface:
*"  IMPORTING
*"     REFERENCE(I_APPSYS) TYPE  /SAPTRX/APPLSYSTEM
*"     REFERENCE(I_EVENT_TYPES) TYPE  /SAPTRX/EVTYPES
*"     REFERENCE(I_ALL_APPL_TABLES) TYPE  TRXAS_TABCONTAINER
*"     REFERENCE(I_EVENTTYPE_TAB) TYPE  TRXAS_EVENTTYPE_TABS_WA
*"     REFERENCE(I_EVENT) TYPE  TRXAS_EVT_CTAB_WA
*"  EXPORTING
*"     VALUE(E_RESULT) LIKE  SY-BINPT
*"  TABLES
*"      C_LOGTABLE STRUCTURE  BAPIRET2 OPTIONAL
*"  EXCEPTIONS
*"      PARAMETER_ERROR
*"      RELEVANCE_DETERM_ERROR
*"      STOP_PROCESSING
*"----------------------------------------------------------------
--

  DATA: lv_low TYPE tvarvc-low,
        lv_auart LIKE vbak-auart,
        lv_kunnr LIKE vbak-kunnr.
  DATA:
*   Sales Document: Header Status and Administrative Data New
    lt_xvbuk TYPE STANDARD TABLE OF vbukvb,
*   Sales Document: Header Status and Administrative Data Old
    lt_yvbuk TYPE STANDARD TABLE OF vbukvb.

  FIELD-SYMBOLS:

*   Work Structure for Delivery Header
    <ls_xlikp>     TYPE likpvb,
```

```
*    Work Structure for Delivery Item
     <ls_xlips>     TYPE lipsvb,
*    Work Structure for Delivery Item old
     <ls_xlips_old> TYPE lipsvb,
*    Work structure for Sales Document: Header Status and Admin Data New
     <ls_xvbuk>  TYPE vbukvb,
*    Work structure for Sales Document: Header Status and Admin Data Old
     <ls_yvbuk>  TYPE vbukvb.


* Read Main Object Table
* Check if Main New table is Delivery Line or not.
  IF i_event-maintabdef >< 'DELIVERY_ITEM_NEW'.
    PERFORM create_logtable_et_rel
      TABLES c_logtable
      USING  i_event-maintabdef
             space
             i_event_types-trrelfunc
             i_event-eventtype
             i_appsys.
    EXIT.
  ENDIF.
  ASSIGN i_event-maintabref->* TO <ls_xlips>.
* Read Master Object Table
* Check if Master New table is Delivery Header or not.
  IF i_event-mastertabdef >< 'DELIVERY_HEADER_NEW'.
    PERFORM create_logtable_et_rel
      TABLES c_logtable
      USING  i_event-mastertabdef
             space
             i_event_types-trrelfunc
             i_event-eventtype
             i_appsys.
    EXIT.
  ENDIF.
  ASSIGN i_event-mastertabref->* TO <ls_xlikp>.
```

```
* read main old object table
* Check if Main Old table is Delivery Line or not.
  IF i_event-mainoldtabdef >< 'DELIVERY_ITEM_OLD'.
    PERFORM create_logtable_et_rel
      TABLES c_logtable
      USING  i_event-mainoldtabdef
             space
             i_event_types-trrelfunc
             i_event-eventtype
             i_appsys.
  EXIT.
ENDIF.
ASSIGN i_event-mainoldtabref->* TO <ls_xlips_old>.
e_result = false_condition.

CHECK <ls_xlips> IS ASSIGNED.
CHECK <ls_xlikp> IS ASSIGNED.
CHECK <ls_xlikp>-lfart = 'ZULF'.  "Outbound delivery

SELECT SINGLE low INTO lv_low
CHECK sy-subrc = 0.

SELECT SINGLE auart INTO lv_auart
  FROM vbak
  WHERE vbeln = <ls_xlips>-vgbel.

CHECK sy-subrc = 0.

SELECT SINGLE low INTO lv_low
CHECK sy-subrc = 0.

* <1> Read necessary application tables
* <1-1> From table reference
  PERFORM read_appl_tables_del_status
    TABLES lt_xvbuk
```

255

```
            lt_yvbuk
      USING   i_all_appl_tables.



* <3-2> Check Status - If Picking Status is completed &
* Total goods movement status is completed.
    READ TABLE lt_xvbuk ASSIGNING <ls_xvbuk>
      WITH KEY vbeln = <ls_xlikp>-vbeln
      BINARY SEARCH.
    CHECK sy-subrc IS INITIAL.
    IF ( <ls_xvbuk>-kostk = 'C' AND
          <ls_xvbuk>-wbstk = 'C' ).
*      Check Status Before - If GI Status is completed
      READ TABLE lt_yvbuk ASSIGNING <ls_yvbuk>
        WITH KEY vbeln = <ls_xlikp>-vbeln
        BINARY SEARCH.
      CHECK sy-subrc IS INITIAL.
      IF <ls_yvbuk>-wbstk <> 'C'.
        e_result = true_condition.
      ENDIF.
    ENDIF.
  ENDIF.
ENDFUNCTION.
```

Invoice Event Type

The Sales & Distribution invoice event type sends the invoice created information to SAP Event Management. The event type requires BAdI (BADI_SD_BILLING) implementation with the invoice document add method. Figure 8.10 shows the configuration for the event type.

Shipment Event Type

The shipment event type sends the POD received information to SAP Event Management. The event type requires BAdI (BADI_LE_SHIPMENT) implementation with the save and publish document method. Figure 8.11 shows the configuration for the event type.

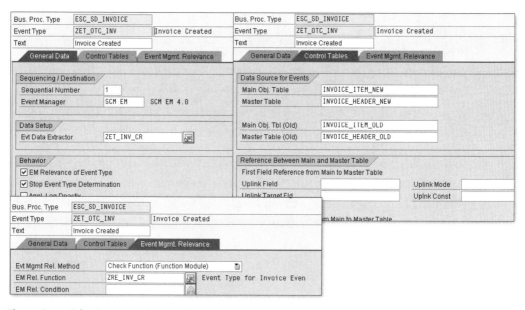

Figure 8.10 Sales Document Invoice Event Type

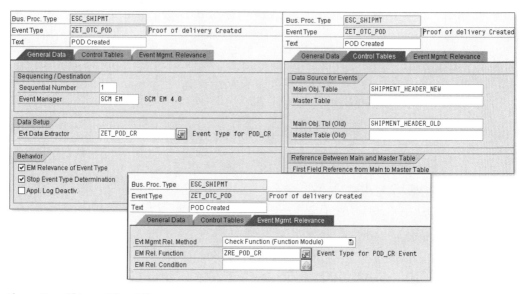

Figure 8.11 Shipment Event Type

8.3   Event Posting Techniques

In Section 6.3 we looked at the event posting technique through BAPI posting. In this section, we'll see the functioning of IDOC EVMSTA02, which serves a similar function as the BAPI. The primary difference is that the IDOC has a hierarchical structure, whereas the BAPI has a flatter structure. The IDOC structure (Figure 8.12) shows the mandatory and optional segments for the IDOC.

You use function module `/SAPTRX/IDOC_INPUT_EVMSTA` to process the IDOC. This function module converts the IDOC input data into the BAPI tables shown in Figure 8.12 and calls function module `/SAPTRX/BAPI_EH_ADDEVENTMSG_02` in asynchronous mode. The two mandatory segments are header `E1EVMHDR02` and tracking ID `E1EVMTID`, which needs the definition of event code `EVTCOD` and a unique tracking ID `TRXID` for the posting of an event message to the SAP Event Management system.

Let's now see the steps for configuring an example proof of delivery (POD) event posting in our order-to-cash scenario, where the IDOC function module triggers the creation of the IDOC and posts the event message in the SAP Event Management system.

The scenario requires the configuration of an IDOC partner profile (Transaction WE20) in both the SAP ECC and SAP SCM systems. Configure the following settings in both systems (Figure 8.13):

- SAP ECC application system – outbound partner profile
  - Message Type : EVMSTA
  - Basic Type : EVMSTA02
- SAP SCM system – inbound partner profile
  - Message Type : EVMSTA
  - Process Code : EVMI

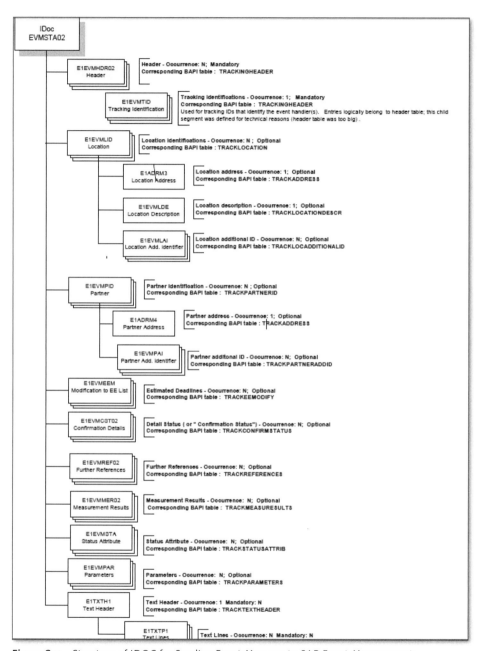

Figure 8.12 Structure of IDOC for Sending Event Message to SAP Event Management

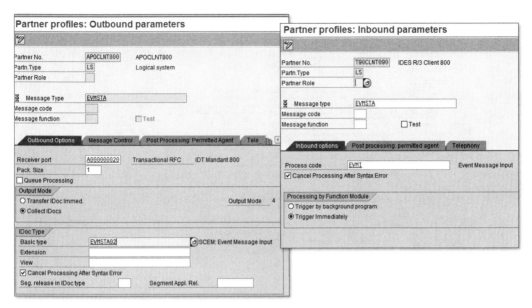

Figure 8.13 IDOC Partner Profile Configurations in SAP ECC (Outbound) and SAP SCM (Inbound)

You need a function module in SAP ECC to create an event using an IDOC (EVM-STA). The sample code may look like the following.

```
FUNCTION ZSAPTRX_SEND_IDOC.
*"--------------------------------------------------------------------
--
*"*"Local Interface:
*"  IMPORTING
*"     REFERENCE(VBELN) LIKE  VBAP-VBELN
*"     REFERENCE(POSNR) LIKE  VBAP-POSNR
*"--------------------------------------------------------------------
--
  DATA:
*    System Timezone
      lv_timezone       TYPE timezone.
*----> get the receiver system
  SELECT SINGLE rcvprn
    FROM   edp13
```

```
      INTO    edp13-rcvprn
      WHERE   mestyp = z_mess_type.
*----> only proceed if there is a receiver system
    IF sy-subrc = 0.
      z_idoc_receiver-logsys = edp13-rcvprn.
      APPEND z_idoc_receiver.
*     Get System TimeZone
      CALL FUNCTION 'GET_SYSTEM_TIMEZONE'
        IMPORTING
          timezone            = lv_timezone
        EXCEPTIONS
          customizing_missing = 1
          OTHERS              = 2.
      CLEAR: elevmhdr02, elevmtid.
      elevmhdr02-evtid  = gc_event_podcreated.
      elevmhdr02-evtdat = sy-datum.
      elevmhdr02-evttim = sy-uzeit.
      elevmhdr02-evtzon = lv_timezone.
      z_idoc_data-segnam = z_hdr_seg.
      z_idoc_data-sdata  = elevmhdr02.
      APPEND z_idoc_data.
      elevmtid-trxcod = 'SO_LINE'.
      CONCATENATE 'VB' vbeln posnr INTO elevmtid-trxid.
      z_idoc_data-segnam = z_tid_seg.
      z_idoc_data-sdata  = elevmtid.
      APPEND z_idoc_data.
*----> set up idoc_control
      z_idoc_control-mestyp = z_mess_type.
      z_idoc_control-idoctp = z_idoc_type .
      z_idoc_control-serial = sy-datum.
      z_idoc_control-serial+8 = sy-uzeit.
      CALL FUNCTION 'ALE_IDOCS_CREATE'
        EXPORTING
          idoc_control                = z_idoc_control
```

```
    TABLES
      idoc_data                     = z_idoc_data
      receivers                     = z_idoc_receiver
      created_idocs                 = z_comm
    EXCEPTIONS
      idoc_input_was_inconsistent = 1
      OTHERS                        = 2.
  IF sy-subrc <> 0.
    MESSAGE i999(b1) WITH 'Idoc failed to create!!!'.
  ELSE.
    COMMIT WORK.
  ENDIF.
ENDIF.
ENDFUNCTION.
```

8.4   SAP SCM Configuration

The configuration on SAP SCM can be divided into four components:

► **Event handler**
Monitoring of planned events and reporting of unplanned events

► **Reaction to event**
Identifying follow-up activities after event message posting in SAP Event Management

► **Web communication**
Displaying and reporting events on the Web

► **Analytics**
Measuring metrics in an order-to-cash business process

8.4.1   Event Handler

An event handler represents the business process objects in an application system, and SAP Event Management monitors and manages this business process. The event handler has various components (Figure 8.14) that all need to be integrated for better event reporting purposes. The application object ID together with the application object type and the business process type serve as a reference between the event handler in SAP Event Management and the corresponding application object in the application system.

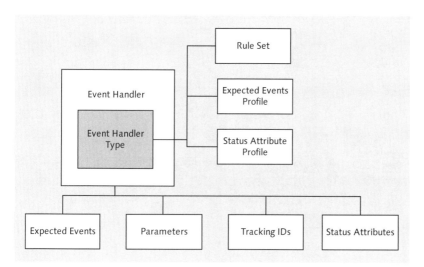

Figure 8.14 SAP Event Management Event Handler Components

Event Codes

Event codes are defined for both planned and unplanned events in SAP Event Management. The event message posting from the application system (SAP ECC) contains the event code that is matched in the SAP Event Management event code during the event posting. Before defining the event code, we must first define the application object code and Tracking ID (Figure 8.15), which serves as a key during the event handler creation or update in SAP Event Management. In Transaction SPRO, follow the menu path EVENT MANAGEMENT • EVENT HANDLERS AND EVENT HANDLER DATA • CODES • DEFINE CODE SETTING CUSTOMIZING).

Next, define the expected event codes for the scenario (Figure 8.16): consisting of sales order, delivery, invoice, and shipment information from application system. The nomenclature of the event code can be similar to the event code that's posted in the event message from the application system. In Transaction SPRO, follow

the menu path EVENT MANAGEMENT • EVENT HANDLERS AND EVENT HANDLER DATA •
CODES • EVENT CODES.

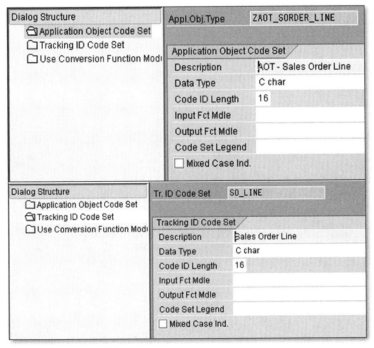

Figure 8.15 Event Code Settings

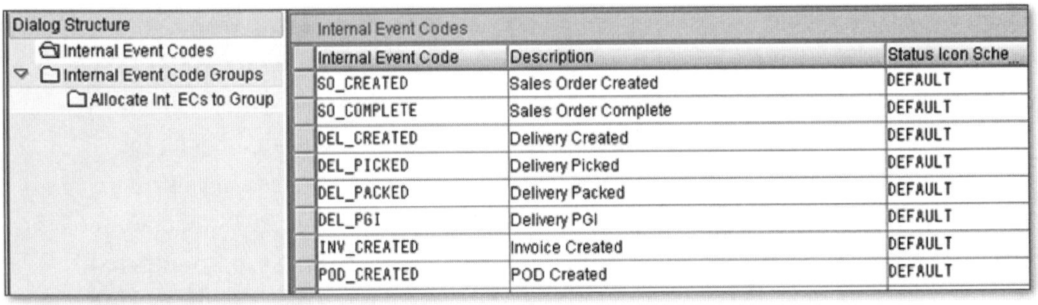

Internal Event Code	Description	Status Icon Sche...
SO_CREATED	Sales Order Created	DEFAULT
SO_COMPLETE	Sales Order Complete	DEFAULT
DEL_CREATED	Delivery Created	DEFAULT
DEL_PICKED	Delivery Picked	DEFAULT
DEL_PACKED	Delivery Packed	DEFAULT
DEL_PGI	Delivery PGI	DEFAULT
INV_CREATED	Invoice Created	DEFAULT
POD_CREATED	POD Created	DEFAULT

Figure 8.16 Internal Event Codes

Expected Event Profile

An expected event profile is configured to define the sequence of the event activity for the scenario. The event code of SAP Event Management and event code of SAP ECC (Figure 8.17) are matched to report the event in the event handler during the event message posting. Within the profile, an expected event monitor activity is also defined to check the current status of the order-to-cash business process and report overdue if the business events are not reported within a tolerance window.

Dialog Structure									
▽ ☐Update Expected Event F		Expected Event Profile	ZEEP_SALESORDERLINE						
▽ ☐Update Profile Group		Description		Expected Event Profile - Sales Order Line					
☐Update Profile Ite		Display Profile							
▽ ☐Display Expected Event F		Group	Item	Event Code	Description	Prio	Requireme	Generated From	Message D	Event Date Rule
☐Display Profile		10	10	SO_CREATED	Sales Order Created	0	R Require	SO_CREATED	No date 1	From Application System
		10	20	SO_COMPLETE	Sales Order Complete	0	R Require	SO_COMPLETE	No date 1	From Application System
		10	30	DEL_CREATED	Delivery Created	0	R Require	DEL_CREATED	No date 1	From Application System
		10	40	DEL_PICKED	Delivery Picked	0	R Require	DEL_PICKED	No date 1	From Application System
		10	50	DEL_PACKED	Delivery Packed	0	R Require	DEL_PACKED	No date 1	From Application System
		10	60	DEL_PGI	Delivery PGI'd	0	R Require	DEL_PGI	No date 1	From Application System
		10	70	INV_CREATED	Invoice Created	0	R Require	INV_CREATED	No date 1	From Application System

Figure 8.17 Expected Event Profile

Parameter Mapping

Parameters are used to store attributes for the event handler. Three types of parameters are stored in SAP Event Management. Control parameters (Figure 8.18) primarily determine the process steps once the event is posted in SAP Event Management. Info parameters are for reporting or selection criteria. System parameters are stored in extension tables for indexing purposes. The parameters configured in SAP Event Management are mapped with the application system parameters and are updated during the event type posting from SAP ECC.

Status Attributes

The status attribute profile (Figure 8.19) helps provide visibility of the business process status toward the order fulfillment. Statuses are set when the transaction is recorded in the application system. Table 8.2 lists the statuses you can configure in SAP Event Management.

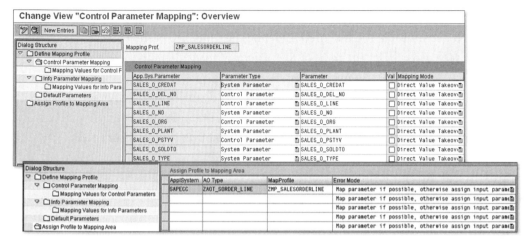

Figure 8.18 Control Parameter and Parameter Mapping with Application System

Change View "Status Attribute Profile Items": Overview

Dialog Structure	Stat.Attr.Prof.	ZSAP_SALESORDERLINE
▽ ☐ Status Attribute Profiles	Description	OTC Status Attribute Profile
🗁 Status Attribute Profil		

Status Attribute Profile Items

StatusAtt. Name	Description	St. Attr. Value	Description
Z10TC_SO	OTC Sales Order Status	SO_NO	No Sales Order
Z20TC_DEL	OTC Delivery Status	DEL_CR_NO	No Delivery Created
Z30TC_INV	OTC Invoice Status	INV_CR_NO	No Invoice
Z40TC_POD	OTC POD Status	POD_NO	No POD

Figure 8.19 Status Attribute Profile

Business Process	Status
Sales order	Sales order created: expected
	Sales order complete: expected
	Sales order blocked: unexpected
	Delivery date late: unexpected

Table 8.2 Status for Order-to-Cash Scenario in SAP Event Management

Business Process	Status
Delivery	Delivery created: expected
	Delivery picked: expected
	Delivery packed: expected
	Delivery post goods issued: expected
	Delivery late: unexpected
Invoice	Invoice created: expected
	Invoice late: unexpected
Proof of Delivery	Proof of delivery received: expected
	Proof of delivery late: unexpected
	Proof of delivery not received: Unexpected

Table 8.2 Status for Order-to-Cash Scenario in SAP Event Management (Cont.)

8.4.2 Reaction to Event

In the rule set we define how the system reacts to a reported and unreported event. In Transaction SPRO, follow the menu path EVENT MANAGEMENT • REACTION TO EVENT • DEFINE RULE SET. A rule set consists of three parts:

▸ **Rules**
Determine how to react to an event and defines the activities and the conditions

▸ **Activities**
Defines how the event messages are processed — in single or multiple steps

▸ **Conditions**
Define which tasks need to be executed in the rule set

You can configure the condition either with the condition editor or with a function module. To create the function module, use the copy of /SAPTRX/RULE_COND_TEMPLATE. Rules (Figure 8.20) are created based on the expected event, and activities are built based on each event. A generic event EVM_EE_UPDATE is included in the rules to update the Expected Event dates as a true rule. The activities can include the task of updating the status of the event handler, creating alert notification for any unexpected event reporting (e.g., delivery late), updating parameters from the application system, or initiating business workflow for rescheduling of orders in case of delays.

Dialog Structure	Rule Set		ZRS_SALESORDER		Sales Order Rule Set			
▽ ☐ Rule Sets								
☐ Rules	**Rules**							
☐ Activity Functions	Rule Se	Rule	Condition	Activity	True Rule	False Rule	Description	
☐ Activity Methods	10	SO_COMPLETE	ZRC_SO_COMPLETE	SO_COMPLETE	EVM_EE_UPDATE		Sales Order Complete	
▽ ☐ Multitask Activities	20	DEL_CREATED	ZRC_DEL_CREATED	DEL_CREATED	EVM_EE_UPDATE		Delivery Created	
☐ Tasks	30	DEL_PICKED	ZRC_DEL_PICKED	DEL_PICKED	EVM_EE_UPDATE		Delivery Picked	
☐ Rule Conditions	40	DEL_PACKED	ZRC_DEL_PACKED	DEL_PACKED	EVM_EE_UPDATE		Delivery Packed	
☐ Rule Condition Functions	50	DEL_PGI	ZRC_DEL_PGI	DEL_PGI	EVM_EE_UPDATE		Delivery PGI	
▽ ☐ Rule Condition Sets	60	INV_CREATED	ZRC_INV_CREATED	INV_CREATED	EVM_EE_UPDATE		Invoice Created	
☐ Condition Set Items	70	POD_RECEIVED	ZRC_POD_RECEIVED	POD_RECEIVED	EVM_EE_UPDATE		POD RECEIVED	
	900	EVM_EE_UPDATE		EVM_UPDATE			EE update	

Figure 8.20 Rule Set Based on the Expected Events

8.4.3 Web Communication

The web customization (Figure 8.21) involves the following configuration objects:

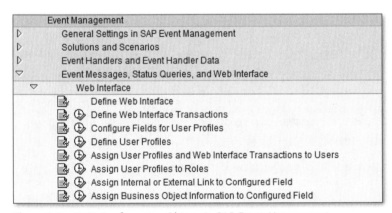

Figure 8.21 WCL Configuration Objects in SAP Event Management

▶ Define Web Interface Transactions

   ▶ Create a user transaction WCL_OTC linked with your tracking scenario.

▶ Configure Fields for User Profiles

- ▶ Configure fields for display: The fields can be either from event handler header or event message data. Each field defined is mapped with an event management (EM) attribute ID.

- ▶ Parameters start with `CNTR_*`, `INFO_*` or `SYST_*`.

- ▶ Event details start with `EVENT*` and `EVENT MSG*`.

- ▶ Status details start with `STATUS*`, `STATUS_ICON*` and `STATUS_TYPE*`.

- ▶ Configure fields for selection: The fields defined are from the event handler. You must also define the event handler type for each field.

- ▶ Parameters start with `CNTR_*`, `INFO_*` or `SYST_*`.

- ▶ Status details start with `STATUS_TYPE*`.

- ▶ Must have an EH ACTIVE field.

- ▶ Configure fields for event message: The fields defined are from the event handler or event message. Define the event parameter and tracking ID.

- ▶ Build groups of configured fields: This allows you to display them together in one column.

▶ Define User Profiles

- ▶ We define three profiles (selection profile, display profile, event message profile) and attach them to create the user profile.

▶ Assign User Profiles and Web Interface Transactions to Users

- ▶ Combine the user profile and web Transaction WCL_OTC defined earlier for the web display.

8.4.4 Analytics

SAP offers standard business content (Figure 8.22) in SAP NetWeaver BW, where you can activate the BW objects to see what it offers, determine whether it can reduce the amount of customization you need to do, perform gap analysis, and produce a prototype to show the business users on available reports and queries.

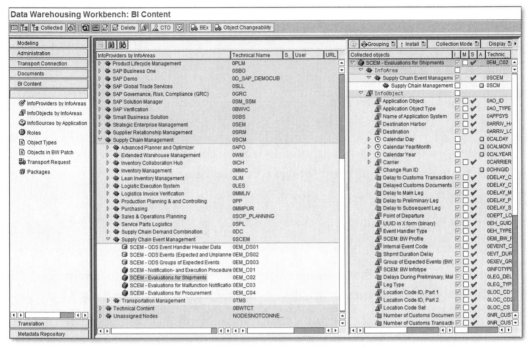

Figure 8.22 Standard Business Content in SAP NetWeaver BW for SAP Event Management

The BW extraction process for the order-to-cash business visibility scenario is similar to the steps described in Chapters 6 and 7.

8.5   Scenario Monitoring in SAP Event Management 5.1

SAP Event Management aims to fill the gap business users have that's due to the lack of near real-time visibility in the end-to-end order-to-cash business process. Even with current reporting tools, companies are constantly challenged by an inability to sense upstream and downstream changes, and the dynamic data is not easily linked in the process. Delays in the transactional order-to-cash process are opaque and lead to customer dissatisfaction, lost sales, excessive supply chain costs, and poor use of working and fixed capital.

The SAP Event Management event handler (Figure 8.23) manages and monitors the sales order per line item transaction and reports on exceptions to the business users. The event handler tracks the order fulfillment to completion and resolves disruptions and discrepancies effectively through real-time information and minimizes downtime by getting to root causes faster.

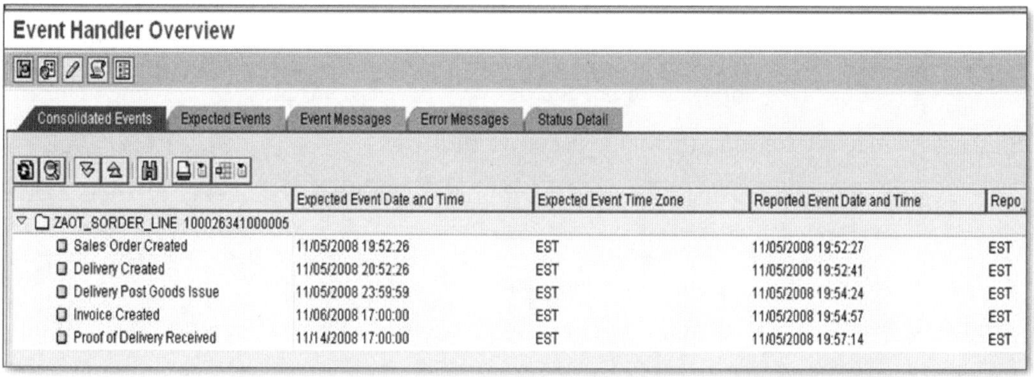

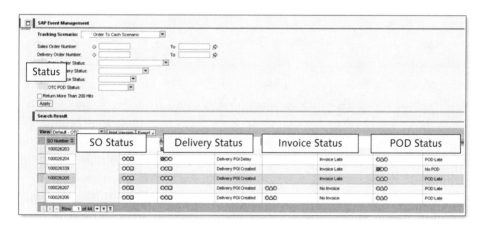

Event Handler Overview
Consolidated Events
Expected Events
Event Messages
Error Messages
Status Detail
Expected Event Date and Time
Expected Event Time Zone
Reported Event Date and Time
Repo
ZAOT_SORDER_LINE 100026341000005
Sales Order Created 11/05/2008 19:52:26 EST 11/05/2008 19:52:27 EST
Delivery Created 11/05/2008 20:52:26 EST 11/05/2008 19:52:41 EST
Delivery Post Goods Issue 11/05/2008 23:59:59 EST 11/05/2008 19:54:24 EST
Invoice Created 11/06/2008 17:00:00 EST 11/05/2008 19:54:57 EST
Proof of Delivery Received 11/14/2008 17:00:00 EST 11/05/2008 19:57:14 EST

Figure 8.23 Order-to-Cash Event Handler Showing Expected Events

SAP Event Management status reporting (Figure 8.24) offers the ability to view and enter event messages for internal and external business partners. The functionality helps order management, warehousing, accounts payable, and transportation functional divisions with integrated supply chain visibility.

SAP Event Management
Tracking Scenario:
Order To Cash Scenario
Status
Search Result
SO Status
Delivery Status
Invoice Status
POD Status

Figure 8.24 Status Reporting in SAP Event Management Web Dynpro

The visibility eliminates many of the additional costs associated with rectifying defective or mishandled orders, such as the need to expedite shipments or incur overtime.

This visibility offers the business opportunities listed below using the SAP Event Management solution:

▶ Monitoring and controlling the delivery process (supplier)

▶ Actively tracking the delivery (customer)

▶ Reporting business events (suppliers, external business partners, and customers)

▶ Notifying the business partners involved in the process

▶ Triggering of subsequent business events (for example, sending an email to a customer if a delay occurs)

▶ Evaluating the business process in SAP NetWeaver Business Warehouse (BW)

▶ Improving back office execution and awareness of order processing needs based upon end-to-end order requirements

SAP Event Management contains an interface to SAP NetWeaver BW as part of analytical SCEM. Data that is collected from various sources within operational SCEM is transferred from SAP Event Management to SAP NetWeaver BW after the business process has been completed. You can then use this information to evaluate key performance indicators (KPIs) and/or indicators that measure collaboration between partners (Collaboration Performance Indicators - CPIs). KPIs measure the extent to which company targets have been met, whereas CPIs help determine why targets have not been met. An example of a company target is improving the overall lead time. This is measured using the Overall Lead Time KPI. You can use the Transportation Service Provider Reliability CPI to find out why the target was not met.

SAP Event Management provides a digital visibility solution that supports real-time order status, integrating the visibility engine with sell-side websites that allow customers to obtain online order status information — a weakness in many current e-commerce applications. Although a supply chain encompasses numerous processes, there are several reasons why the unique order-to-cash process strongly demonstrates the value of SOA and BPM. There is no other process in a manufacturing organization that spans more work groups, departments, business units, and even enterprises than this one, especially if the company outsources and if the product has even a modicum of complexity. Coordination, collaboration, and a shared understanding of expectations become critical components of this process. In addition, there is seldom a single, one-size-fits-all order-to-cash process across the entire organization. There are differences by business unit, by geography, and even by customer that create additional challenges in managing this process.

8.6   Summary

This chapter gave an overview of how to set up an order-to-cash business scenario in SAP Event Management to gain supply chain visibility of what is happening across your supply chain network. SAP Event Management offers capability beyond just status visibility but also has the ability to respond. A common example is deadline management. Customers expect on-time deliveries based on the promised date given to them. However, any number of events can occur that put these expected delivery dates in jeopardy. The key is to monitor progress continuously and alert the appropriate person in the supply chain operation when events occur or when the trend is not positive.

The chapter also provided detailed insights on the sample template custom codes for configuring event messages and IDOC setup for sending event messages from the application system to SAP Event Management. The next chapter looks at the transportation visibility business process and how to integrate SAP Event Management within the overall transportation management solution.

SAP Event Management offers a visibility process that covers various complex transportation networks. This chapter describes in detail the transportation scenarios that SAP Event Management 5.1 supports.

9 Setting Up a Transportation Scenario

Maximizing the effectiveness of your supply chain requires an emphasis on transportation visibility. By improving the supply chain visibility, logistics service providers, consignees, and shippers derive economic value for their organizations. Transportation business processes are critical success factors for manufacturing firms where transportation is required for inflows and outflows of materials.

The objective of this chapter is to highlight various visibility scenarios where SAP Event Management integrates within an end-to-end transportation business process to provide near real-time visibility across the supply chain network.

9.1 Transportation Business Processes

Excellent transportation execution is a powerful competitive differentiator. This helps companies reduce transportation costs and increase service levels while functioning in today's single and multimode, multi-business networks. End-to-end transportation business processes consist of tightly integrated core processes for planning, execution, monitoring, and controlling. This section describes the flow of business processes, events, and system applications allowing the process to flow smoothly.

9.1.1 Transportation Planning

Transportation planning serves as a foundational step for the overall transportation management process. The primary task in transportation planning (Figure 9.1) consists of combining the orders to deliveries and then preparing shipping documents. The important functions are grouping of inbound and outbound deliveries, carrier selection, leg determination, freight costs estimations, and shipment tendering.

Figure 9.1 Transportation Planning Functionalities

The transportation process (Figure 9.2) starts with combining deliveries (inbound or outbound), which are relevant for shipment. Shipments can be a combination of inbound delivery documents (with reference to purchase orders) or a combination of outbound delivery documents (with reference to sales orders). After a planned shipment creation, transportation routes and stages are planned. Subsequently, a carrier is selected that's appropriate for that route, stage, or group of products for the means of transport selected. After the carrier selection, the shipment costs calculation process takes place for the estimation of transportation costs. These costs are then transferred into the customer billing documents to be included in the invoice to the customer. Later, the settlement is completed with service through the payment of the invoice or creation of a credit memo. The shipment cost settlement takes place either by billing (for outbound) or by invoice verification (for inbound).

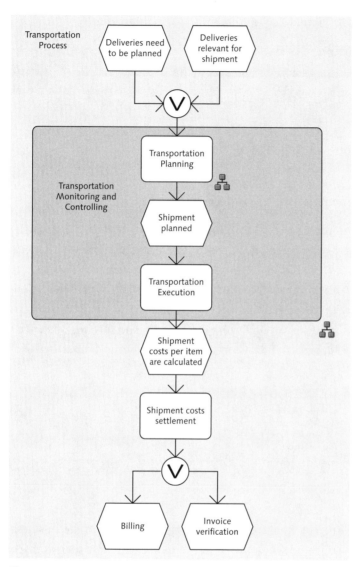

Figure 9.2 Transportation Process

9.1.2 Transportation Execution

Transportation execution starts with the actual creation of shipment documents and movement of goods. It has similar functions like transportation planning and goes toward realization of the following functions:

- Combining deliveries (inbound or outbound) to form shipments
- Assigning service agents, modes of transport, and shipment types
- Planning and monitoring deadlines and specifying shipment stage
- Cross-delivery packing and creation of handling units
- Creating output and shipping papers
- Freight cost estimating and shipment tendering

9.1.3 Transportation Monitoring and Controlling

The transportation monitoring and controlling process (Figure 9.3) is a supportive process for planning and execution. Its main task is to monitor the shipment process, ensure that all of the shipments are planned efficiently (and if they aren't, proposes a new plan), and monitors the control shipment tendering process. After completion of the overall transportation process, the information generated during the process is collected and used for analyzing the process, and this helps in creating effective planning methods and decision-making processes in the future.

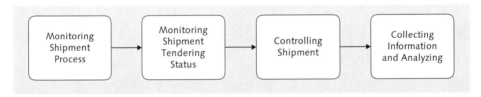

Figure 9.3 Transportation Monitoring and Controlling

Transportation controlling is a function for managing exceptions on the business process. The process is triggered when the carrier reports exceptions such as truck delays, bad weather, and goods damaged during transport. The exceptions come as alerts to the transport controller, who works with the transport planner to reschedule the overall transportation process. The entire transportation planning process is performed again, including carrier selection. In this process the same forwarding agent can accept the job, or the supplier can arrange for the retendering process to find alternative forwarding agents.

9.1.4   Transportation Tendering

Tendering is a process where a suitable forwarding agent or transport agent is identified who can take up the transportation task efficiently. Then the transport requests are sent for acceptance by the transport agent. If the agent does not get feedback within the acceptance period, the request expires and is sent to next best forwarding agent. Once the transport is accepted by the transport agent, the normal transportation execution process takes place, followed by shipment cost settlements. SAP Event Management provides the following alerts that can be triggered during the tendering process:

▸ Proposed shipment rejected by the transportation service provider (TSP)

▸ Proposed dates and times changed by the TSP

▸ Transferred shipment: proposed dates and times changed by the TSP

▸ Transferred shipment: proposed dates and times rejected by the TSP

▸ No response from the TSP

The retendering process (Figure 9.4) is one of the sub-functions of the controlling shipment function that starts when an operational exception is reported on the transportation execution business process. The retendering process is important because transportation time is short, and the planner or controller needs to be quick in selecting and confirming the available forwarding agent to fulfill the shipment. With SAP Event Management and a collaborative transportation planning process in place, the retendering process can become more dynamic and reduce the effort and cycle time required for the agent search.

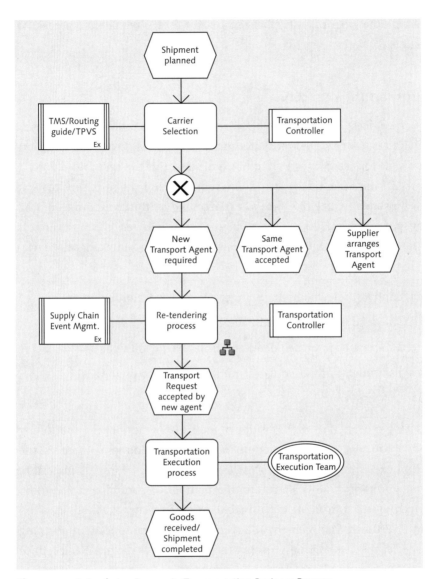

Figure 9.4 Retendering Process in Transportation Business Process

9.1.5 Transportation Scenarios

Many transportation scenarios have the tracking (i.e., equipment) and tracing (i.e., location) functional requirements. The scenarios can be:

▶ **Parcel shipping**

Performing parcel consolidation, rules-based parcel to Less Than Truckload (LTL) decision making, rate-shopping parcel carriers, labeling and operational manifesting, tracking, and freight costing.

▶ **LTL and Truck Load (TL) shipping**

Order consolidation, load planning, manual and optimized routing and scheduling, carrier collaboration, appointment scheduling, tracking, and freight costing.

▶ **Bulk products**

Similar to LTL and TL, but with liquid bulk materials such as chemicals, oil and gas, using single- and multi-compartment equipment and freight costing.

▶ **Rail transportation**

Managing the fixed route and costs associated with movements, limited sophisticated planning requirements, and tracking.

▶ **Ocean shipping**

Containerized and break bulk international shipping, booking space on vessels, arranging for domestic and international freights, and freight costing.

▶ **Inbound logistics**

Managing inbound routing either internationally for finished goods or domestically for raw materials or intermediate suppliers, routing, tracking. and freight costing.

▶ **Private and dedicated fleets**

Managing the dispatching of drivers and equipment, usually along fixed routes and schedules.

▶ **Third Party Logistics (3PL)**

Buying and selling transportation services while performing all of the previously listed activities. These service provider do not usually own their equipment. They are primarily service focused and perform goods tracking freight costing, and billing activities.

▶ **Carrier management**

Similar to 3PL, but own their equipment and are mostly asset based. Can include all elements of the areas mentioned above, tracking, and freight billing.

9.2 Visibility Export Scenario I – Road and Sea Shipments

The SAP Event Management transportation visibility process covers transportation and customs issues for inbound and outbound goods flows. Because international sea shipments play a large role, the visibility process concentrates mainly on transportation chains for sea processes and on collective road shipments. The visibility process demonstrates the following functions:

- Monitor and control the transportation process
- Actively track the delivery (customer)
- Report events, both within the company and by business partners
- Notify the business partners involved in the process
- Trigger follow-up activities on exceptions cases
- Analyze the business processes in the SAP NetWeaver Business Warehouse

9.2.1 Scenario Monitoring

Two sub-processes are considered in the visibility process (Figure 9.5):

- **International road shipment**
  Describes a collective shipment and may consist of several inbound and outbound deliveries that are collected from or delivered to various locations.

- **International sea shipment**
  Describes a transportation chain that consists of at least three legs consisting of (a) a preliminary leg that transports the deliveries to the port of departure (road); (b) a main leg that transports the deliveries by sea, and (c) subsequent legs that transport the deliveries from the destination harbor to the recipients (road).

The visibility of the business process in SAP Event Management is achieved by creation of three shipment types (pre-carriage land, main carriage water, on carriage land) in SAP ECC and subsequent triggering of three event handlers (Figure 9.6) in SAP Event Management.

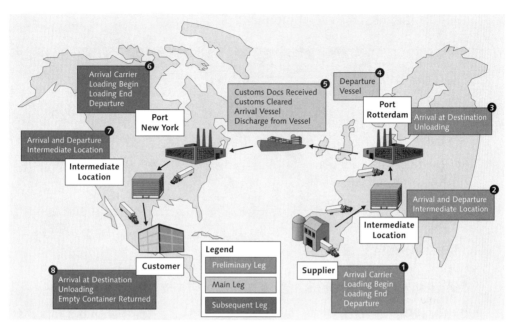

Figure 9.5 Transportation Export Scenario

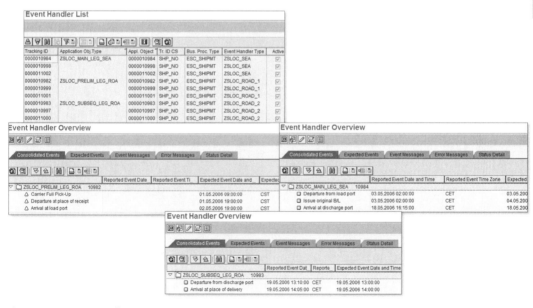

Figure 9.6 Event Handler List

Table 9.1 lists all of the events covered in the scenario.

Business Process Event	Type of Event	Event Status
Road Shipment - First Leg Carrier full pick-up Departure at place of receipt Arrival at load port	Expected	**Delivery Status** On time Delay **Transportation Status**
Sea Shipment - Second Leg Departure from load port Issue original Bill of Lading Arrival at discharge port	Expected	Not started Arrived In transit Loading Unloading
Road Shipment - Third Leg Departure from discharge port Arrival at place of delivery	Expected	

Table 9.1 Transportation Status for Export Scenario

SAP Event Management offers an event handler set (Figure 9.7) that consolidates all three event handlers based on a common outbound delivery number and gives the overall status of the scenario.

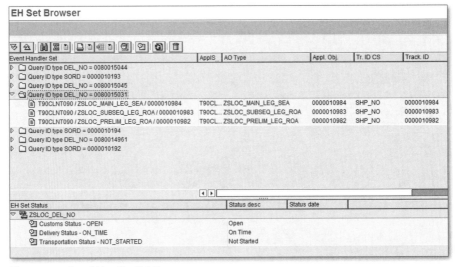

Figure 9.7 Event Handler Set Browser

9.2.2 Configuration Steps

In SAP ECC, we need to configure the business process type, application object types, and the event type. The business process type for the scenario is shipment. The primary application tables (Figure 9.8) used for the scenario are VTTK, VTSP, VTTP, VTTS, VEKP, VEPO, VBPA, LIKP, and LIPS.

Next we need to define three application object types (AOTs). The primary reason for creating three AOTs (Figure 9.9) is to have distinct SAP Event Management relevancy conditions and event types defined for the three legs.

Structure Name	DDIC Definition	DB Struc. Name	Bus.	Updte Fld Name	No Ch	Insert	Updat	Delete
ADDRESS_NEW	SADRVB	SADR	☐					
ADDRESS_OLD	SADRVB	SADR	☐					
DELIVERY_HEADER	VTRLK	LIKP	☐					
DELIVERY_ITEM	VTRLP	LIPS	☐					
HU_HEADER_NEW	VEKPVB	VEKP	☐	UPDKZ		I	U	D
HU_HEADER_OLD	VEKPVB	VEKP	☐	UPDKZ		I	U	D
HU_ITEM_NEW	VEPOVB	VEPO	☐	UPDKZ		I	U	D
HU_ITEM_OLD	VEPOVB	VEPO	☐	UPDKZ		I	U	D
PARTNER_NEW	VBPAVB	VBPA	☐	UPDKZ		I	U	D
PARTNER_OLD	VBPAVB	VBPA	☐	UPDKZ		I	U	D
SHIPMENT_HEADER_NEW	VTTKVB	VTTK	☑	UPDKZ		I	U	D
SHIPMENT_HEADER_OLD	VTTKVB	VTTK	☐	UPDKZ		I	U	D
SHIPMENT_ITEM_LEG_NEW	VTSPVB	VTSP	☐	UPDKZ		I	U	D
SHIPMENT_ITEM_LEG_OLD	VTSPVB	VTSP	☐	UPDKZ		I	U	D
SHIPMENT_ITEM_NEW	VTTPVB	VTTP	☐	UPDKZ		I	U	D
SHIPMENT_ITEM_OLD	VTTPVB	VTTP	☐	UPDKZ		I	U	D
SHIPMENT_LEG_NEW	VTTSVB	VTTS	☐	UPDKZ		I	U	D
SHIPMENT_LEG_OLD	VTTSVB	VTTS	☐	UPDKZ		I	U	D

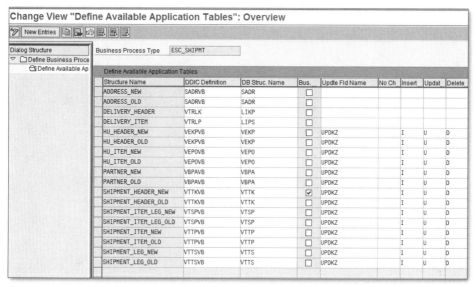

Figure 9.8 Application Tables for Shipment Document Business Process Type

Appl.Obj.Type	Seq. No.	Description	Event Mgr	Object Type	BO S	EM Relev.	Info Relev	Stop AO
ZSLOC_MAIN_LEG_SEA	10	Ocean Carrier Main leg Sea Shipment	EM_01_800			☑	☐	☐
ZSLOC_PRELIM_LEG_ROA	10	Ocean Carrierr Prelim. Leg Road Shipment	EM_01_800			☑	☐	☐
ZSLOC_SUBSEQ_LEG_ROA	10	Ocean Carrierr Subsequent Leg Road Shipment	EM_01_800			☑	☐	☐

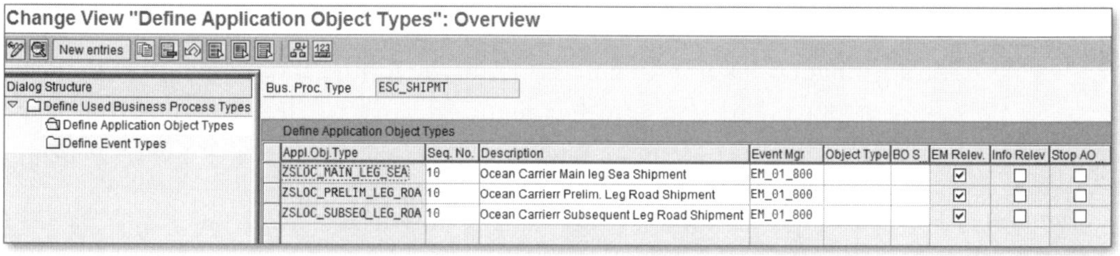

Figure 9.9 Three Application Object Types for the Scenario

In the application object type, attach the SAP-delivered extractors for the parameters and expected events. You can further enhance the SAP-delivered extractors TRA10*_ to include customer fields.

On the SAP SCM configuration side, we need to set up an event handler, an event handler set, status attributes, and a rule set.

Within the transportation visibility process, SAP delivers document flow (Figure 9.10), which provides a graphical display of the network of business objects that are related to the monitored object or process. Document flow uses the object link model with a concept that a relationship always exists between two documents and links can be formed across documents with a successor or predecessor.

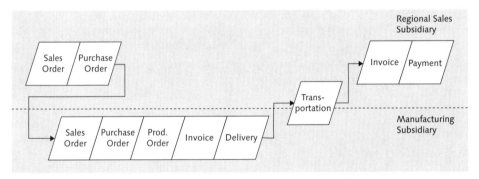

Figure 9.10 Document Flow for Tracking Business Process Across Boundaries

Below are the configuration steps for setting up document flow in SAP Event Management:

▶ **Customize document category for SAP Event Management**
(Transaction /SCMB/DF_CUST)
The document categories (Figure 9.11) are the technical representation of documents or document items. A document category has to be defined for every business object. SAP delivers few predefined categories. SAP Event Management relevant category objects start with numerical digit 1.

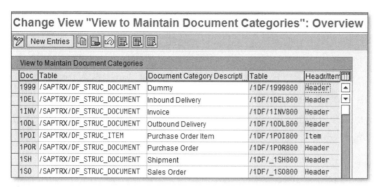

Figure 9.11 Document Category for SAP Event Management

▶ **Maintain document flow object link model for SAP Event Management**
(Transaction SOBL_MODEL)

A role category is defined first in the object link model (Figure 9.12). The role category can group multiple document categories. Also, two role categories can only be connected with each other by one link type.

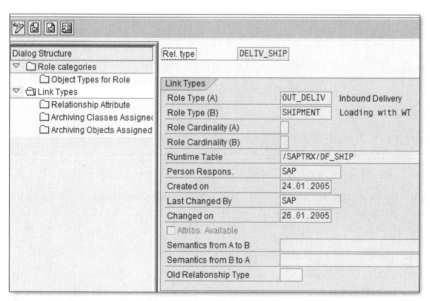

Figure 9.12 Document Flow Object Link Model

▶ **Maintain document flow group for SAP Event Management**
(Transaction/SAPTRX/TSCODF)
This allows us to map the generic SAP Event Management objects to the document flow. This customizing is pre-delivered for the transportation visibility scenario. A group can be assigned to different event handler type activities or an event message rule. The settings for the document flow group (Figure 9.13) are defined as follows:

▶ **DF Target Level**
Helps define whether the document for which we want to create a node is the network, a header, or an item document.

▶ **EM Level for DF**
Used to decide whether the business document is sent by an event handler or an event message. If a business document is sent via an event message, the system also offers some event message tables for the source or predecessor mapping.

▶ **EM Source Level**
Used to maintain the source level.

▶ **Document**
Document categories of the source and predecessor category and the relation type between these two documents.

▶ **DF Pred. Search**
Identifies how to find a predecessor. Four options are available: no search (first document in net), mapping search (the predecessor is mapped in the following configuration), customer function (a function for the search can be implemented), and sequence search (if more than one entry exists per one group and one of them is predecessor).

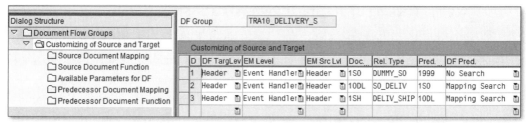

Figure 9.13 Document Flow Category Fields for Transportation Scenario

▸ **Define condition for the document flow** (Transaction /SAPTRX/TSC0TC6)
We can define conditions if we want SAP Event Management to create or update the network under only certain circumstance. To define conditions, use either the condition editor or a function.

▸ **Define multitask activity for event handler** (Transaction /SAPTRX/TSC0TP)
You must define a multitask activity in the rule set. It calls for the activity function DF_UPDATE_FROM_EH and can contain two parameters: the name of the corresponding DF group and a condition

▸ **Assign multitask activity to event handler** (Transaction /SAPTRX/TSC0TT)
The multitask activity create is assigned to the EH Upd. Acty 2 field so that the document flow net is created or updated.

▸ **Create a new rule for event message** (Transaction /SAPTRX/TSC0TR)
You can use the activity DF_UPDATE for creating or updating a document flow net with an event message.

▸ **Delete document flow net**
No archiving functionality exists for document flow. Instead, deletion report /SAPTRX/DELETE_DF is available. The deletion report deletes a net only if every event handler that belongs to the net is deleted or the deletion flag is selected.

9.3 Visibility Scenario II – Transportation Management

This scenario offers visibility processes that integrate SAP Transportation Management (TM) with SAP Event Management. Each visibility process enables us to track different business objects and transportation processes.

9.3.1 Tracking of Shipment Requests and Shipments

In this order, taking the visibility process, the internal company transportation dispatchers and shipper can track and monitor events for shipment requests in transportation planning and events for shipments in transportation execution. Also, the transportation service providers (TSPs) and consignee can track and monitor events for shipments in transportation execution and report actual events.

During the transportation planning, the shipper or ordering party sends requests to transport goods from the source to a target location. On receiving the order, the transportation dispatcher creates a shipment request in SAP TM. Once saved, the shipment request status can be tracked in SAP Event Management on any further progress on the request. You can track the following events in this shipment request process:

▶ Receive shipment request

▶ Prepare planning

▶ Start planning

▶ Finish planning

▶ Confirm

▶ Block for planning and execution

▶ Block for execution

▶ Cancel

▶ Assign shipment

After the transportation planning, SAP TM creates freight units and shipments for the execution of the shipment request. You can track this execution phase of the shipment request in the shipment event handler (Figure 9.14) in SAP Event Management.

Below is the list of the expected events for shipments tracking in SAP Event Management:

▶ Loading

▶ Proof of pickup

- Departure
- Arrival at destination
- Unloading
- Proof of delivery

In addition to normal expected events, SAP Event Management can also track unexpected events or other normal business events, for example:

- Delay
- Cargo split
- Shipment blocked
- Customs in (export)
- Clear customs (export)
- Customs in (import)
- Clear Customs (Import)

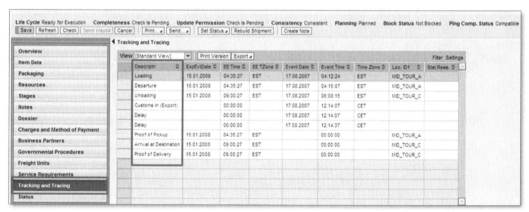

Figure 9.14 Event Handler in Transportation Menu – Tracking and Tracing

These events can be reported in two ways:

- When a TSP sends an event message from the SAP Event Management web user interface to SAP TM (Figure 9.15), the shipment is updated with information in an event message.

▶ When the shipment is updated directly in SAP Event Management, the event message is sent to SAP Event Management.

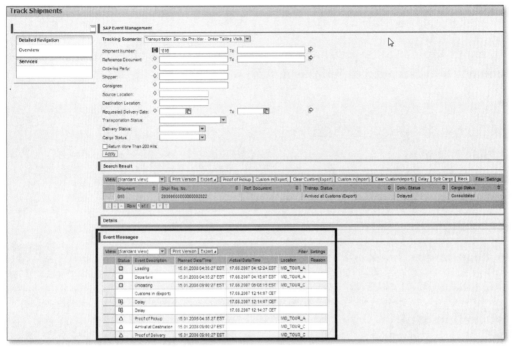

Figure 9.15 Event Message Reporting via SAP Event Management Web Interface

The business goals achieved in this scenario are:

▶ The shipper or ordering party can monitor the status changes of shipment requests.

▶ The transportation dispatcher, shipper, consignee, and transportation service provider can monitor the expected and actual events for shipments from loading the goods to the proof of delivery at the consignee.

▶ The consignee can report proof of delivery.

▶ The transportation service provider can report events, including unexpected events during the execution, for example, a delay.

▶ The transportation dispatcher can receive an alert when an unexpected event is reported, for example, a delay.

9.3.2 Tracking of Tours

In this transportation execution visibility process, the internal company transportation dispatchers and shipper can track and monitor events for tours during the execution process. The capability also exists for your TSPs to monitor events for tours and report actual events.

You can track the following expected events for tours in SAP Event Management:

▶ Departure

▶ Arrival

In addition to the expected events, the process can also report below unexpected events and trigger alerts to SAP TM:

▶ Skip Location

▶ Delay

▶ Block

These events can be reported in two ways:

▶ When the TSP sends an event message from the SAP Event Management web user interface to SAP TM, the tour is updated with information in an event message.

▶ When the tour is updated directly in SAP Transportation Management, the event message is sent to SAP Event Management.

The business goals achieved in this scenario are:

▶ The shipper or ordering party can monitor the expected events for their tours.

▶ Transportation dispatchers can monitor all events including unexpected events concerning tours and receive alerts about delays.

▶ TSPs can monitor all events including unexpected events concerning tours in which they are involved and report these events.

9.3.3 Tracking of Transportation Unit and Vehicle Resources

This transportation resource enables internal company transportation dispatchers to track and monitor events for transportation unit resources and vehicle resources in transportation execution. The transportation execution clerk can also report the actual events for execution.

The resources are tracked via their assignment on the tour. When an event occurs for the assigned tour, an event may also be registered for the resource. SAP Event Management can track following events for resources:

▶ Departure

▶ Arrival at destination

▶ Assign tour

▶ Remove assignment

In addition to expected events, we can also track below unexpected events for resources:

▶ Sighting

▶ Damage

▶ Skip location

These events can be reported in two ways:

▶ The transportation execution clerk can send an event message from the SAP Event Management web user interface to SAP TM.

▶ When a tour is assigned to resources directly in SAP TM, the event message is sent to SAP Event Management.

The business goals achieved in this scenario are:

▶ Transportation dispatchers can monitor actual events concerning their resources within their tour planning and can receive alerts in case of damages.

▶ The transportation execution clerk can report actual events such as departure, arrival, sighting, damage, and skip location directly through the SAP Event Management web interface.

9.3.4 Tracking of Supplier Shipment and Freight Quotes

This tendering visibility process enables internal company transportation dispatchers to track and monitor requests for supplier shipment quote (RSSQ) and requests for supplier freight quote (RSFQ) in the tendering process of SAP TM. This scenario helps transportation dispatchers track and monitor their requests for quotations.

SAP Event Management can track following events for this scenario:

▶ Send request for quote

▶ Receive response (Messages can be quote acceptable or quote not acceptable or reject request for quote or require quote for review.)

▶ Select quote

▶ Accept quote

▶ Cancel tendering (occurs when tendering process is cancelled and event handler in SAP Event Management is deactivated.)

9.3.5 Configuration Steps

There are three configuration steps involved in this scenario:

SAP Transportation Management–SAP Event Management integration

Configure the EM relevance (Figure 9.16) for all transportations scenarios.

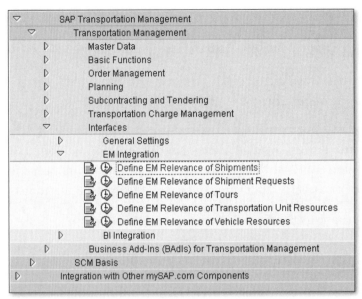

Figure 9.16 Configurations for Transportation EM Integration

Maintain the following SAP Event Management application objects (Figure 9.17) for each relevance:

- Define EM Relevance of Shipments: ODT10_HSH

- Define EM Relevance of Shipment Requests: ODT10_SRQ

- Define EM Relevance of Tours: TEX10_TOUR

- Define EM Relevance of Transportation Unit Resources: RES10_VEHICLE_RES

- Define EM Relevance of Vehicle Resource: RES10_TU_RES, RES10_VEHICLE_RES

Each configuration item is marked Active for object tracking in SAP Event Management.

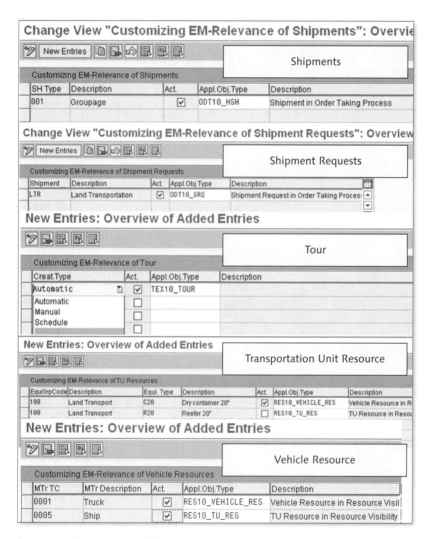

Figure 9.17 Transportation EM Integration Relevance

SAP Event Management Application System Configuration

For application system configuration, we need to maintain business process types (BPTs), application object types (AOTs), and event types (ETs).

The BPTs (Figure 9.18) that are used for this scenario are:

- Tracking of shipments: TMS_HSH

- Tracking of shipment requests: TMS_SRQ

- Tracking of tours: TMS_TOUR

- Tracking of transportation unit resource and vehicle resource: TMS_RESOURCE

- Tracking of supplier shipment and freight quote: TMS_RFQ

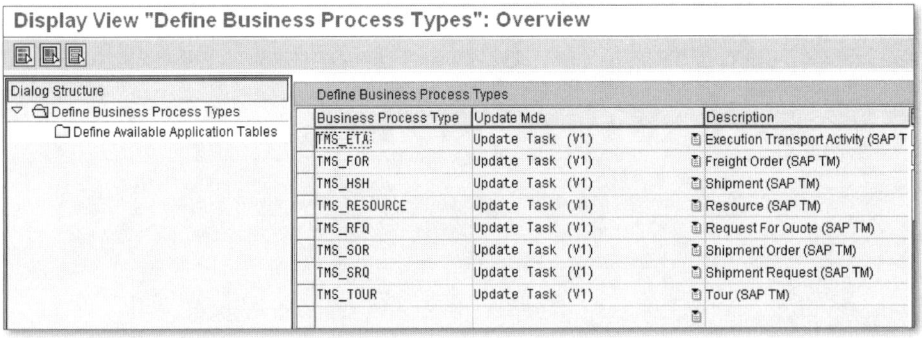

Figure 9.18 Business Process Types for Transportation Scenario

Table 9.2 lists the SAP-delivered event types for the corresponding AOTs and BPTs.

Business Process Type	Application Object Type	Event Type(s)
TMS_HSH	ODT10_HSH	ODT10_ASSIGN_HSH
		ODT10_BLOCK
		ODT10_CANCEL

Table 9.2 Delivered Event Types for SAP TM Scenarios

Business Process Type	Application Object Type	Event Type(s)
TMS_SRQ	ODT10_SRQ	ODT10_BLOCK_EXEC
		ODT10_BLOCK_PLAN
		ODT10_CANCEL
		ODT10_CONFIRM
		ODT10_FINISH_PLAN
		ODT10_PREPARE_PLAN
		ODT10_RECEIVE_SRQ
		ODT10_START_PLAN
		ODT10_UNBLOCK
TMS_TOUR	TEX10_TOUR	TEX10_CANCEL
TMS_RESOURCE	RES10_VEHICLE_RES	RES10_DELETE_TU
		RES10_DELETE_VEH
TMS_RFQ	TND10_RSFQ	TND10_CANCEL_RSFQ
	TND10_RSSQ	TND10_CANCEL_RSSQ
		TND10_SEND_RSFQ
		TND10_SEND_RSSQ

Table 9.2 Delivered Event Types for SAP TM Scenarios (Cont.)

SAP Event Management Configuration

SAP Event Management configuration involves maintenance of event handler types, unexpected events, expected event profiles, status attributes, the web interface, and rule sets.

Let's take the example of the tracking of shipment scenario. Begin with the Event Handler definition (Figure 9.19) with the assignment of the shipment business process type. Assign the standard ODT10_HSH profile to the rule set, expected event profile, and status attribute profile. Next, define the unexpected event codes (Figure 9.20) for the scenario for the event handler type. You use the expected event profile to monitor the expected events during the tolerance time window defined. You use the rule set to define the activities when event message is posted from SAP TM and the reaction to that event message. A list of multitask activities are defined for both expected and unexpected event messages.

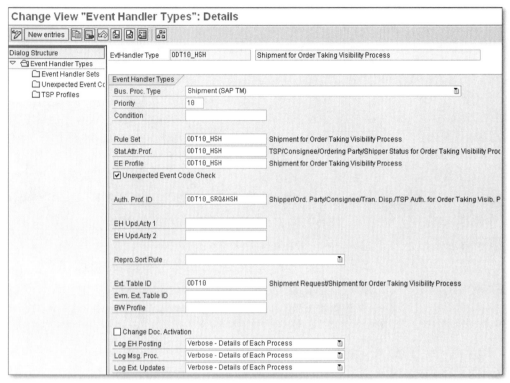

Figure 9.19 Event Handler Type for Shipment Tracking

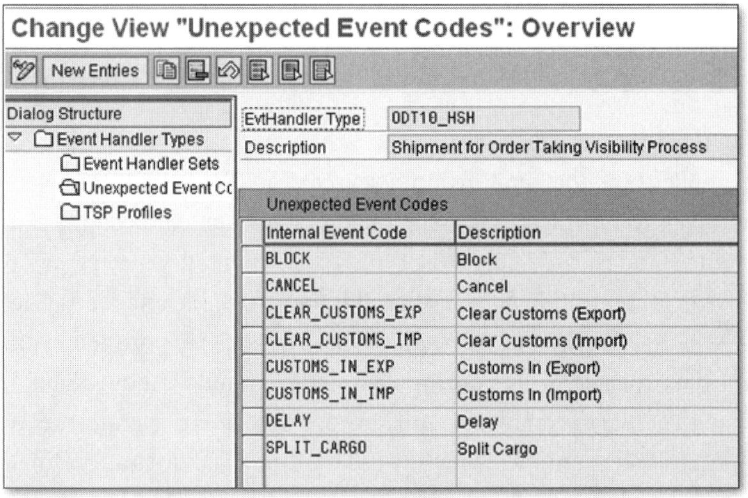

Figure 9.20 Unexpected Event Codes for Shipment Tracking Scenario

9.4 Visibility Scenario III – SAP APO TP/VS Shipments and Tendering

The SAP Advanced Planner and Optimizer (APO) component Transportation Planning and Vehicle Scheduling (TP/VS) is used to plan and optimize shipment for orders (sales orders, purchase orders, stock transport orders) and deliveries. The transportation planners create shipments and assign vehicles to them. During the planning, the planner can model various constraints, for example, requested delivery date or transportation capacities when assigning the shipments to vehicle resources. The result of TP/VS is the creation of a planned shipment. The core features of TP/VS are:

▶ **Interactive planning**
Used to plan shipments for orders and deliveries and process them manually. The planner can also use an interactive planning board to schedule the shipments or vehicle resources.

▶ **Optimization**
Primarily for optimizing the shipment on the basis of the cost and to determine the optimal delivery sequence and transportation dates and times.

▶ **Transportation service provider (TSP) selection**
Assignment of the TSP to the shipments, either manually or automatically. For automatic assignment the system assigns the transportation service providers based on a profile where they can define criteria of assignment, for example, costs or priority.

▶ **Releasing planned shipments**
Used to fix the planned shipment after completing the planning.

▶ **Transportation tendering (collaborative transportation planning)**
Used to tender released shipments to external transportation service providers using electronic data Interchange (EDI) or the Internet. The transportation service provider can react to the tender in various ways: accept the offer, reject the offer, or suggest changes to deadline dates.

▶ **Monitoring exceptional situation**
If problems arises during the planning, TSP selection or transportation tender-

ing, the exceptions alert helps the planner display and resolve the issues in interactive planning.

The integration of TP/VS and SAP Event Management (Figure 9.21) comes in the monitoring transportation execution. You can use SAP Event Management not only for monitoring the fulfillment of shipment orders, but also during the tendering process with forwarding agents or transport agents.

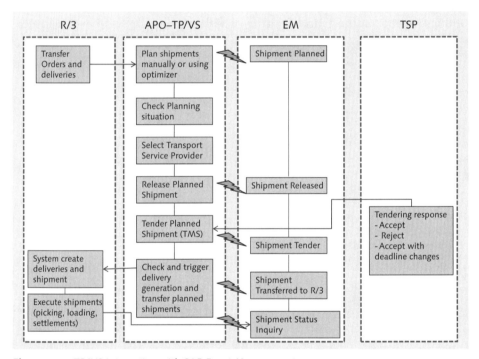

Figure 9.21 TP/VS Integration with SAP Event Management

The process flow steps for the integration are:

▶ Transactional data (sales orders and deliveries) is transferred from SAP R/3 to SAP APO via the Core Interface (CIF).

▶ The transportation planner executes planning in TP/VS and assigns the orders to vehicle resources. The system uses this assignment to generate a planned shipment automatically. While creating the shipments, TP/VS can take various constraints such as vehicle capacities and delivery dates into account. A event can also be triggered to SAP Event Management for shipment planned creation.

▶ The planner can check the planning situation on the planning board by displaying all planning objects (orders, resources, and planned shipments).

▶ Before releasing the planned shipment, the planner assigns a transportation service provider to the shipment and issues a new tender to TSP. Events can be triggered to SAP Event Management for updating the shipment status to release and tendered. If the company uses EDI, it sends EDI outbound message number 204.

▶ The TSP can either accept, reject, or accept with changes in deadline. If EDI is the communication means used, the TSP sends EDI inbound message number 990. The status response is updated in TP/VS and accordingly updated in SAP Event Management.

▶ On planning completion, the planner triggers generation of deliveries of SAP R/3 for the orders for which planned shipments exist.

▶ Once the delivery creation is complete, the planned shipment is transferred to SAP R/3 either manually or in the background. The shipments are created automatically in SAP R/3.

▶ The SAP R/3 Logistics Execution (LE) component is used for processing transportation execution. This involves picking, loading, freight costing, and printing shipping documents. Shipment status can be inquired between SAP R/3 and SAP Event Management for current shipment status. Once EDI inbound message 214 is received for proof of delivery in SAP R/3, the status in SAP Event Management shows proof of delivery completion.

9.4.1 Configuration Steps

The configuration for this scenario involves defining the shipment business process types in the SAP SCM system. Figure 9.22 shows the application tables associated with the two business process types defined in the SAP SCM system.

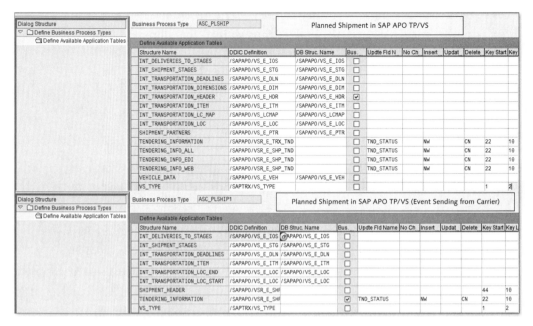

Figure 9.22 Business Process Types for Integration with SAP APO TP/VS

In addition to the BPT configuration, you need to implement a set of business add-ins (BAdIs) in SAP APO TP/VS. You can find these BAdIs in the menu path shown in Figure 9.23. The purposes of these BAdIs are outlined below:

▶ Definition name /SAPAPO/VS_CLP1

If data that is relevant for collaboration with a transportation service provider is changed in a TP/VS process step, this data is made available for other applications using this BAdI. The scenarios in which it can be used are:

▶ A shipment is released from planning for further process steps (for example, delivery generation in an Online Transaction Processing (OLTP) system). This leads to a bid invitation for a transportation service provider.

▶ A shipment that has already been released is returned to the planning stage. Undoing the release leads to the rejection of the transportation service provider.

▶ If a shipment has already been tendered, a rejection can be sent manually to the transportation service provider.

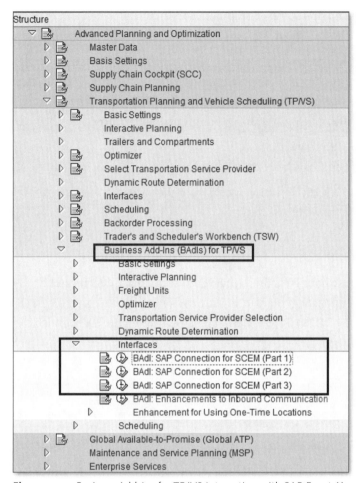

Figure 9.23 Business Add-Ins for TP/VS Integration with SAP Event Management

▶ After a transportation service provider has been rejected, if a shipment is assigned to the next transportation service provider from the results list of the TSP selection, a new bid invitation is also sent.

▶ If a shipment that has already been released and tendered is manually assigned to a new transportation service provider, the old transportation service provider is sent a rejection, and the new one is sent a bid invitation.

▶ Definition name /SAPAPO/VS_CLP2
The scenarios in which this BAdI can be used are:

> ▶ The collaboration engine selects a shipment for tendering to send an IDoc or EDI. As a result, the shipment is classified as tendered for the transportation planning process.

> ▶ A shipment is selected by a transportation service provider who is connected to SAP APO using Internet Transaction Server (ITS). As a result, the shipment is classified as tendered for the transportation planning process.

▶ Definition name /SAPAPO/VS_CLP3
The scenarios in which this BAdI can be used are:

> ▶ Shipments for which the bid invitation was either accepted or rejected by the transportation service provider.

> ▶ Shipments for which the bid invitation was accepted by the transportation service provider with changes.

For this scenario, we also configure the SAP APO alert monitor, which can be triggered via the SAP Event Management rule set activity function SEND_VS_APO_ALERT. The available SAP APO TP/VS alerts are shown in Figure 9.24 under the Alert Monitor transaction (/SAPTRX/AMON1).

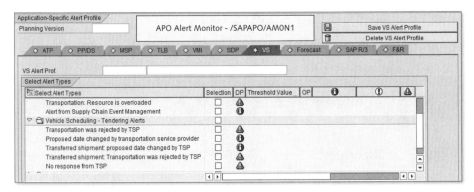

Figure 9.24 APO Alert Monitor for Shipment and Tendering tracking in SAP Event Management

For further monitoring of shipments, the event handler list for shipments (Figure 9.25) is available in the SAP ECC system, which can be accessed via Transaction code /SAPTRX/ASEHVIEW.

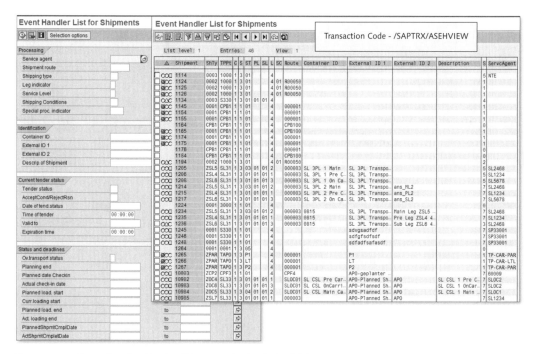

Figure 9.25 Event Handler List for Shipments in the SAP ECC System

9.5   Transportation Analytics

The SAP Event Management event handler contains event data that can be transferred to SAP NetWeaver BW for analytics. The information can be used to evaluate key performance indicators (KPIs) and/or indicators that measure collaboration between partners (CPIs). An example KPI that can be measured is overall transportation cycle time, whereas you can use the measurement of the transportation service provider reliability CPI to find out why the target was not met. For the transportation visibility process, the sea shipment is Business Warehouse business content example for analyzing data in SAP NetWeaver BW. The following evaluations are available in SAP NetWeaver BW content:

▸ Adherence to the planned duration of the entire shipment (transportation chain)

- Adherence to the planned durations for preliminary, main, and subsequent legs
- Duration of custom processing
- Arrival of customs documents

In addition to measuring transportation duration, you can use the analytics to measure the execution and reporting compliance in the transportation scenario. The execution compliance helps us evaluate deviations between the planned and actual occurrence of an event in the transportation scenario. The reporting compliance evaluates the planned and actual arrival of the event message for the events. Whereas the former helps us answers questions such as What was the reason for delays? Was plant departure late? and Does this delay occur frequently for a group of carriers?, the latter compliance measure helps us evaluate how reliable the carrier is on reporting actual events.

9.6 Summary

Transportation visibility plays a major role in fulfilling orders in an extended, competitive supply chain environment. This chapter highlighted the transportation business processes that SAP supports and the integration of SAP Event Management as a visibility tool with SAP Transportation Management (TM) and a planning tool with Transportation Planning and Vehicle Scheduling (TP/VS). The chapter summarized the key configuration objects, monitoring tools, and reporting analytics that can support an overall transportation business process.

The next chapter looks at monitoring of returnable transportable items (RTIs) using RFID technology. The RFID-enabled transport item visibility process enables the outbound, inbound, and return execution, as well as location and status tracking of returnable items typically circulating between business partner locations.

Returnable transport items are key elements for enabling the smooth flow of goods throughout the supply chain. This chapter highlights the integration of SAP Event Management with the SAP Auto-ID infrastructure for enabling business processes supported by radio frequency identification (RFID). We also describe system customization and monitoring procedures.

10   Setting Up a Returnable Transportable Scenario

Returnable transport items (RTIs) include pallets, plastic crates, containers, and industry-specific transport items varying in size and value that are reused. These items may circulate across specific location boundaries or across business partner locations or within one business entity managed by an RTI pool.

This chapter highlights how you can set up the RTI business process in SAP Event Management for tracking and monitoring purposes. The chapter also demonstrates the capability of SAP Event Management to integrate with industry-specific solutions such as the SAP Auto-ID infrastructure (SAP AII). SAP AII uses RFID technology to provide a powerful means to counter inefficiencies in the RTI management process and improve the overall effectiveness of the RTI supply chain network.

10.1   Business Scenario

Despite their importance in supply chain goods flow, RTIs can be prone to high loss and breakage rates. Today's RTI management processes are rather inefficient and are based on estimates about when, where, and how RTIs are utilized. This limited visibility inevitably causes the involved parties to feel less responsible for the proper management of RTIs. As a consequence, inefficiencies created by a single party can result in a significant cost burden for the whole supply chain. The RFID-enabled transport items process enables the outbound, inbound, and return execution and location and status tracking of returnable containers and pallets typically circulating between two business partner locations.

The SAP Event Management visibility process aims to enable the tracking of RTI cycles in locations across business partners. With the help of SAP Event Management, we can monitor a single RTI cycle with its status and material associations across different business partner locations. For scenarios where SAP AII technology is not available, the users can report the events manually in SAP Event Management. The RTI process aims to provide visibility into RTI processing, from the time an RTI tag is commissioned until the asset is decommissioned. Figure 10.1 shows the example of RTI cycle with container items. The key business execution activities for the scenario are:

► RTI initial commissioning, tracking of shipping, and location and maintenance status tracking by supplier

  ► Commission of Global Returnable Assets Identifier (GRAI) encoded by suppliers

  ► Management of available and restricted (damaged) tagged RTI stock

  ► Visibility of empty RTI stock levels

  ► Track and trace of RTI stock with their shipping and location ID and document and maintenance status

► RFID enables outbound processing by the supplier

  ► RFID-enabled or barcode packing (filling) of RTIs

  ► RFID-enabled internal move transactions for empty and packed (filled) RTI units

  ► Manual document assignment for delivery

  ► RFID-enabled loading of RTIs for shipment to business partner

► RFID enabled inbound processing by the customer

  ► Unloading of the packed RTI at the customer location

  ► Moving of the packed RTI to a consumption location at the customer's location

▶ Unpacking of the RTI or disassociation of the RTI with the material at the consumption station

▶ RFID-enabled returns processing of the empties by the customer to the supplier

 ▶ Move of the RTI empties to an RTI empties location awaiting return to the issuing business partner location

 ▶ Assignment of an outbound reference document to the RTI empties for return to the supplier

 ▶ Loading of the empties back to the supplier

▶ RFID-enabled inbound processing of the returned empties by the supplier

 ▶ Unloading of the empties back to the vendor's location

 ▶ Physical inspection of the returned RTIs by the vendor to decide whether the RTIs are in good or damaged condition, enabling the decision about whether the RTIs can be assigned to available to restricted stock status

 ▶ Confirmation of the return of the empties

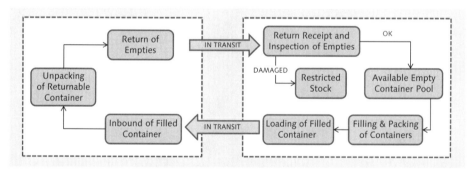

Figure 10.1 Returnable Transport Item (e.g., Container) Process Flow

RFID is fast becoming an important method for automatic identification (auto-ID) of goods, especially for supply chain visibility. Goods containing a small chip with an antenna (RFID tag) are detected at several points along the supply chain. In contrast to barcode strategies that typically identify only the material (for example, the International article numbering (EAN) ID), most RFID applications focus on the identification of each object (pallet, case, or individual item), giving you much more detailed information than barcodes alone. Figure 10.2 shows how the RFID tag can be integrated within SAP technology of SAP AII, SAP R/3, and SAP Event Management.

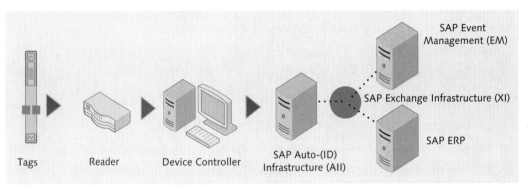

Figure 10.2 RFID Technology with SAP Landscapes

The functions of each component in a landscape are:

▶ Tags
Hold data and transmit data using radio waves.

▶ Readers
Read, write, and transmit data to systems.

▶ Device controller
Manage multiple readers and standardize data.

▶ SAP Auto-ID infrastructure
Store and translate raw electronic product code (EPC) data to business data.

▶ SAP Exchange Infrastructure
Route business data and events to applications.

▶ SAP ERP and SAP Event Management
Provide decision support and execute transactions.

The SAP Auto-ID infrastructure (SAP AII) is essentially a mapping engine, using condition techniques and contextualizing EPC data captured through RFID with business process steps. SAP AII provides logic to map EPC identification data, together with their physical and logical reading location, into business process contexts with the attendant creation or update of business documents such as deliveries and objects such as handling units. The SAP Auto-ID infrastructure also features a database in which the EPC IDs are stored with their associated current and historic states, such as read points, handling unit associations, time stamps, and contexts.

The RTI scenario provides visibility across a closed loop returnable transport item process covering the outbound, inbound, and return process and can be broadly divided into three parts — commissioning, processing, and decommissioning. The key features of this visibility process that supports Global Returnable Assets Identifier (GRAI) encoding are:

- Track and trace RTIs
- Monitor RTIs (internal and business partners)
- Record current and historic cycles
- Monitor RTI status (full, empty)
- Process status (outbound, inbound, return)

10.1.1 Commission RTI Tag

When commissioning a tag, the system determines whether the object is SAP Event Management relevant. The configuration shown in this chapter looks at the product category returnable as the relevancy. A tag for an RTI object is commissioned in SAP AII, and the corresponding event handler is created in SAP Event Management.

10.1.2 Process RTI

The first relevant process step in a cycle occurs when the RTI is moved or packed. A new cycle begins when an empty RTI or a damaged RTI that still may be filled is unloaded at the supplier.

▶ Pack
Packing can be done for both EPC and non-EPC objects. A packing hierarchy is created that sends a Packing event message to SAP Event Management, where it is processed for the event handler type RTI10_EPC. The packing hierarchy is reflected as attributes. The Filling status is set to Not Empty.

▶ Move
A movement can take place at the supplier and at the original equipment manufacturer (OEM) site. This means the RTI is taken to a different sub-location without the contents or status being affected. The event message Movement is sent to SAP Event Management, where it is processed for the event handler type RTI10_EPC. The current location is updated accordingly.

▶ Load
During loading, the RTI is put in transit to another location with (optionally) another SAP AII system. As a consequence, it is no longer an active object in the previous SAP AII system. The Loading event message is sent to SAP Event Management, where it is processed for the relevant event handler with the type RTI10_EPC. The shipping status is set to In transit.

▶ Unload
During unloading, the RTI and its content are received at the destination with (optionally) another SAP AII instance. Therefore, a new active object is created in the related SAP AII system. The Unloading event message is sent to SAP Event Management, where it is processed for the event handler type RTI10_EPC. The shipping status is set to Delivered.

▶ Unpack child objects
Unpacking the child objects removes all of the contents from the related RTI. The Unpacking event message is sent to SAP Event Management, where it is processed for the event handler type RTI10_EPC. The filling status is copied

from SAP AII with the value Empty. If we want to unpack only specific objects from the RTI, we need to perform an unpack action. This way the child objects can be identified with the help of a tag or barcode. Only scanned objects are then removed from the RTI. Any other objects are left untouched. Once the last child object is unpacked, the Empty indicator must be selected manually to be seen in SAP Event Management.

▶ Return
Return means sending the RTI back to the originator. Usually, the RTI is empty, but when damage to the RTI or its contents has been discovered, the physical condition status can be Damaged with a filled RTI.

▶ Confirm return
Confirming the return means getting the RTI back. SAP AII sends the Unloading event message to SAP Event Management, where it is processed for the relevant event handler with the type RTI10_EPC. When unloading an empty RTI or a damaged, filled RTI, it is assumed that the RTI is back at the origin and available for a new cycle. To indicate this, another event message Confirm Return is triggered from SAP Event Management. This deactivates he current event handler and creates a new event handler with a cycle counter increment of 1.

10.1.3 Decommission RTI Tag

When an RTI tag is decommissioned, the relevant event handler is deactivated in SAP Event Management. The information about former RTI cycles is still available in the system, but it is no longer possible to report events for this RTI.

Because there are no planned dates for the activities within SAP AII, no expected events are defined for the RTI scenario. Actual business events are reported either from SAP AII to SAP Event Management or via a web interface when SAP AII is not available.

Table 10.1 lists the events for the scenario.

Event Code	Type of Event	Source
Commission_Tag	Unexpected	SAP AII
Decommission_Tag		SAP AII
Packing		SAP AII
Loading		SAP AII
Confirm_Return		SAP AII
Movement		SAP AII
Unloading		SAP AII, web interface
Unpacking		SAP AII, web interface
Unpacking_Child_ Obj		SAP AII
Update_Attribute		SAP AII

Table 10.1 Event Codes Related to the Scenario

10.2 SAP ECC Configuration

This section details the SAP ECC configuration of three objects: business process type, application object type, and event type.

10.2.1 Business Process Type

Data is transferred from the SAP AII object tables, EPC detailed information, product, object context, location, activity context, and document. This data is contained in the event handler in SAP Event Management. Various application tables (Figure 10.3) reside within the business process type. The primary tables for business process type (BPT) are:

▸ AII_OBJECT
/AIN/DM_ACT_OBJ, /AIN/DM_DEV, /AIN/DM_DEVCTR, /AIN/DM_DEVGRP, /AIN/DM_LOC, /AIN/ID_DATA_STR, /AIN/DM_DOC_STR, /AIN/DM_OBJECT_STR, /AIN/DM_PROD_ALL_STR

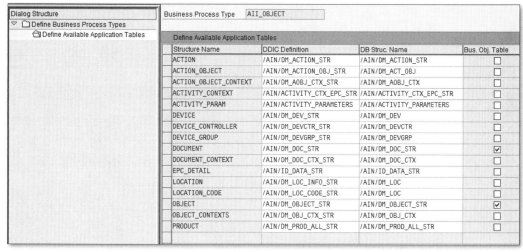

Figure 10.3 Business Process Type(AII_OBJECT) Application Tables

The BPT is made active (Figure 10.4) in Transaction /SAPTRX/ASC0AO. The communication means between SAP ECC and SAP EM is set as update.

Bus. Proc. Type	Update Mode	BPT Process Mode	Description
AII_OBJECT	Update Task (V1)	Active	SAP All Object
EPL_NOTIF	Dialog Update	Inactive	Notification in SAP R/3 Enterprise
ESC_DELIV	Update Task (V1)	Inactive	Delivery in SAP R/3 Enterprise
ESC_FI_CLEARING	Determined by Application	Inactive	FI Clearing in SAP R/3 Enterprise
ESC_MATDOC	Update Task (V1)	Active	Material Document in SAP R/3 Enterprise

Figure 10.4 Business Process Type Activation in Update Mode

10.2.2 Application Object Type

Application object types are used to check the SAP Event Management relevancy and pass parameters, tracking, and ID queries to the SAP Event Management event handler. The two parameters defined are info and control. Info parameters are informative in nature and are displayed, for example, in web queries. Examples of info parameters are order number and the material text. Control parameters are used for control purposes, for example, to define conditions or, in case of an email address to send electronic notifications. Figure 10.5 shows the standard extractors SAP provides for the scenario.

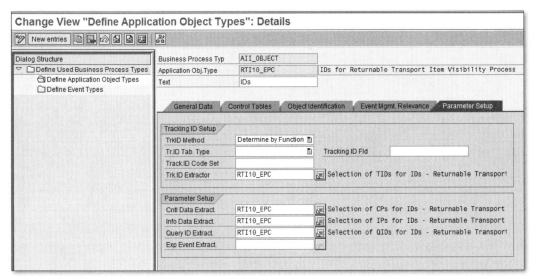

Figure 10.5 Business Process Type Extractors

We need a tracking ID and a query ID to report events and to query statuses. These are also transferred from SAP AII and created together with the event handler. Table 10.2 lists the tracking ID and query ID used in the scenario.

ID	Parameter
Tracking ID	EPC
	EPC URN format
Query ID	Asset type
	Filter

Table 10.2 List of Tracking and Query IDs for the Scenario

The parameters provided in this visibility scenario are shown in Figure 10.6.

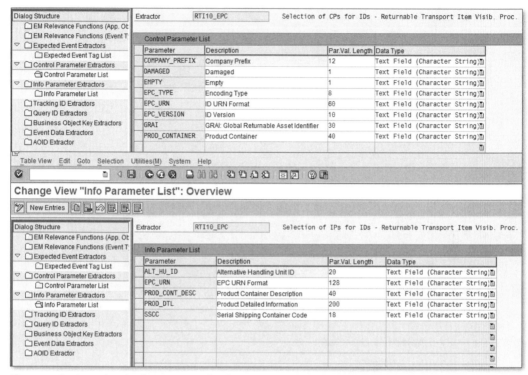

Figure 10.6 Control and Info Parameters for the Scenario

The SAP Event Management relevancy (Figure 10.7) is provided in the form of the function module, and it looks at the combination of the main object table — object and activity parameter — and checks if the product category is returnable.

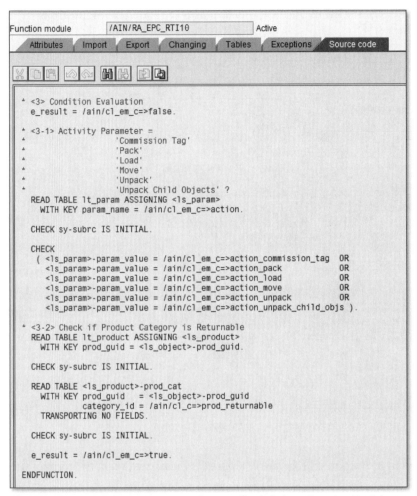

```
Function module        /AIN/RA_EPC_RTI10              Active
  Attributes    Import    Export    Changing    Tables    Exceptions    Source code


* <3> Condition Evaluation
  e_result = /ain/cl_em_c=>false.

* <3-1> Activity Parameter =
*                 'Commission Tag'
*                 'Pack'
*                 'Load'
*                 'Move'
*                 'Unpack'
*                 'Unpack Child Objects' ?
  READ TABLE lt_param ASSIGNING <ls_param>
    WITH KEY param_name = /ain/cl_em_c=>action.

  CHECK sy-subrc IS INITIAL.

  CHECK
    ( <ls_param>-param_value = /ain/cl_em_c=>action_commission_tag  OR
      <ls_param>-param_value = /ain/cl_em_c=>action_pack            OR
      <ls_param>-param_value = /ain/cl_em_c=>action_load            OR
      <ls_param>-param_value = /ain/cl_em_c=>action_move            OR
      <ls_param>-param_value = /ain/cl_em_c=>action_unpack          OR
      <ls_param>-param_value = /ain/cl_em_c=>action_unpack_child_objs ).

* <3-2> Check if Product Category is Returnable
  READ TABLE lt_product ASSIGNING <ls_product>
    WITH KEY prod_guid = <ls_object>-prod_guid.

  CHECK sy-subrc IS INITIAL.

  READ TABLE <ls_product>-prod_cat
    WITH KEY prod_guid   = <ls_object>-prod_guid
             category_id = /ain/cl_c=>prod_returnable
    TRANSPORTING NO FIELDS.

  CHECK sy-subrc IS INITIAL.

  e_result = /ain/cl_em_c=>true.

ENDFUNCTION.
```

Figure 10.7 SAP Event Management Relevancy Check Code as Function Module

10.2.3 Event Types

Event types post the event messages to SAP Event Management. For the RTI scenario, multiple event messages (Figure 10.8) are assigned to the business process type AII_OBJECT.

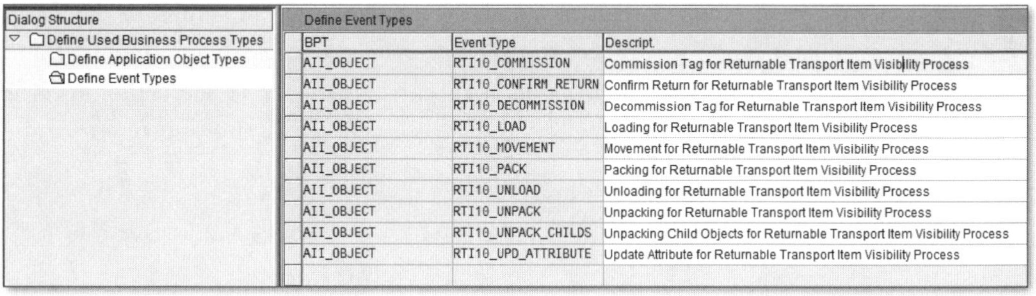

Figure 10.8 Event Types for RTI Scenario

In the Event Data Extractor field, maintain the function module listed in Table 10.3, which primarily passes the event message (code) to SAP Event Management based on the tracking ID of the EPC number. The event message also passes the location code to the SAP Event Management event handler.

Event Types	Event Data Extractor	Function Module
RTI10_COMMISSION	RTI10_COMMISSION	/AIN/ET_COMMISSION_TAG_RTI10
RTI10_CONFIRM_RETURN	RTI10_CONFIRM_RETURN	/AIN/ET_CONFIRM_RETURN_RTI10
RTI10_DECOMMISSION	RTI10_DECOMMISSION	/AIN/ET_DECOMMISSION_TAG_RTI10
RTI10_LOAD	RTI10_LOAD	/AIN/ET_LOAD_RTI10
RTI10_MOVEMENT	RTI10_MOVEMENT	/AIN/ET_MOVEMENT_RTI10
RTI10_PACK	RTI10_PACK	/AIN/ET_PACK_RTI10
RTI10_UNLOAD	RTI10_UNLOAD	/AIN/ET_UNLOAD_RTI10
RTI10_UNPACK	RTI10_UNPACK	/AIN/ET_UNPACK_RTI10
RTI10_UNPACK_CHILD	RTI10_UNPACK_CHILD	/AIN/ET_UNPACK_CHILDOBJS_RTI10
RTI10_UPD_ATTRIBUTE	RTI10_UPD_ATTRIBUTE	/AIN/ET_UPDATE_ATTRIBUTE_RTI10

Table 10.3 Function Modules Associated with Event Types

The SAP Event Management relevancy for the event type is similar to the application object type. In addition to checking whether the activity parameter and the product category are returnable, a check is also made to see if the object is empty or damaged. the following sample code represents all event types for the scenario.

```
DATA:
    lt_param     TYPE /ain/activity_parameters_tab,
    lt_product   TYPE /ain/dm_prod_all_tab,
    lt_obj_ctx   TYPE /ain/dm_obj_ctx_tab.


  FIELD-SYMBOLS:
    <ls_object>  TYPE /ain/dm_object_str,
    <ls_param>   LIKE LINE OF lt_param,
    <ls_product> LIKE LINE OF lt_product,
    <ls_obj_ctx> LIKE LINE OF lt_obj_ctx.

* <1> Read necessary application tables
* <1-1> Activity Parameter
  PERFORM read_appl_table_act_param
    USING     i_all_appl_tables
    CHANGING lt_param.


* <1-2> Product
  PERFORM read_appl_table_product
    USING     i_all_appl_tables
    CHANGING lt_product.


* <1-3> Object Contexts
  PERFORM read_appl_table_obj_ctx
    USING     i_all_appl_tables
    CHANGING lt_obj_ctx.


* <2> Check if Main table is Object.
  IF i_event-maintabdef >< /ain/cl_em_c=>bpt_object.
```

```
    PERFORM create_logtable_et_rel
      TABLES c_logtable
      USING  i_event-maintabdef
             space
             i_event_types-trrelfunc
             i_event-eventtype
             i_appsys.
    EXIT.
  ENDIF.
* Read Main Old Object Table (Object)
  ASSIGN i_event-maintabref->* TO <ls_object>.


* <3> Condition Evaluation
  e_result = /ain/cl_em_c=>false.


* <3-1> Activity Parameter = 'Update Attribute'?
  READ TABLE lt_param ASSIGNING <ls_param>
    WITH KEY param_name = /ain/cl_em_c=>action.

  CHECK sy-subrc IS INITIAL.
  CHECK <ls_param>-param_value = /ain/cl_em_c=>action_update_attribute.

* <3-2> Check if Product Category is Returnable
  READ TABLE lt_product ASSIGNING <ls_product>
    WITH KEY prod_guid = <ls_object>-prod_guid.

  CHECK sy-subrc IS INITIAL.

  READ TABLE <ls_product>-prod_cat
    WITH KEY prod_guid  = <ls_object>-prod_guid
             category_id = /ain/cl_c=>prod_returnable
    TRANSPORTING NO FIELDS.
  CHECK sy-subrc IS INITIAL.
```

```
* <3-3> Check if Object Context 'EMPTY' or 'DAMAGED' exist.
  LOOP AT lt_obj_ctx ASSIGNING <ls_obj_ctx>
    WHERE obj_guid  = <ls_object>-obj_guid
      AND ( field_name = /ain/cl_prf_c=>mc_elem_empty
       OR  field_name = /ain/cl_prf_c=>mc_elem_damaged ).
    e_result = /ain/cl_em_c=>true.
  ENDLOOP.
```

10.3   SAP SCM Configuration

The configuration of SAP SCM can be divided into five components.

▶ **Event handler**
  Monitoring of events.

▶ **Status**
  Providing the current status for shipping, filling, or physical condition.

▶ **Reaction to event**
  Rule sets for identifying follow-up activities after the event message is posted to SAP Event Management.

▶ **Parameter mapping**
  Mapping the SAP ECC fields with SAP SCM fields for info and control parameters.

▶ **Web interface**
  By providing a connection to Internet, SAP Event Management allows all parties in the supply chain network to gain and flexible access to data for display and confirmation purposes.

10.3.1   Event Handler

The defined event handler type is tied to the application object type. In the event handler type (Figure 10.9) we describe the rule set, the status profile, and the authorization profile. Also in the event handler type we define the unexpected events for the scenario. For our scenario, all of the events are reported as unexpected events (Figure 10.10) from SAP AII.

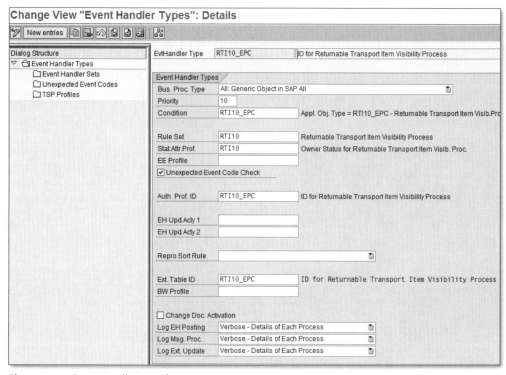

Figure 10.9 Event Handler Type for RTI Scenario

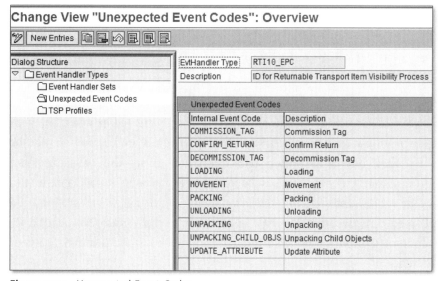

Figure 10.10 Unexpected Event Codes

Parameter Mapping

Via Transaction /SAPTRX/TSCOPDM we can define how the parameter information from the application system is mapped with parameters in SAP Event Management. After mapping the control and info parameter, the profile (Figure 10.11) is linked with application object type RTI10_EPC and the SAP AII application system.

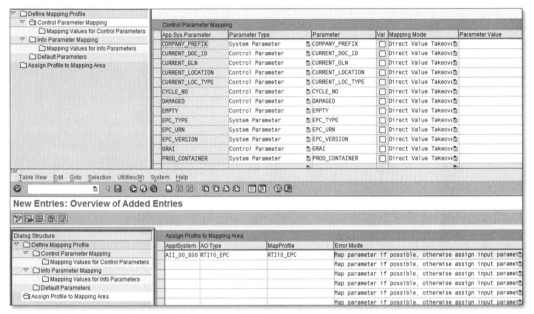

Figure 10.11 Parameter Mapping for RTI Scenario

Status

Statuses are also determined when an event handler is created or when an event message is posted from the SAP AII application. These statuses provide a quick overview of the event handler when status queries are made. Also, the statuses can be used for selecting event handlers. Table 10.4 lists the status RTI scenario and the possible values. The status values change when particular events are reported or are copied directly from SAP AII. In addition to the status, the location ID and document ID updates are also integrated between SAP AII and SAP Event Management.

▶ The shipping status provides information about the progression of the RTI cycle.

▶ The filing status provides information about whether the RTI is empty or filled.

▶ The physical condition status indicates possible damage to the RTI or its content.

Status Attribute	Status Attribute Values
RTI10_SHIPPING	Delivered
	In transit
	New
	Return confirmed
RTI10_FILLING	Empty
	Non_empty
RTI10_MAINTENANCE	Damaged
	OK

Table 10.4 Status Attributes and Status Values

10.3.2 Reaction to Event

The rule set in SAP Event Management is triggered when an event message arrives. This in turn triggers follow-up activities. Figure 10.12 shows an example rule set for an RTI scenario configured for the event messages posted in SAP Event Management. A good example of a rule set in action is the status value update in the event handler. Table 10.5 shows rule set status update that follows the arrival of an event message.

Reported Event	Status Change in Event Handler
Commission	Shipping status: new
Load	Shipping status: in transit
Unload	Shipping status: delivered
Confirm return	Shipping status: return confirmed

Table 10.5 Example of Rule Set on Status Update

At the start of a new cycle, a new event handler with an incremental cycle counter is created. The shipping status is set to New. The filling and physical condition statuses are always copied directly from SAP AII.

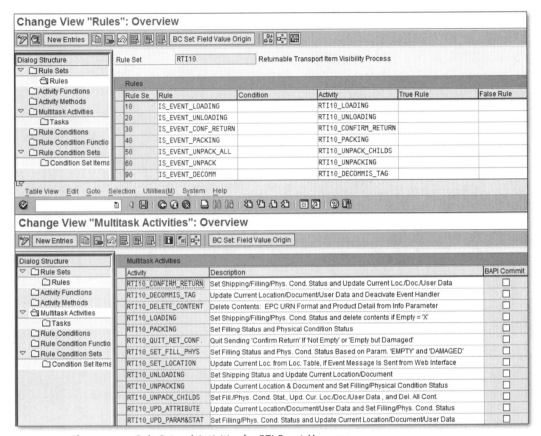

Figure 10.12 Rule Set and Activities for RTI Event Messages

10.3.3 Setting Up the Web Interface

We can customize both the web layout structure and the page contents in SAP Event Management. The screen sequence in the SAP Event Management Web Communication Layer (WCL) of the individual pages is predefined and cannot be changed in the configuration. When the user calls the web link, the logon screen appears, and the pages display in the following order:

- Logon screen for entering the user and password
- Selection screen that displays the web interface transaction in the upper section and the fields that can be selected in the lower section
- List screen with all objects that have been selected
- Screen with detailed information about the relevant object
- Buttons on various screens to navigate to the screen for confirming current events
- Detail screen for confirming actual events with the button for sending actual events

We can also define the following settings for customization:

- Web interface transaction definition
- User profile definition

Both the settings are assigned to the user in SAP Event Management. Whenever the user logs on to the web interface, the settings specified for him are used to determine the following:

- The layout of all web screens (specified in the selection profile, display profile, and event message profile)
- The choice of selection parameters (specified in the selection profile)
- The field contents that are displayed (specified in the display profile)
- The possibility to confirm actual events (specified in the event message profile)

We can use the authorization and filter profiles to customize the contents that are displayed and the options for confirming events. If changes are made to the layout in customizing, the profiles must be reloaded in the web interface. The profiles can be manually reloaded on the Web interface admin page. We can also automatically trigger the reload by selecting parameter /SAPTRX/WCLNOCACHING under Parameter in the user master (Transaction SU01) and by setting the value to X. As a result, each time a web interface action is called, the most recent setting in the user profile is displayed.

Defining Web Interface Transactions

Web interface transactions are used in the web interface selection screen. We can assign several combinations of a web interface transaction and a user profile to a user. The web interface transactions delivered in this visibility process include RTI10_OWNER and RTI10_CUSTOMER.

Configuring Fields for the User Profile

The parameters (info, control, system), status profiles, and event message data fields for the web interface are configured in relation to already known fields in SAP Event Management. The configured fields are then assigned in the display profile, the selection profile, and the event message profile. Info, control, and system parameters are listed with the prefixes Info_, control_ or system_. All of the configured fields that are relevant to this visibility process are prefaced with RTI10_.

Defining User Profiles

The display profile, selection profile, and event message profile are joined together in a user profile. When assigned to a user profile, the user can select and display data and confirm events when logged on to the web interface. The event message profile is optional and can be left if the user does not want to confirm the events in the web interface. A user profile is delivered in this visibility process for both the supplier (RTI10_Owner) and customer (RTI10_Customer).

Assigning User Profiles to Users

A user can only log on to the web interface when he has been assigned a user profile. You can make this assignment in Transaction code /SAPTRX/UCUSER.

Assigning User Profiles to Roles

Alternatively, the assignment can take place with the help of a user role. You can make this assignment in Transaction code /SAPTRX/UCROLE.

10.3.4 BAdI Activation for SAP AII

Business add-in (BAdI) implementation /SAPTRX/RTI10_EHUPD needs to be active in SAP Event Management for communication with SAP AII.

10.4 Scenario Monitoring in SAP Event Management 5.1

SAP AII enables backend systems such as SAP ERP and supply chain visibility tools such as SAP Event Manager to leverage RFID technology. SAP AII connects the physical world, as observed by RFID devices, with the business-oriented document view of an SAP ERP system. For example, the RFID detection of pallets and cases at a gate in the warehouse can confirm that an expected inbound delivery is complete.

The scenario commences by writing a new tag in SAP AII Auto-ID Cockpit (Figure 10.13) for your Global Returnable Asset Identifier (GRAI). A new tag is necessary for using the returnable transport item for first time. The commission tag is reported to an SAP Event Management event handler.

An operator uses a web browser on the handheld mobile RFID device to access the SAP AII mobile UI. After logon, the operator can access a transaction for writing RFIDs (tag commissioning) or a transaction that involves reading RFIDs (pack, move, and load). The operator can interact with these transactions using a keyboard and function keys ($\boxed{\text{Enter}}$, $\boxed{\text{F1}}$ – $\boxed{\text{F10}}$). Typically, the operator initiates RFID reading or writing by pulling the trigger on the mobile RFID device while a tag is in the scanning field.

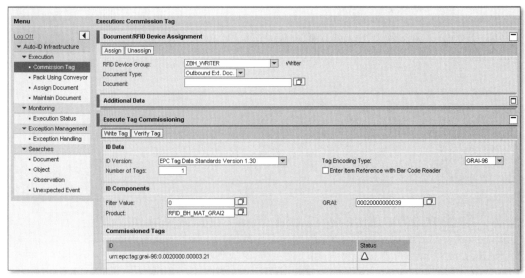

Figure 10.13 Auto-ID Cockpit for Writing New Commission Tag

Using the auto-ID mobile device, the operator enters the device group and commences the pack process (Figure 10.14). The event is seen in Web Communication Layer (WCL) with a new filling status update.

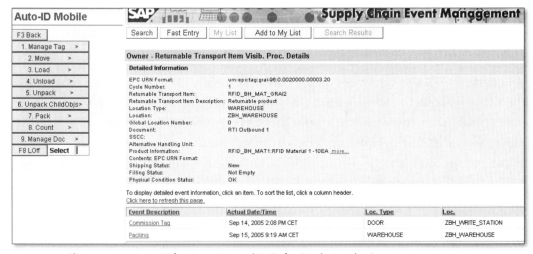

Figure 10.14 Auto ID for Reporting and WCL for Displaying the Event

Using the device controller and device ID, we can report the loading status in the SAP AII Auto ID test tool simulation. The loading event (Figure 10.15) is displayed in the WCL with the updated shipping status.

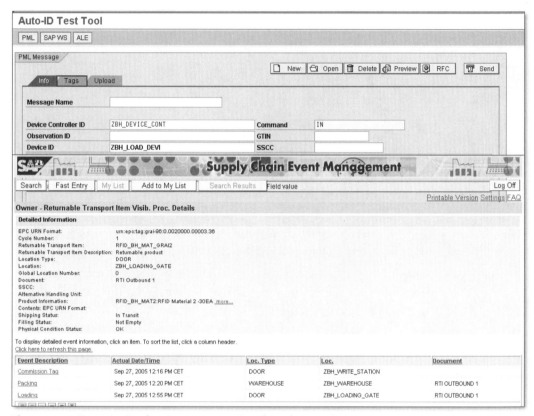

Figure 10.15 Reporting Loading Event in Auto-ID and Display in WCL

After the goods arrive at the customer site, the unloading process commences. The customer may want to report the event online via WCL (Figure 10.16). The shipping status is updated to Delivered status. The customer unpacks the products and again reports the unpacking status.

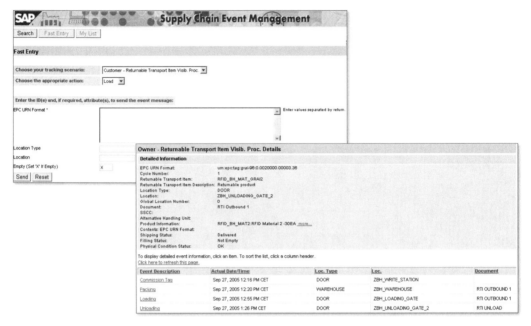

Figure 10.16 Unloading at Customer Site and Reporting via WCL

The movement of an empty container is reported again via the auto-ID mobile device, and the filling status is updated in WCL.

Figure 10.17 Movement of Container Back from Customer to Warehouse

The GRAI is loading in SAP AII to return the device to the vendor.

Once the unloading event is reported in the vendor side, the confirm return is immediately reported as well. When this last event the cycle is complete and now again if we pick material for this transport item, the system generates a new event handler (Figure 10.18). SAP EM automatically creates a new event handler for a GRAI if the existing event handler status is Confirm Return. For every event handler, a new cycle number is created automatically.

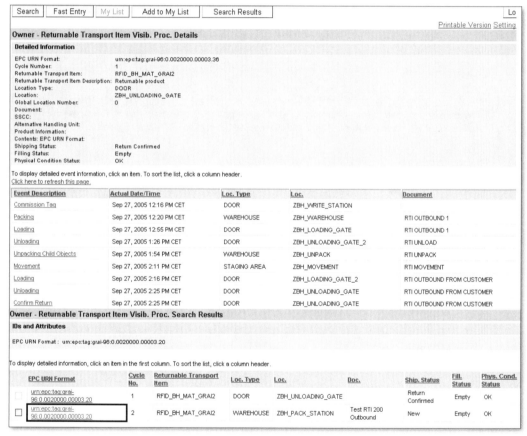

Figure 10.18 Completion of RTI Event Cycle and Creation of New Event Handler

In addition to WCL, the RTI event cycles can also be seen in an SAP Event Management event handler (Figure 10.19) via Transaction /SAPTRX/EH_LIST.

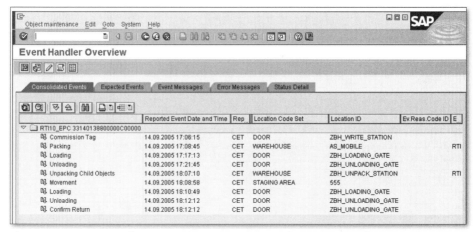

Figure 10.19 Event–Handler–Reported Unexpected Events for RTI Event Cycle

Two user profile–web transaction combinations are available for the RTI process: RTI10_Owner for the owner of the RTI and RTI10_Customer for the posting of the event messages (without SAP AII) at the customer site.

10.4.1 Analytics and Reporting

SAP Auto-ID infrastructure 4.0 features direct extractors to SAP NetWeaver Business Warehouse. Preconfigured BW query reports with corresponding KPIs are offered that enable the reporting on the quality of reads and quality of writes, the current state of RTI objects, the cycle time across locations (with and without ID), and movements across locations (with and without ID), as well as stock situations at different locations and movements at locations by action type.

In addition, SAP Auto-ID infrastructure enables (through the implementation of a BAPI) the upload of observed EPC events by business partners. This enables (in addition to offering extended reporting capabilities) checking that the business partners have received all tagged products issued.

10.5   Summary

With the advancement in radio frequency identification (RFID) technology, the vision of tracking the flow of goods along the complete supply chain in real time is becoming a reality. SAP Auto-ID infrastructure integrates SAP ERP solutions with RFID technologies seamlessly and provides near real-time visibility with SAP Event Management. This chapter described how returnable transportable items (RTIs) can be modeled in SAP AII and SAP Event Management applications. Configuration steps in SAP ECC and SAP SCM were highlighted with detailed descriptions of steps during the scenario execution.

The next chapter focuses on the integration of SAP Event Management with other SAP solutions. The integration provides real-time supply chain visibility to customers and capabilities of tracking vehicles and cargo. SAP Event Management condenses the various physical events received into a meaningful business context. Integrating with both frontend and backend applications, SAP Event Management event handling capabilities enable action to take place in a proactive versus reactive mode.

This chapter deals with the optimal integration of SAP Event Management with other SAP solutions. It introduces integrated SAP solutions that are beneficial for high-performance supply chain visibility processes.

11   Integrating SAP Event Management with other SAP Solutions

Supply chain visibility means a supply chain manager can identify purchased materials as they move through the suppliers' production flow and transportation networks to the company's receiving docks. In the same context, the company must have the same visibility into outbound goods as they are manufactured, assembled, stored in inventory, and shipped through the transportation network to customers' receiving docks. SAP Event Management integrates with other SAP applications to identify disruptions in the flow of materials and uses workflow and modeling abilities to improve a supply chain manager's ability to respond and take proactive actions.

This chapter illustrates how SAP Event Management integrates with other SAP solutions supporting business processes to provide supply chain visibility on overall business processes.

11.1   SAP Supply Network Collaboration

SAP SNC 5.1 supports supplier collaboration business processes in the area of procurement planning, procurement processing, and billing. The individual areas within the supplier collaboration are:

► **Collaborative forecasting**
Used in procurement planning where the supplier monitors the planning figures and replenishes the manufacturer. The supplier can adjust his capacity and avoid any excess inventories.

► **Order-based collaboration**
Scenario where customer uses individual orders to inform the suppliers about net demands. Processes covered can be work order or kanban process.

► **Demand-related collaboration**
Unlike the previous scenario, the customer transfers the gross demand to the supplier and gets timely replenishment of stocks.

► **Replenishment execution**
The execution is carried out by creating advanced shipping notifications (ASNs) in SAP SNC and integrating third-party logistics service providers using the Supply Network Inventory (SNI) functionality.

► **Invoice collaboration**
Invoices can be covered independently for all business processes by using invoice collaboration in SAP SNC 5.1. The supplier can create invoices in SAP SNC, or the customer can carry out automatic receipt settlement.

SAP Event Management supports all supplier collaboration business processes in SAP SNC, with a primary focus on the purchase order and responsive replenishment monitoring scenarios. Below are some examples of SAP SNC and SAP Event Management integration for supplier collaboration business processes delivered in SAP SCM 5.1:

► **Purchase order (business process type: SNC_PURORD)**
The supplier needs to acknowledge the receipt of a purchase order within a specified time window. An event is automatically generated from SAP SNC during the purchase order creation (Figure 11.1). The subsequent process of process receipt and confirmation is also reported from SAP SNC to SAP Event Management.

▶ **Replenishment order (business process type: SNC_RPLORD)**

The replenishment process can function for purchase orders or sales orders. SAP Event Management can monitor the creation, publication, and sending of replenishment orders (customer or supplier). It can also monitor the confirmation for purchase orders (customer) or confirmation for sales orders (supplier).

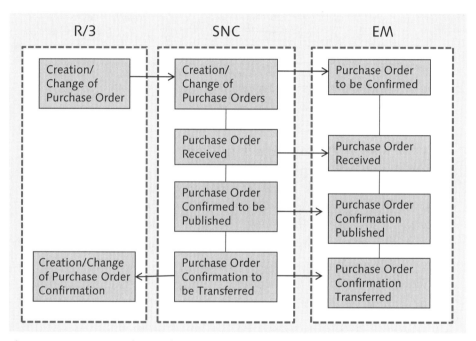

Figure 11.1 SAP SNC Purchase Order Integration with SAP Event Management

▶ **Expected XML messages for SMI (business process type: SNC_MSGIN)**

In SAP SNC the customer routinely transmits the ProductActivityNotification message for sending the forecast and inventory-level information to suppliers. SAP Event Management helps in monitoring that the expected event is generated by report /SCA/EM_MSG_EE_CREATE for SAP SNC messages (Figure 11.2). If the event is not received within a specified time window, an alert is created that is visible in the SAP SNC Alert Monitor.

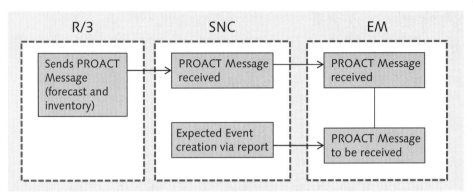

Figure 11.2 SAP SNC XML Message Monitoring in SAP Event Management

11.2 SAP Transportation Management

SAP Transportation Management (TM) provides integrated transportation planning and execution functionality. The target customers for SAP TM functionalities are shippers (companies that either manufacture or distribute products) and logistics service providers (LSPs) (companies that manage the movement of goods for the shippers). SAP Event Management is an integral part of SAP TM for tracking and tracing functionalities. SAP Event Management supports the following transportation business processes (explained previously in Chapter 9, Section 9.3):

▶ **Order taking**
Helps in tracking and monitoring events for shipment request in transportation planning and events for shipments in transportation execution.

▶ **Transportation execution**
Helps in tracking and monitoring events for tours in transportation execution processes.

▶ **Resource**
Helps in tracking and monitoring events for transportation unit resources and vehicle resources in transportation execution processes.

▶ **Tendering**
Helps in tracking and monitoring requests for supplier shipment quotes and requests for supplier freight quotes in the transportation tendering process.

The SAP TM solution is built on ABAP Web Dynpro user interfaces with enhanced usability features, portal integration, and a role-based dashboard. SAP Event Management key transactions are available as part of Personal Object Worklist Tracking (POWL) with alert inbox and role-based Web Dynpro status tracking for shipments, tours, resources, and quotation requests.

Figure 11.3 shows the document flow in SAP TM and the creation of various documents by SAP TM planning engines (tour builder, planning, shipment builder, freight builder, charge engine, shipment freight order). All of the business documents highlighted in Figure 11.3 are tracked in SAP Event Management for shipment fulfillment. SAP Event Management provides complete visibility of end-to-end transportation processes and monitors critical events.

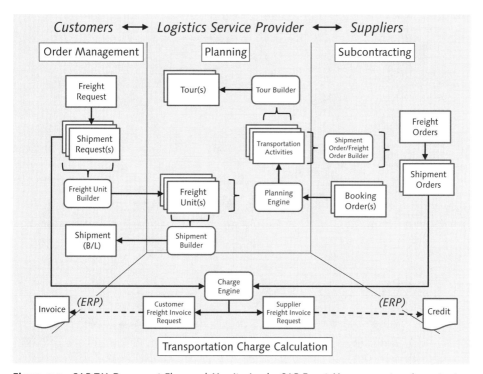

Figure 11.3 SAP TM Document Flow and Monitoring by SAP Event Management on Important Process Documents

11.3 SAP NetWeaver Business Warehouse

SAP NetWeaver Business Warehouse (BW) provides business content for various visibility scenarios. The business content delivers a preconfigured set of role- and task-relevant information models. The information models include all of the technical objects such as workbooks, queries, info sources, data sources, info cubes, key figures, characteristics, update rules, and extractors.

SAP Event Management provides the expected event and actual event date and time stamp that can be used for measuring the cycle time in supply chain processes. In addition to information on measuring cycle times, we can also extract information on recorded reason codes for exceptions in supply chains and the number of occurrences of a particular event. You can use SAP NetWeaver BW for measuring the following supply chain visibility key performance metrics:

▶ On-time delivery

▶ Perfect order

▶ Inventory turns finished goods

▶ Fill rate

▶ Lost sales

▶ Inventory turns raw materials

SAP NetWeaver BW also integrates with SAP TM and SAP Event Management to provide various business content metrics on shipments, carriers, and customers.

11.4 SAP NetWeaver Portal

SAP NetWeaver Portal provides small programs called iViews. iViews are self-contained web documents that are provided via a Uniform Resource Locator (URL) managed by the SAP portal framework. The resource itself can be anywhere on the Web and accessible by internal or external business partners. From the user perspective, the iView is a mini-app that appears through a portal. The user logs on via a portal, and the portal server communicates directly with SAP Event Management

(Figure 11.4). SAP Event Management events' visibility with status integrated in SAP Portal can be shared between manufacturers, suppliers, retailers, and distributors for providing near real-time visibility of the order fulfillment. You can also use the SAP Portal for posting various event messages by business partners and exchanging backend data and documents among business partners.

SAP NetWeaver Portal can group together process steps that are required for the complete process flow by providing visibility of end-to-end business processes. Some of the business activities you can see in SAP Portal are:

▶ Delivery of work-item by workflow for follow-up activities from SAP Event Management.

▶ List of expected events for the day. This helps operations to prioritize the activities scheduled for the day.

▶ Overdue list report highlighting the expected events that didn't occur as planned.

▶ Alert inbox giving the notification of supply chain exceptions.

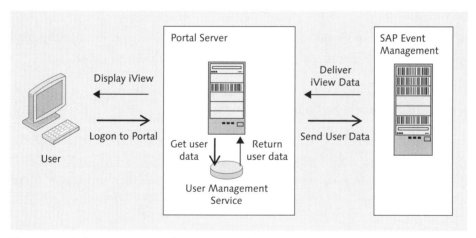

Figure 11.4 SAP NetWeaver Portal Integration with SAP Event Management

11.5 SAP Advanced Planning and Optimization

SAP Advanced Planning and Optimization (APO) offers a planning tool for managing sales and operation planning (SOP) business processes. The functionality covers strategic, tactical, and operational levels of business processes. Whereas SAP APO balances supply and demand, the supply-chain planning system benefits from the constant plan monitoring with SAP Event Management. SAP Event Management enables rapid responses to surplus or shortage conditions in the supply chain network. SAP Event Management can send alerts to SAP APO Alert Monitor for consolidating alerts from planning situations. SAP Event Management capabilities provides early warning capabilities to help effectively execute the established supply chain plans. In Chapter 9, Section 9.4 we gave an example of SAP APO TP/VS integration with SAP Event Management where the transportation shipment lifecycle can be tracked and monitored in SAP Event Management. SAP Event Management can also proactively monitor measurement values of equipment (for example, refrigerated containers) and give notifications if the measurements (temperatures) are outside tolerance limits. SAP Event Management serves as a mechanism for fine-tuning the gap between planning and execution with process efficiency improvement initiatives. SAP Event Management helps in decision-making support by identifying the root cause of supply chain exceptions such as inaccurate forecasts, product out of stock, and shipment delays.

SAP Event Management can also be a central place for consolidating events happening in different applications.

An example (Figure 11.5) is new product introduction (NPI), where different product lifecycle activities are planned in SAP PLM, SAP R/3 and SAP APO. SAP Event Management can serve as a progress report to track the execution of these plans.

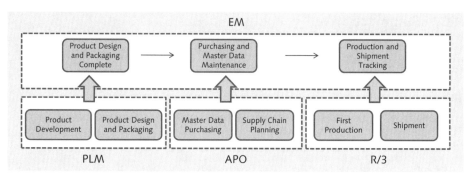

Figure 11.5 New Product Introduction (NPI) Process Monitoring

Figure 11.6 shows the integrated view of SAP Event Management and SAP solutions in providing supply chain visibility among internal and external business partners. This integrated view can be made accessible to both internal and external business partners for business event tracking all time towards balancing demand and supply in the company.

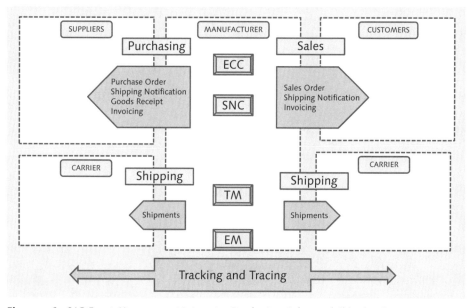

Figure 11.6 SAP Event Management integrates Purchasing, Sales, and Shipping Processes

11.6 Summary

The key drivers of supply chain visibility are tracking of inventory flow, updating of order status in real time, and managing exceptions in the supply chain. This chapter highlighted SAP Event Management integration points with other SAP solutions to provide end-to-end visibility of supply chain business processes.

The next chapter focuses on the monitoring, error handling, and escalation procedures for an SAP Event Management production environment.

This chapter describes the system administration procedures for monitoring, error handling, and escalation management for the SAP Event Management 5.1 system.

12 Monitoring Procedures for SAP Event Management

Monitoring procedures ensure smooth and reliable flow and handling of the event management business process. The objective of this chapter is to provide insight into the production environment for monitoring procedures, error handling, and escalation management for the SAP Event Management system.

12.1 Monitoring

SAP Event Management offers various tools for monitoring your SAP Event Management system. This section describes four different monitoring methods in SAP Event Management.

12.1.1 Processing Control

The following monitors are available for analyzing in SAP Event Management:

▶ **Event handler list** (Transaction code /SAPTRX/EH_LIST)
The event handler list provides details about event handlers. You can see the status of expected events, unexpected events, error messages, rule set processing, and parameter details in the list.

▶ **Event message processing status** (Transaction code /SAPTRX/EVM_STATUS)
This list shows system-generated messages and points out whether objects are processed correctly in SAP Event Management. The list reflects only data errors — not business process issues.

▶ **Expected event monitor** (Transaction code /SAPTRX/EE_MON)
The expected event monitor is a background report that checks whether an expected event that should have been reported within a specific period has become overdue. If the monitor discovers an overdue event, SAP Event Management reacts according to the rules that have been defined. Within a rule, activities are provided for performing specific tasks (for example, comparing two fields or activating an event handler set). A follow-up activity can be sending email notification or generating a daily overdue report for business users. Customers can also use this report to identify the aging profile of open transactions toward order fulfillment.

▶ **Process messages for locked event handler**
(Transaction code /SAPTRX/LOCKED_PROC)
This report triggers subsequent processing of event messages awaiting posting in an event handler that was locked earlier in an initial posting attempt.

▶ **Process locked event handler sets** (Transaction code /SAPTRX/LOCKED_PSET)
The report assigns an event handler once again to an event handler set that SAP Event Management is locking.

▶ **Resend application object data for event handler**
(Transaction code /SAPTRX/EMJOBS)
The report resends the application object date for the event handler. This can occur when the event handler is locked during the processing of the event message. To ensure that the system updates the event handler with the data sent once the lock is released, it temporarily stores the data in a database table. A routine background job can be set for checking event entries in a database and processing them for posting in an event handler. It updates the event handler that was previously locked with the data.

▶ **Remote function call (RFC) monitor** (Transaction code SM58)
If you use tRFC (asynchronous communication) to communicate with SAP Event Management from the application system, then use this to work through any errors in this process.

12.1.2 Application Logs

The application log is available in both application systems (SAP ECC) and SAP Event Management. You can access the logs via Transaction code /SAPTRX/ASAP-LOG for the application log interface. The application log (Figure 12.1) documents messages, exceptions, and fields. The data provides information on communication processes and problems that occurred on the application side when event handlers were created or event messages were processed in SAP Event Management and when information queries were made to SAP Event Management.

▶ The application log in the application system provides an overview of all of the activities relevant to an application object and the appropriate event messages. You can reduce the memory space for the application log by deactivating it per business object.

▶ The SAP Event Management application log provides an overview of all activities for an event handler and for its corresponding event messages that have occurred during the event handler processing.

You can define the following when creating an event handler:

▶ The objects that are logged, such as event handler creation, event message processing, and updating data from an external source

▶ The level of detail the system should use when logging (from high-level process logging to details of each business process)

Application logs can be switched off in SAP ECC via Transaction /SAPTRX/ASCOAO. In the General Data tab, select Appl. Log. Deactive. In event handlers the following fields can configure the log level:

▶ **Log EH Posting**
Writes an application log for an event handler when posting updates from an application system.

▶ **Log Msg. Proc**
Writes an application log during event message processing.

▶ **Log Ext. Update**

Writes an application log for external updates and manual changes done in Transaction /SAPTRX/EH_LIST.

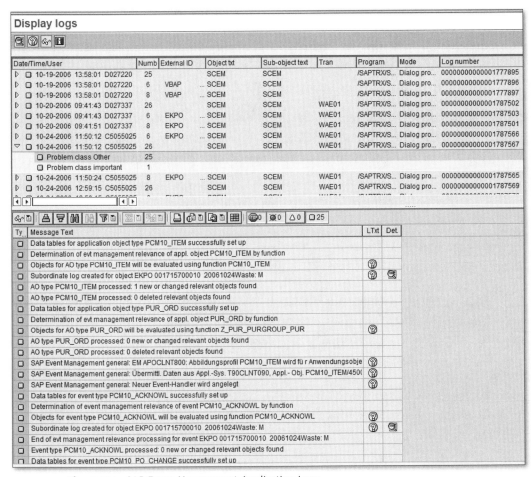

Figure 12.1 SAP Event Management Application Logs

12.1.3 Alert Monitoring with CCMS

Proactive automated monitoring is required for monitoring operations in the SAP Event Management environment. The Computing Center Management System (CCMS) provides a range of monitors for monitoring the SAP environment and its components. These monitors are indispensable for understanding and evaluating the behavior of the SAP processing environment. In the case of poor performance values, the monitors provide you with the information required to fine-tune your SAP system and therefore to ensure that your SAP system installation is running efficiently. The CCMS analysis monitors provide functions for:

▶ Checking the system status and the operating modes

▶ Detecting and correcting potential problems as quickly as possible

▶ Making an early diagnosis of potential problems, such as resource problems in a host or database system, which could affect the SAP system

▶ Analyzing and fine-tuning the SAP system and its environment (host and database system) to optimize the throughput of the SAP system

To use the specific SAP Event Management monitor in the CCMS, you must first do the following:

▶ Run reports /SAPTRX/SLG1_LINK & /SAPTRX/SCHEDULE-EM_JOBS_NODE once before calling the SAP Event Management monitor. This is to ensure that the functions for evaluating the application log and scheduling SAP Event Management jobs appear in the choice of functions for the SAP Event Management monitor.

▶ Schedule a list of SAP Event Management batch jobs (Table 12.1) that you want to set as monitoring functions in the CCMS. The system displays the background job in the dialog structure of the SAP Event Management monitor.

Background Job	Purpose
/SAPTRX/COLLECT_LOCKED_EH	Number of locked event handlers in the SAP Event Management client
/SAPTRX/COLLECT_LOCKED_EHSETS	Number of locked event handlers sets in the SAP Event Management client
/SAPTRX/COLLECT_UNPROC_EVMSG	Number of unprocessed event messages in the SAP Event Management client

Table 12.1 SAP CCMS Monitoring Jobs

12.1.4 Interface Monitoring

Interface monitors are essential for analyzing problems with interfaces such as RFC, IDOC, and HTTP. SAP Event Management uses the standard tools available in SAP Web Application Server 6.40 and does not require any application-specific tool. If the scenario requires qRFC (synchronous) processing, you can monitor the inbound and outbound RFC queues using Transactions SMQ1 and SMQ2.

12.2 Archiving and Deletion

Events in SAP Event Management can no longer be either archived or deleted. The data archiving process not only consistently removes data from the database, but also ensures data availability for future business requirements. This section describes the archiving and deletion process for SAP Event Management.

12.2.1 Archiving

SAP Event Management contains archiving tools to save SAP Event Management data on external media and delete them from the database. SAP delivers the following archiving objects for SAP Event Management:

▶ Event handler tables (object /SAPTRX/A0)

▶ Event handler sets (object SAPTRX_A2)

▶ Event messages tables (object /SAPTRX/A1)

To archive SAP Event Management–relevant objects and delete them from database:

▶ Specify the archiving objects in the customizing (Transaction /SAPTRX/AOBJ).

▶ Deactivate the event handler and the event handler sets before archiving (via rule in rule set).

▶ Specify the time intervals (residence time) for the archiving objects.

We can trigger the archiving and/or deletion of the event handler in one of the ways described below:

▶ Archive an event handler that belongs to one or more event handler sets by deactivating and archiving the entire set.

▶ Specify that event handlers and event handler sets are archived automatically by defining appropriate activity parameters and using them in plug-in function modules within a rule. To automatically archive event handlers or event handler sets, define an activity in a rule set that is triggered by a received event (e.g., ARCHIVE). This activity deactivates the event handler and archives it. You then need to ensure that the ARCHIVE message is sent to SAP Event Management when the appropriate time has come to archive the event handler. Another way is to have an expected event defined when the event handler is created, and when the date becomes overdue the overdue monitor processes a similar activity to the one described above.

▶ The system checks if the difference between the date on which the objects were created and the current date is greater than the residence time. If this is the case, the event handlers and the event messages along with all data belonging to them are archived.

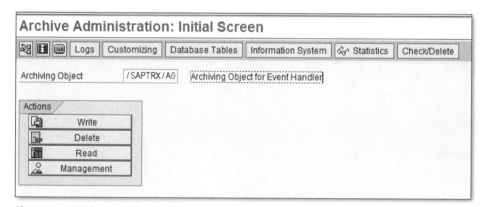

Figure 12.2 Archiving Object in SAP Event Management

▶ The archiving process in SAP Event Management is done via Transaction SARA (Figure 12.2), which is used to:

▶ Write the archive

▶ Delete the data in SAP Event Management

▶ Read event handler and message data from the archive

▶ Reload the event handler and message back to SAP Event Management

If you have the Web Communication layer (WCL) logging manager configured to collect a lot of detail on transactions, then you will need to review archiving in this area as well.

The configuration involves defining archiving objects and residence times for archiving. In Transaction SPRO, follow the menu path EVENT MANAGEMENT • ARCHIVE OR DELETE EVENT HANDLERS AND EVENT MESSAGE.

▶ **Archiving object**
Define the archiving objects as shown in Figure 12.3.

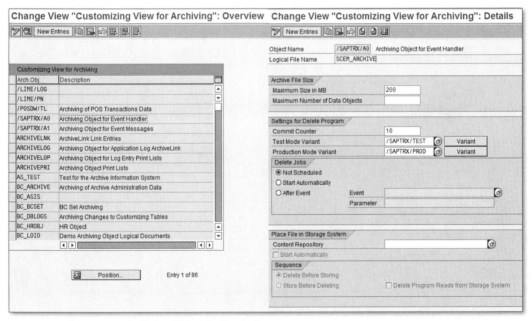

Figure 12.3 Archiving Object Customization

▶ **Residence time** (Figure 12.4)

If the customizing table is blank, then the system default for archiving is 100 days. That means all events will automatically be archived after 100 days. The default value for the event handler residence time is the date when the event handler was created. You can also select the date when an event handler is deactivated. It is also possible to specify that that once a week all event handlers that are older than 3 months and whose indicators have been set to inactive should be archived.

Figure 12.4 SAP Event Management Archiving Residence Time

12.2.2 Growing Tables for SAP Event Management

You need to watch some tables in your SAP Event Management solution because they can grow large depending on your rules, parameters (how many you have), and expected events.

▶ Event handler tables to monitor:

  ▶ /SAPTRX/EH_INFO (info parameters)

  ▶ /SAPTRX/EH_CNTRL (control parameters)

  ▶ /SAPTRX/EH_EXPE (expected events)

  ▶ /SAPTRX/EH_STHST (status history)

  ▶ /SAPTRX/EH_TASK (tasks performed if logging is on)

- Event message tables to monitor:

  - /SAPTRX/EVM_AFB (attachment contents of binary file)

  - /SAPTRX/EVM_AFC (attachment contents)

  - /SAPTRX/EH_EVMSG (event message header)

12.2.3 Deletion

The deletion of an event handler or event message is possible in the following ways:

- When you delete an application object in the application system, the corresponding event handlers is deleted in SAP Event Management.

- By specifying an appropriate rule in the rule set to delete the events that are older than specific weeks.

- By executing one of the following deletion reports:

  - The report for deleting inactive event handlers (/SAPTRX/DELETE_EH) that should not be archived Report /SAPTRX/DELETE_EH for deleting inactive event handlers belonging to an event handler set

  - The report for deleting event messages (/SAPTRX/DELETE_EVMSG) that should not be archived

The configuration involves defining residence times for deletion. In Transaction SPRO, follow the menu path EVENT MANAGEMENT • ARCHIVE OR DELETE EVENT HANDLERS AND EVENT MESSAGE.

12.3 Regular Batch Jobs

Table 12.2 lists the scheduled batch jobs for SAP Event Management. These jobs helps process any locked event messages, monitor overdue events, and error-handle any blocked communication queues between the application system and SAP Event Management.

Monitoring Object	Transaction/ Report	Monitor Frequency	Monitoring Activity or Error Handling Procedure
Set up of monitoring	/SAPTRX/SLG1_ LINK	Once before starting to work the first time with SAP Event Management	Schedule background jobs for each client that wants to be monitored in CCMS
Set up of monitoring	/SAPTRX/ SCHEDULE_EM_ JOBS_NODE	Once before starting to work the first time with SAP Event Management	Schedule background jobs for each client that wants to be monitored in CCMS
Processor of locked event handler	Report- /SAPTRX/ PROCESS_ LOCKED_EHS	Six times per day	Schedule a regular job in Transaction / SAPTRX/EMJOBS
Processor of locked event handler sets	Report - /SAPTRX/ PROCESS_ LOCKED_SETS	Six times per day	Schedule a regular job in Transaction / SAPTRX/EMJOBS
Resend application object data for event handlers	Report - /SAPTRX/R_ REPOST_AI_LOGS	Six times per day	Schedule a regular job in Transaction / SAPTRX/EMJOBS
Number of locked event handlers in the desired client	/SAPTRX/ COLLECT_ LOCKED_EH	Six times per day	Schedule a regular job in Transaction / SAPTRX/EMJOBS
Number of locked event handlers sets in the desired client	/SAPTRX/ COLLECT_ LOCKED_EHSETS	Six times per day	Schedule a regular job in Transaction / SAPTRX/EMJOBS
Display application log in SAP Event Management	Transaction / SAPTRX/ASAPLOG	Daily	Display the application log in the SAP Event Management

Table 12.2 SAP Event Management Monitoring Batch Jobs

Monitoring Object	Transaction/ Report	Monitor Frequency	Monitoring Activity or Error Handling Procedure
Evaluation of application log	Transaction SLG1	Daily	Display the application log in the SAP Event Management
Continuously identifies expected events that are overdue	Report /SAPTRX/EE_ MONITOR	Every 5-15 minutes based on the event-posting frequency	Display functionality
Status of events and error messages shown	/SAPTRX/EH_LIST		Display functionality
List to see if objects are processed correctly. The list reflects only data issues — not business process issues	/SAPTRX/EVM_ STATUS		Display functionality
Inbound and outbound queue monitoring	Transaction SMQ1 /SMQ2	Daily	Status of the inbound and outbound queues
Consistency check in SAP Event Management	Report /SAPTRX/EH_ CONSISTENCY_ CHECK	Periodically	Checks the application system against SAP Event Management parameter mapping for any customizing inconsistencies

Table 12.2 SAP Event Management Monitoring Batch Jobs (Cont.)

12.4 Sizing

The SAP Event Management sizing check (Figure 12.5) helps determine whether there are enough hardware and application server resources in the SAP SCM system to handle the SAP Event Management expected workload. This check is important to prevent any severe performance problems that can be caused by underestimating the hardware requirements.

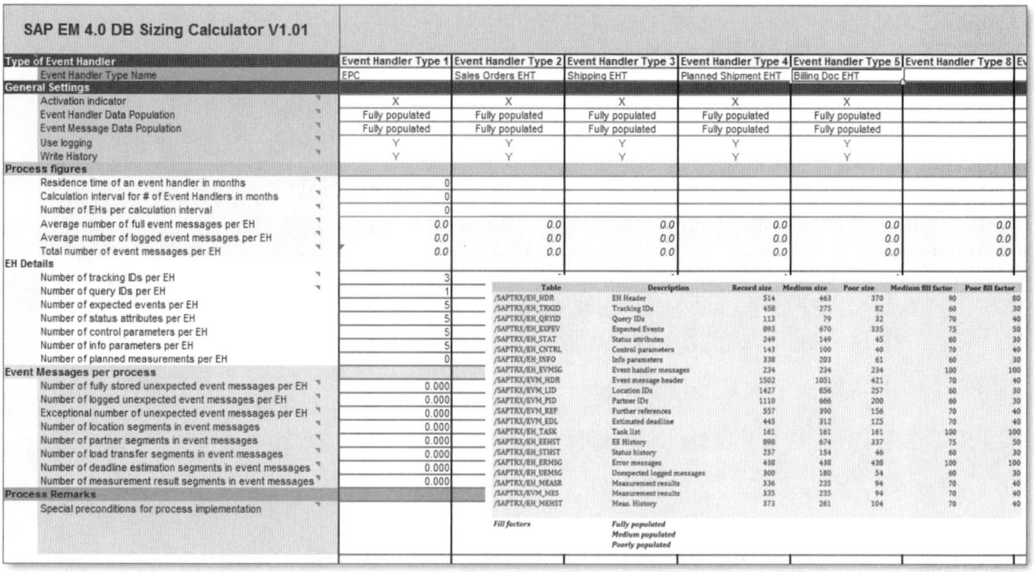

Figure 12.5 SAP Event Management Quick Sizer for Database Requirement Calculation

12.4.1 Sizing CPU and Memory

SAP memory consumption depends on the size of the packages that contain event messages. The most efficient size is recommend is 100 event messages in a single transmission from the application system. As the size of the event handler package increases, the average memory consumption per package decreases. CPU consumption, however, increases slightly. Table 12.3 shows the SAP recommendation for CPU and memory per event handlers posted in SAP Event Management. The assumptions are four event messages per event handler.

Category	Event Handler per day	CPU in SAPS	Memory in GB
Small	100,000	300	1
Medium	250,000	600	2
Large	500,000	1250	4
Extra large	1,000,000	2500	8

Table 12.3 SAP Event Management Sizing CPU and Memory

12.4.2 Sizing the Disk

Table 12.4 shows SAP recommendations for disk sizing. The assumption is residence time of one month. A higher residence time leads to larger disk requirements. Also, it is assumed that the event processing and event handler creation are logged because this contributes to disk size as well.

Category	Number of Events per Year	Disk in GB
Small	30,000,000	70
Medium	75,000,000	190
Large	150,000,000	390
Extra large	300,000,000	780

Table 12.4 SAP Event Management Sizing the Disk

12.5 Event Handler Processing

This section describes the event handler processing and simulation capabilities.

12.5.1 Event Handler Reprocessing

If the expected events of an event handler are changed (for example, milestone added) the original event handler is technically deleted and recreated. All event messages that have been posted to this event handler are then processed again. This behavior can be suppressed by the use of the activity method (Figure 12.6)

CHECK_REPROCESS_FLAG. This method identifies if you are in reprocessing mode or not. You can then skip some of the activities that have already been performed during the creation of the original event handler and not perform them again.

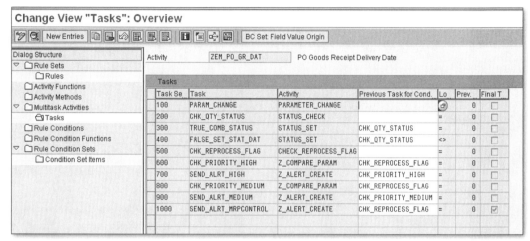

Figure 12.6 Event Handler Reprocessing Activity in Rule Set

12.5.2 Simulation of Event Handler Processes

In the application system (SAP ECC), we can switch on the simulation mode to get detailed information on how data is extracted and posting takes place. The simulation tool helps:

▶ Identify the impact of a customizing change

▶ Analyze a problem

▶ Step through and view the result of the event message processing

During the simulation in the application system, dialog boxes are seen for every step:

▶ No data is written to the database.

▶ Simulation mode in SAP Event Management is called automatically.

▶ Simulation is available for event handler posting and for event message processing.

The simulation process can be done in SAP Event Management (Figure 12.7), directly in the event handler, or by setting the import parameter SIMULATE in the BAPI to X.

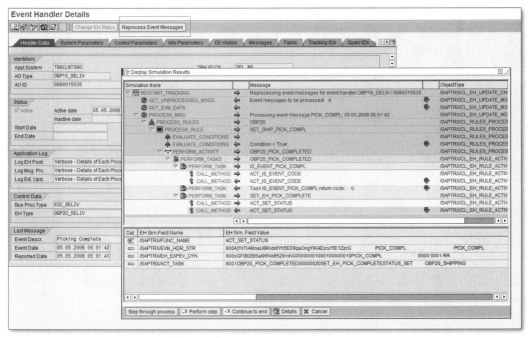

Figure 12.7 Event Handler Simulation in SAP Event Management

12.6   Summary

This concluding chapter of the book looked at system administration and gave insights into the monitoring and error handling procedures for SAP Event Management. The maintenance procedures for routine archiving, deletion, hardware sizing, and scheduling monitoring batch jobs are imperative for better performance management and stability of SAP Event Management functionality.

Appendices

SAP Event Management uses rule sets and expected event monitor profiles to control how event handlers are processed. In the rule set and expected event monitor profile we define the activities for performing follow-up activity for posted event messages.

A   Activities for SAP Event Management

A.1   Rule Activity Function

Activity Name	Description	Method/Function module name	Method (M) / Function (F)
510_ARCH_EH_DEACT	Deactivation of the event handler during the archiving of the PO	/SAPTRX/FS_ARCH_EH_DEACT	F
510_CHECK_ACKNOWL	Verify confirmed quantity	/SAPTRX/FS_ACKNOWL_CHECK	F
510_CHECK_REPROCESS	Check whether messages were reprocessed during event handler update	/SAPTRX/FS_CHECK_REPROCESS	F
510_DATE_SEND_TO_APP	Publish event date in application system	/SAPTRX/FS_DATE_SEND_TO_APP	F
510_GR_QTY_CHECK	Check GR quantity against PO quantity	/SAPTRX/FS_GR_QTY_CHECK	F
510_PARAM_UPDATE	Parameter update for purchase order (seasonal procurement)	/SAPTRX/FS_PARAM_UPDATE	F

Activity Name	Description	Method/Function module name	Method (M) / Function (F)
ALERT_CREATE	Integration of alert framework	/SAPTRX/CREATE_ALERT	F
BW_UPLOAD	Upload Business Information Warehouse	/SAPTRX/BW_EXTRACTION2	F
CHECK_AND_SET_EH_SET	Check notification status & set event handler set notification status	/SAPTRX/CHECK_AND_SET_EH_SET	F
DF_UPDATE	Update document flow	/SAPTRX/DF_UPDATE	F
EH_AUTO_ARCH	Event handler automatic archiving	/SAPTRX/EH_AUTO_ARCH	F
EH_AUTO_ARCH_SET	Event handler set automatic archiving	/SAPTRX/EHSET_AUTO_ARCH	F
ID_MAPPING	Call ID mapping functionality and set rule processing parameters	/SAPTRX/ID_MAPPING	F
PCM10_DF_CHECK	Check if document flow is enabled in procurement visibility process	/SAPTRX/PCM10_DF_CHECK	F
RESEND	Resend event messages to another event handler	/SAPTRX/RESEND	F
RESEND_EVTMSG_SUBSEQ	Resend an event message to subsequent leg	/SAPTRX/RESEND_TO_SUBSEQ_LEG	F

Activity Name	Description	Method/Function module name	Method (M) / Function (F)
RESEND_ MULTIPLE	Resend event messages to other event handlers	/SAPTRX/RESEND_ MULTIPLE	F
SEND_POD	Send a proof of delivery	/SAPTRX/SEND_ POD	F
SEND_PPDS_APO_ ALERT	Send PP/DS alert to SAP APO alert monitor	/SAPTRX/SEND_ PPDS_APO_ALERT	F
SEND_SNC_DOC_ ALERT	Send document-related alert to SAP SNC	/SAPTRX/SEND_ SNC_DOC_ALERT	F
SEND_SNC_MSG_ ALERT	Send XML-message-related alert to SAP SNC	/SAPTRX/SEND_ SNC_MSG_ALERT	F
SEND_VS_APO_ ALERT	Send VS alert to SAP APO alert monitor	/SAPTRX/SEND_ VS_APO_ALERT	F
SHIPMENT_DATE_ UPDATE	Update actual dates in the SAP R/3 shipment	/SAPTRX/SET_ ACT_SHIPMENT_ DDL	F
SHPMT_DATE_ UPDATE	Update actual dates in the SAP R/3 shipment (as of SAP SCM 4.0 with PI2003.1)	/SAPTRX/SET_ ACT_SHIPMENT_ DDL1	F
SHPMT_ ENDDATE_ UPDATE	Update actual shipment end date in the SAP R/3 shipment	/SAPTRX/ SET_SHIPMENT_ ENDDATE	F
TM_MAINTAIN_ ETA	Create/update ETA with or without reference to PTA(s) in SAP TM	/SAPTRX/TMS_ CHANGE_ETA	F

Activity Name	Description	Method/Function module name	Method (M) / Function (F)
TM_SET_HSH_STATUS	Set life cycle status in shipment in transportation management	/SAPTRX/TMS_SET_HSH_STATUS	F
WORKFLOW_START	Create the event Start_workflow in the BO /SAPTRX/EH to trigger the workflow	/SAPTRX/CREATE_BO_EVENT	F

A.2   Rule Activity Method

Activity Name	Description	Method/Function Module Name	Method (M) / Function (F)
ADD_EHS_TO_PROCESS	Add additional related event handler GUIDs from further reference data	ACT_ADD_EHS_TO_PROCESS	M
ADD_TO_SET	Add current event handler to event handler sets	ACT_ADD_TO_SET	M
ARE_PRIOR_REQS_MET	Have prior required expected events been reported for an event?	ACT_PRIOR_REQS_REPORTED	M
CHECK/SET_PARAM_VALS	Check parameter values in event message against info/control parameter values and set the result	ACT_CHECK_AND_SET_PARAM_VALUES	M
CHECK_EH_IN_SETS	Check the status of event handlers in event handler set	ACT_CHECK_EH_IN_SET	M

Activity Name	Description	Method/Function Module Name	Method (M) / Function (F)
CHECK_PARAM_ VALUE	Check value of system, control, info, or rule processing parameter	ACT_CHECK_ PARAMETER_ VALUE	M
CHECK_RELATED_ EH	Check status of related event handlers	ACT_CHECK_ RELATED_EH	M
CHECK_ REPROCESS_FLAG	Check value of class attribute MY_REPROCESS	ACT_CHECK_ REPROCESS_FLAG	M
CHECK_ SYSPARAM_VALUE	Check parameter values in event message against system parameter values	ACT_CHECK_ SYSTEM_PARAM_ VALUE	M
COMPARE	Compare two fields	ACT_COMPARE	M
EE_ALL_REQS_ MET	Have all required expected events been reported?	ACT_ALL_REQS_ REPORTED	M
EE_EXP_DATES_ CLEAR	Clear the expected dates for an expected event	ACT_CLEAR_ EXPECTED_DATES	M
EE_PROCESS	Process expected events	ACT_PROCESS_EE	M
EE_RESET	Reset the actual dates and status for an expected event	ACT_RESET_EE	M
EHSET_ACTIVATE	Activate event handler set	ACT_SET_EHSET_ ACTIVE	M
EHSET_SET_ INACTIVE	Deactivate event handler set	ACT_SET_EHSET_ INACTIVE	M

Activity Name	Description	Method/Function Module Name	Method (M) / Function (F)
EHSET_STATUS_CHECK	Check status records for status attribute name & value for event handler set	ACT_CHECK_EHSET_STATUS	M
EHSET_STATUS_SET	Create or update a status attribute name for event handler set	ACT_SET_EHSET_STATUS	M
EH_ACTIVATE	Activate event handler	ACT_ACTIVATE	M
EH_DEACTIVATE	Deactivate event handler	ACT_DEACTIVATE	M
EH_GUID_SET	Retain event handler GUID currently being processed	ACT_SET_EH_GUID	M
EH_HIERARCHY_UPDATE	Update event handler hierarchy table	ACT_UPDATE_EH_HIERARCHY	M
ERROR_MESSAGE_CLEAR	Clear (deactivate) error messages	ACT_CLEAR_ERR_MSGS	M
ERROR_MESSAGE_LOG	Log an error message	ACT_LOG_ERROR_MSG	M
EVENT_CODE_CHECK	Does internal event code equal <parameter>?	ACT_IS_EVENT_CODE	M
EVM_EE_UPDATE	Update expected event list from event message EE MODIFY table (from SAP SCM 4.0)	ACT_EE_MODIFY	M

Activity Name	Description	Method/Function Module Name	Method (M) / Function (F)
EVM_ETA_UPDATE	Update expected date for an event with estimated deadlines (only SAP Event Management 1.1)	ACT_ETA_EVENT_ MSG	M
HDR_EXT_VALUE_ UPDATE	Updating field value in header extension table	ACT_UPDATE_ HDR_EXTENTION	M
IS_EE_EARLY	Is the event date prior to the earliest expected date?	ACT_IS_EE_EARLY	M
IS_EE_IN_DATE_ SEQ	Is this event and all prior events in chronological order?	ACT_IS_EE_IN_ DATE_SEQ	M
IS_EE_LATE	Is this event date after the (latest) expected date?	ACT_IS_EE_LATE	M
IS_EE_MSG_EARLY	Is the event message date prior to the earliest expected date?	ACT_IS_EE_MSG_ EARLY	M
IS_EE_MSG_LATE	Is this event message date after the (latest) expected date?	ACT_IS_EE_MSG_ LATE	M
IS_EE_ REPROCESSED	Has this expected event been reported previously?	ACT_IS_EE_ REPROCESSED	M
IS_EQUAL	Equate two fields	ACT_IS_EQUAL	M
IS_EVENT_ EXPECTED	Is the event an expected event (= EE code, partner, location)?	ACT_IS_EVENT_ EXPECTED	M

Activity Name	Description	Method/Function Module Name	Method (M) / Function (F)
IS_EVENT_IN_GROUP	Is the internal event code in group <parameter>?	ACT_IS_EVENT_IN_GROUP	M
IS_EVENT_REPORTED	Was event message already reported for same event handler?	ACT_IS_EVENT_REPORTED	M
IS_EVM_CODE_EXPECTED	Is the internal event code one of the expected event codes?	ACT_IS_EVM_CODE_EXPECTED	M
IS_LAST_EE	Is this event the last expected event?	ACT_IS_LAST_EE	M
IS_MEASUREMENT_CONF	Did the event message confirm an expected measurement result?	ACT_IS_MEASUREMENT_CONFIRMED	M
IS_MSRMNT_NOT_COMPAR	Was event message not comparable to the expected measurement result?	ACT_IS_MSRMNT_NOT_COMPARABLE	M
IS_MSRMNT_OUT_OF_TOL	Did the reported measurement result exceed the expected result?	ACT_IS_MSRMNT_OUT_OF_TOLERANCE	M
IS_ORIG_EE_LATE	Is the event date after the original expected date?	ACT_IS_ORIG_EE_LATE	M
IS_ORIG_EE_MSG_LATE	Is this event message date after the original expected date?	ACT_IS_ORIG_EE_MSG_LATE	M

Activity Name	Description	Method/Function Module Name	Method (M) / Function (F)
IS_REPORTED_FOR_EH	Was event message already reported for another event handler?	ACT_IS_REPORTED_FOR_EH	M
PARAMETER_CHANGE	Add, change, or delete control, and/or info parameter(s)	ACT_CHANGE_PARAM	M
PARAM_CHANGE_CUST	Add, change, or delete control and/or info parameter(s) using customizing	ACT_CHANGE_PARAM_WITH_CUST	M
PROCEDURE_RC_SET	Set return code for multitask activity explicitly	ACT_SET_PROC_RC	M
PROCESS_MEASUREMENTS	Process measurement data	ACT_PROCESS_MEASUREMENTS	M
PROCESS_UNPROCESSED	Check for and process any unprocessed event messages	ACT_PROCESS_UNPROCESSED_MSGS	M
QUIT_EVM_PROCESSING	Quit event message processing and mark as irrelevant	ACT_QUIT_EVM_PROCESSING	M
RETRIEVE_MSG	Retrieve process-related messages for visibility processes	ACT_LOG_MSG	M
SET_RULE_PROC_PARAM	Create, update, or delete a rule processing parameter	ACT_SET_ACTIVITY_PARAM	M

Activity Name	Description	Method/Function Module Name	Method (M) / Function (F)
STATUS_CHECK	Check status records for status attribute name and value for event handler	ACT_CHECK_STATUS	M
STATUS_SET	Create or pdate a status attribute name and update status history for event handler	ACT_SET_STATUS	M
TRACKING_ID_REMOVE	Delete tracking IDs	ACT_REMOVE_TRACKING_IDS	M
TRACKING_ID_SET	Create additional tracking ID(s) from event message further reference data	ACT_SET_TRACKING_ID	M
WEBLINK_SET	Create a web link	ACT_CREATE_WEBLINK	M

A.3 Expected Event Monitor Activity Function

Activity Name	Description	Method/Function Module Name	Method (M) / Function (F)
510_PUR_FASH_OVERDUE	Monitor for overdue expected events for purchase order (seasonal procurement)	/SAPTRX/FS_MONITOR_PURORD	F
ALERT_CREATE	Integration of alert framework	/SAPTRX/CREATE_ALERT	F
SEND_SNC_DOC_ALERT	Send document-related alert to SAP SNC	/SAPTRX/SEND_SNC_DOC_ALERT	F

Activity Name	Description	Method/Function Module Name	Method (M) / Function (F)
SEND_SNC_MSG_ ALERT	Send XML-message-related alert to SAP SNC	/SAPTRX/SEND_ SNC_MSG_ALERT	F
SEND_VS_APO_ ALERT	Send VS alert to SAP APO alert monitor	/SAPTRX/SEND_ VS_APO_ALERT	F
TM_UPDATE_DO_ TENDER	Update the dependent object tendering	/SAPTRX/ TMS_UPD_DO_ TENDERING	F

A.4   Expected Event Monitor Activity Method

Activity Name	Description	Method/Function Module Name	Method (M) / Function (F)
CHECK_PARAM_ VALUE	Check value of system, control, info, or rule process parameter	ACT_CHECK_ PARAMETER_ VALUE	M
COMPARE	Compare two fields	ACT_COMPARE	M
EHSET_ACTIVATE	Activate event handler set	ACT_SET_EHSET_ ACTIVE	M
EHSET_SET_ INACTIVE	Deactivate event handler set	ACT_SET_EHSET_ INACTIVE	M
EHSET_STATUS_ CHECK	Check status records for status attribute name and value for event handler set	ACT_CHECK_ EHSET_STATUS	M
EHSET_STATUS_ SET	Create or update a status attribute name for event handler set	ACT_SET_EHSET_ STATUS	M

Activity Name	Description	Method/Function Module Name	Method (M) / Function (F)
EH_ACTIVATE	Activate event handler	ACT_ACTIVATE	M
EH_DEACTIVATE	Deactivate event handler	ACT_DEACTIVATE	M
ERROR_MESSAGE_ CLEAR	Clear (deactivate) error messages	ACT_CLEAR_ERR_ MSGS	M
ERROR_MESSAGE_ LOG	Log error message	ACT_LOG_ERROR_ MSG	M
IS_EE_MSG_ OVERDUE	Is the expected event message overdue?	ACT_IS_EE_MSG_ OVERDUE	M
IS_EE_OVERDUE	Is the expected event overdue?	ACT_IS_EE_ EVENT_OVERDUE	M
IS_EQUAL	Equate two fields	ACT_IS_EQUAL	M
OVERDUE_EE_ RESET	Reset Overdue expected event status back to Expected	ACT_RESET_ OVERDUE_EE	M
PARAM_CHANGE_ CUST	Add, change, or delete control and/or info parameter(s) using customizing	ACT_CHANGE_ PARAM_WITH_ CUST	M
PROCEDURE_RC_ SET	Set return code for multitask activity explicitly	ACT_SET_PROC_ RC	M
SET_RULE_PROC_ PARAM	Create, update, or delete a rule processing parameter	ACT_SET_ ACTIVITY_PARAM	M
STATUS_CHECK	Check status records for status attribute name and value for event handler	ACT_CHECK_ STATUS	M

Activity Name	Description	Method/Function Module Name	Method (M) / Function (F)
STATUS_SET	Create or update a status attribute name and update status history for event handler	ACT_SET_STATUS	M

A.5   Event Handler Update Activity Function

Activity Name	Description	Method/Function Module Name	Method (M) / Function (F)
510_CHECK_DEL_ELIKZ	Check for deletion and final delivery indicators for PO (seasonal procurement)	/SAPTRX/ FS_UPD2_ PURORD_01	F
ALERT_CREATE	Integration of alert framework	/SAPTRX/CREATE_ ALERT	F
DF_UPDATE_ FROM_EH	Update document flow from event handler creation or update	/SAPTRX/DF_ UPDATE_FROM_ EH	F

A.6   Event Handler Update Activity Method

Activity Name	Description	Method/Function Module Name	Method (M) / Function (F)
CHECK_PARAM_ VALUE	Check value of system, control, info, or rule processing parameter	ACT_CHECK_ PARAMETER_ VALUE	M
COMPARE	Compare two fields	ACT_COMPARE	M

Activity Name	Description	Method/Function Module Name	Method (M) / Function (F)
EHSET_ACTIVATE	Activate event handler set	ACT_SET_EHSET_ACTIVE	M
EHSET_SET_INACTIVE	Deactivate event handler set	ACT_SET_EHSET_INACTIVE	M
EHSET_STATUS_CHECK	Check status records for status attribute name and value for event handler set	ACT_CHECK_EHSET_STATUS	M
EHSET_STATUS_SET	Create or update a status attribute name for event handler set	ACT_SET_EHSET_STATUS	M
EH_ACTIVATE	Activate event handler	ACT_ACTIVATE	M
EH_DEACTIVATE	Deactivate event handler	ACT_DEACTIVATE	M
ERROR_MESSAGE_CLEAR	Clear (deactivate) error messages	ACT_CLEAR_ERR_MSGS	M
ERROR_MESSAGE_LOG	Log an error message	ACT_LOG_ERROR_MSG	M
IS_EQUAL	Equate two fields	ACT_IS_EQUAL	M
PARAM_CHANGE_CUST	Add, change, or delete control and/or info parameter(s) using customizing	ACT_CHANGE_PARAM_WITH_CUST	M
PROCEDURE_RC_SET	Set return code for multitask activity explicitly	ACT_SET_PROC_RC	M
SET_RULE_PROC_PARAM	Create, update, or delete a rule processing parameter	ACT_SET_ACTIVITY_PARAM	M

Activity Name	Description	Method/Function Module Name	Method (M) / Function (F)
STATUS_CHECK	Check status records for status attribute name and value for event handler	ACT_CHECK_ STATUS	M
STATUS_SET	Create or update a status attribute name and update status history for event handler	ACT_SET_STATUS	M

This list contains transactions associated with SAP Event Management in SAP SCM 5.1 and SAP ECC 6.0.

B   Transaction Codes

B.1   SCM Event Manager Transaction Codes

Transaction Code	Description
/SAPTRX/A0RES	Residence times event handler archiving
/SAPTRX/A1RES	Residence times event message archiving
/SAPTRX/AFPD	Alert framework integration
/SAPTRX/ASAPLOG	Application system log for event handling
/SAPTRX/ASC0AO	Define Application object and event types
/SAPTRX/ASC0AP	Define application parameters
/SAPTRX/ASC0SCU	Assign scenario to users
/SAPTRX/ASC0SD1	Define solution/scenario
/SAPTRX/ASC0SD2	Define solution/scenario
/SAPTRX/ASC0TC	Define EM relevance conditions
/SAPTRX/ASC0TE	Define EM extraction
/SAPTRX/ASC0TF	Define EM interface functions
/SAPTRX/ASC0TO	Define business process types
/SAPTRX/ASC0TS	Define event managers (engines)
/SAPTRX/BWCQ	Check SCEM queue for delta extraction
/SAPTRX/BWEX	Definition of SAP NetWeaver BW – profiles

Transaction Code	Description
/SAPTRX/BWGS	General settings for SAP NetWeaver BW upload
/SAPTRX/BWID	Initialization of setup tables
/SAPTRX/BWIU	Initial data upload to SAP NetWeaver BW
/SAPTRX/BWPQ	Process SCEM-queue for delta extract
/SAPTRX/CONS_CHECK	Consistency check
/SAPTRX/DISP_LINK	Show the link to SAP system
/SAPTRX/EE_MON	Expected events monitor
/SAPTRX/EE_OVD_LIST	Expected event overdue list
/SAPTRX/EH_CREATE	Event handler creation
/SAPTRX/EH_LAST_EVT	Event handler list with the last event message
/SAPTRX/EH_LIST	Event handler list
/SAPTRX/EH_LIST_STAT	Event handler list by status
/SAPTRX/EH_SET	Event handler set browser
/SAPTRX/EMJOBS	Scheduling EM-relevant jobs
/SAPTRX/EM_START	Start the WD ABAP-based EM UI
/SAPTRX/ER_MS_LIST	Error messages list
/SAPTRX/EVM_STATUS	Event message status
/SAPTRX/EVM_STAT_ADM	Event messages list – administrator
/SAPTRX/LOCKED_PROC	Locked event handler message processors
/SAPTRX/LOCKED_PSET	Locked event handler set processors
/SAPTRX/MI01	Single event reporting
/SAPTRX/MI02	Expected event reporting
/SAPTRX/MI02B	Expected event reporting
/SAPTRX/MI03	Process buffered messages, SAP SCEM 4.0

Transaction Code	Description
/SAPTRX/MIC01	Event message input: layout and profiles
/SAPTRX/RESTM	Define residence times for archiving
/SAPTRX/RESTMDF	Document flow: residence time deleting
/SAPTRX/RFC	Define own log. sys. and log sys All
/SAPTRX/TSC0AP	Define authorization profiles
/SAPTRX/TSC0AS	Define application systems
/SAPTRX/TSC0AUTHSND	Authorized event message senders
/SAPTRX/TSC0CONS	Define event consolidation profiles
/SAPTRX/TSC0CS	Code set customizing and mapping
/SAPTRX/TSC0DF	Document flow customizing
/SAPTRX/TSC0DOC	Drilldown to application document
/SAPTRX/TSC0DT	Define Internal and external document types
/SAPTRX/TSC0EC	Define internal event codes and groups
/SAPTRX/TSC0EE	Define expected event profiles
/SAPTRX/TSC0EES	Define event status
/SAPTRX/TSC0ERC	Event reason codes
/SAPTRX/TSC0ES	Define event handler set profiles
/SAPTRX/TSC0ET	Define extension tables
/SAPTRX/TSC0ETE	Define extension for event message
/SAPTRX/TSC0EXEV	External event codes and mapping
/SAPTRX/TSC0FASH	Enable fashion procurement contr.
/SAPTRX/TSC0FP	Define filter profiles
/SAPTRX/TSC0FR	Assign filter profiles to roles
/SAPTRX/TSC0FU	Assign filter profile to user
/SAPTRX/TSC0GBPT	Global business process types definition
/SAPTRX/TSC0LINK	URL template for tracking ID provider

Transaction Code	Description
/SAPTRX/TSC0LOC	Location customizing and mapping
/SAPTRX/TSC0MBF	Event message processing criteria
/SAPTRX/TSC0PAR	Partner customizing and mapping
/SAPTRX/TSC0PD	Define parameter dictionary
/SAPTRX/TSC0PDE	Define parameters for event messages
/SAPTRX/TSC0PDM	Define parameter mapping
/SAPTRX/TSC0PDS	Define system parameters
/SAPTRX/TSC0PME	Defining parameter mapping for event message
/SAPTRX/TSC0SCR	Assign scenarios to roles
/SAPTRX/TSC0SCU	Assign scenario to users
/SAPTRX/TSC0SD1	Define scenario mapping
/SAPTRX/TSC0SD2	Define scenario mapping: profiles
/SAPTRX/TSC0SD3	Define scenario mapping: parameter/condition
/SAPTRX/TSC0SD4	Define scenario mapping: functions
/SAPTRX/TSC0SD5	Define scenario mapping: activities
/SAPTRX/TSC0SD6	Define scenario mapping
/SAPTRX/TSC0SD7	Define scenario mapping: document flow
/SAPTRX/TSC0SO	Define solution/scenario
/SAPTRX/TSC0SO1	Define solution/scenario
/SAPTRX/TSC0SO2	Define solution/scenario
/SAPTRX/TSC0SP	Define status profiles
/SAPTRX/TSC0SPROC	Enable seasonal procurement
/SAPTRX/TSC0SQF	Special query functions for event handler data
/SAPTRX/TSC0ST	Define status attributes
/SAPTRX/TSC0STI	Define status icons for events

Transaction Code	Description
/SAPTRX/TSC0TC	Define event handler conditions
/SAPTRX/TSC0TC1	Define rule conditions
/SAPTRX/TSC0TC2	Define condition for event handler type and set
/SAPTRX/TSC0TC5	Define filter conditions
/SAPTRX/TSC0TC6	Document flow: conditions
/SAPTRX/TSC0TF	Define event manager functions
/SAPTRX/TSC0TF1	Define rule activity functions
/SAPTRX/TSC0TF2	Define event handler type condition functions
/SAPTRX/TSC0TF3	Define expected events functions
/SAPTRX/TSC0TF4	Define parameter mapping functions
/SAPTRX/TSC0TF5	Define filter profile functions
/SAPTRX/TSC0TF6	Define SAP NetWeaver BW interface functions
/SAPTRX/TSC0TF7	Document flow: functions
/SAPTRX/TSC0TP	Define activities
/SAPTRX/TSC0TP1	Define rule activities
/SAPTRX/TSC0TP2	Define event hander update activities
/SAPTRX/TSC0TP3	Define EE monitor activities
/SAPTRX/TSC0TR	Rules, activities, and conditions
/SAPTRX/TSC0TRD	Display rule sets
/SAPTRX/TSC0TSCONF	Define system configuration
/SAPTRX/TSC0TT	Define event handler types
/SAPTRX/TSP_SETUP	R/3 workflow parameter definition
/SAPTRX/UCBO	Business object
/SAPTRX/UCCF	Configure fields for user profile
/SAPTRX/UCNAVI	Navigation to other objects

Transaction Code	Description
/SAPTRX/UCROLE	Assign user profiles to a role
/SAPTRX/UCTD	Maintain WCL transactions
/SAPTRX/UCUP	Maintain user profiles
/SAPTRX/UCURL	Internal/external link
/SAPTRX/UCUSER	Assign user profiles to a user
/SAPTRX/WCL_ADMIN	WCL: administration
/SAPTRX/WCL_FAVORITE	WCL: my favorites
/SAPTRX/WCL_QUICK	WCL: quick search
/SAPTRX/WCL_SEARCH	WCL: search
/SAPTRX/WCL_SEND	WCL: direct event sending
/SAPTRX/WFPD	R/3 workflow parameter definition
ALRTINBOX	Trigger alert inbox BSP
ALRTCATDEF	Alert framework categories
SM59	RFC destination maintenance
SARA	Archive administration
SLG1	Application log monitoring
RZ20	CCMS monitoring

B.2 SAP ECC Application System Transaction Codes

Transaction Code	Description
/SAPTRX/ASAPLOG	Application system log for event handling
/SAPTRX/ASC0AO	Define application object and event types
/SAPTRX/ASC0AP	Define application parameters
/SAPTRX/ASC0SCU	Assign scenario to users
/SAPTRX/ASC0SD1	Define solution/scenario

Transaction Code	Description
/SAPTRX/ASC0SD2	Define solution/scenario
/SAPTRX/ASC0TC	Define EM relevance conditions
/SAPTRX/ASC0TF	Define EM interface functions
/SAPTRX/ASC0TO	Define business process types
/SAPTRX/ASC0TS	Define event managers (engines)
/SAPTRX/ASEHVIEW	Event handler list of shipments
/SAPTRX/DISP_LINK	Display show link
/SAPTRX/TSC0GBPT	Global business process types definition
/SAPTRX/TSC0SCR	Assign scenarios to roles
/SAPTRX/TSC0SCU	Assign scenario to users
/SAPTRX/TSC0SO	Define solution/scenario
CFG1	Application log

Various developer notes exist for SAP Event Management, some of which are listed here.

C   SAP Notes on SAP Event Management

C.1   SAP SCM Event Manager

SAP Note Number	Description
1417564	PTA: quantity events cannot trigger event for delivery event handler
1417439	Document references are not populated in alert container II
1417420	WDA UI: Default values missing after change of scenario
1410998	PROC_DATE is missing for several events
1407562	URL in alert mail is not created correctly
1392898	Customizing: activate seasonal procurement Vis. process
1392859	AWD UI: deadlocks on table DDPRH when the UI is started
1388031	Event handler type is not taken into account
1383844	Short dump when simulating reprocessing events
1381618	SAP OER: integration of unpacking step in PTA scenario
1379027	Short dump when creating alert with date system parameter
1361391	SAP OER - how to use custom extensions
1356930	SAP Event Management: define event message senders – IMG text corrections
1356843	Error when confirming multiple events with same event code
1355699	SAP Event Management: Criteria for saving attachments – IMG text correction
1355395	Overdue events and unwanted status changes

SAP Note Number	Description
1353279	WDA UI: short dump occurs when suppressing empty fields
1338999	Document references are not populated in alert container
1330361	CHECK_PARAM_VALUE determines incorrect value
1328626	AWD UI: link navigation in SAP system fails
1328490	Web Dynpro UI: doubled event message sending checkboxes
1321861	AWD UI: error for event message from detail screen
1318327	EM WDA UI: No icons when using link for other event handlers
1317248	Error in SAP Event Management when deleting deliveries
1310789	WD UI: incorrect display of values in dropdown list
1309971	Short dump if event message header ext used in alert text
1306046	Performance during event processing in BAPI
1298260	Termination when system issues an event message
1295177	SAP TM–SAP Event Management Integration on different systems: alerts are empty
1293208	Define connection to external ID mapping
1292574	Location description cannot be displayed in Web Dynpro UI
1291768	Event Status is not in Expected Event Overdue List
1289093	Method to get MY_REPROCESS in /SAPTRX/CL_EH_PROCESS_MODEL
1286367	SAP Event Management 5.1 SP: changing IMG title from English to German
1272463	Hidden configured fields for event message sending not processed
1269470	Web Dynpro UI: selection with leading zeros is wrong
1268038	SAP Event Management 7.0: SOA documentation corrections
1266541	Web Dynpro UI – fast entry: required input field does not work
1266011	New event for SAP TM: order taking visibility process

SAP Note Number	Description
1260127	SAP Event Management Web UI comparison
1260125	Configuring search fields for the web interface
1259989	Location name and data code set missing in consolidated events
1254943	/SAPTRX/EH_LIST: reprocessing event messages
1253917	Wrong interface parameter in parameter mapping template
1253438	EM WDA UI: no icons in header data of event handler
1252795	SAP Event Management web UI comparison
1251397	/SAPTRX/EH_LIST: invalid short text for status attribute
1250228	BI update for undoing event handler deletion fails
1248309	Typed fields are displayed incorrectly in Alert Framework
1247537	SAP Event Management—SAP TM integration: tendering (end of receive response)
1246273	Wrong event code when using external event code
1239387	Short dump in web UI with certain configured fields
1236057	How to run WCL on multiple Java instances
1172722	Parameters are not filled in function /SAPTRX/CREATE_ALERT
1153145	Short dump in new web interface after SP04 (SCEMSRV5.1)
1144099	Own activity methods when upgrading SAP Event Management
1141578	Composite note for document changes in SAP Event Management 5.1 (as of SP06)
1127053	Wrong status attribute name in rule set
1124226	Additional information for the SAP Event Management eSOA-Services eSOA mapping
1122318	SAP Event Management 5.1: deployment options
1116656	Release restrictions for SAP Event Management 5.1
1111908	Multiple rows for one event handler in Web Dynpro UI

SAP Note Number	Description
1110940	Dump SAPSQL_ARRAY_INSERT_DUPREC with table /SAPTRX/EH_SETEH
1104443	Performance problem with /SAPTRX/EH_LIST
1100582	How To... troubleshoot WCL's connection settings
1088715	Error in activity STATUS_CHECK when recreating event handlers
1069155	User role for SAP Event Management user: wrong menu added
1056154	Event message sending
1052746	Incorrect return code for activity WORKFLOW_START
1038078	SAP Event Management 5.1 SP1 corrections
1005601	Error when parameter is transferred to the workflow
988027	SAP Event Management: IMG and Duet integration enhancement
955940	Missing descriptions in Transaction /SAPTRX/EH_LIST
941801	Alert Framework: additional tracking IDs not available
897217	WCL: selection by EXPECTED EVENT REPORTING TIME/DATE
863551	Event message table /saptrx/evm_unpr not archived correctly
858905	Buffering of table /SAPTRX/AOTREF not necessary
853741	Passing parameters to the workflow
849268	Activity OVERDUE_EE_RESET does not reset overdue flag
839899	Parameters and file attachments are not processed
822831	Incompatible structure /SAPTRX/BAPI_EH_EXPECTED_EVENT
815682	SCEM: preventing updates to the application log
814065	Termination during the initial upload using /SAPTRX/BWIU
805298	Selection criteria for event handler set archiving not working
805294	Short dump CONVT_NO_NUMBER when archiving event handler sets

SAP Note Number	Description
793979	Cross transport of SAP NetWeaver BW procurement development
787694	Endless loop when displaying event handler data in application system
760035	Query ID contains log. system instead of application system name
757146	System parameters as selection fields in WCL
755397	Monitoring WCL in CCMS
752661	Deletion of event handler and SAP NetWeaver BW upload: performance improvement
746256	Alternative BPT is not considered when creating event handler
738947	Build tool for WCL.
737042	Activity PARAMETER_CHANGE deletes wrong parameter
726740	Send proof of delivery from SAP Event Management does not work.
724520	Event message BAPI performance enhancement
718697	Application log settings are not working after upgrade
716176	Memory problems when using application log
703342	Error in Transaction /SAPTRX/BWCQ
700742	Wrong customizing setting: IDoc EVMSTA01, EHPOST01
685871	Production malfunction visibility: PP/DS alerts
683503	Changing expected event date/time in expected event list
677373	Release restrictions visibility processes
664072	Application object ID extractor
651747	Simulation mode not correctly processed
562993	Release of BAPIs for business object /SAPTRX/EH
545166	Transaction /saptrx/mi02: partner info and status reason

SAP Note Number	Description
77305	Archiving: deletion program runs slowly
69143	Archiving: deletion program terminates

C.2   SAP ECC Application System

SAP Note Number	Description
1377325	Checkman correction /SAPTRX/VEXTRACT
1339856	SAP Event Management: /SAPTRX/ASC0TSAI define SAP Event Management: IMG text corrections
1336887	EM parameters: index is missing
1335170	RTI event message extractors: missing location data
1317248	Error in event management when deleting deliveries
1273445	Event management: production malfunction scenario correction
1256056	Missing accessibility settings for /SAPTRX/VEXTRACT
1179634	Missing authorization checks when calling transactions
1176679	Duplicate entries when using data extraction in application system
1174066	Error when maintaining event management relevance condition (event type)
1168318	ESC_SORDER: table SALES_ORDER_HEADER_NEW not filled
1158683	Missing transaction code maintenance with SU22
1137318	Composite note: Doc. changes for PI Basis 2006_1 SP05 and above
1126673	Missing event management documentation in PI_BASIS
1122318	SAP Event Management 5.1: deployment options
1121551	Deadlock occurs during deletion in table /SAPTRX/APPTALOG
1057626	Syntax error in function module /SAPTRX/EVENT_DATA_SETUP

SAP Note Number	Description
993439	EDI ORDRSP: event manager is not called
956887	Tracking ID extractor is called if condition is false
947215	Event handler creation: short dump DATA_UC_STRUCT_C_OFFSET_LENGTH
933506	Queues hang if event manager communication cancelled 2
922815	Remaining queues with canceled event manager communication
896191	FAQ: event manager seasonal procurement (consulting, tips, customizing)
881931	Additional check for dates without predecessors
871818	Application log entries for event manager displayed in another appl.
858905	Buffering of table /SAPTRX/AOTREF not necessary
846914	Unnecessary error messages in application log
802454	Update indicator for PO items not set correctly
787694	Endless loop when displaying event handler data in application system
780064	Syntax error in program /SAPTRX/SAPLSD_INVOICE_EXIT
775723	Original expected date not displayed in EH_List
775317	Termination in /SAPTRX/XET_LE_ROAD_TRA10
773781	SAP Best Practice for SAP SCM: fulfillment visibility scenario
769138	Event type extractors include wrong old table data
719910	Incompatible structure /SAPTRX/BAPI_EVM_EE_MODIFY
716535	Link of event manager in billing for Release 4.6C
710912	Wrapper module for SAP Event Management SD invoice exit
691810	SAP Event manager communication does not work in SAP R/3 4.6C
667692	Purchase order BADI for event manager connection
651910	Does not display the log entry in /saptrx/asaplog

SAP Note Number	Description
648814	Event type – event sending for better performance
643146	Error V0104 during refresh of SCEM data in process order
642856	Change the message text for SAP event manager communication
642741	RFC error occurs during event sending
619492	BADI delivered inactive

D   The Author

Sandeep Pradhan is an SAP solution architect in the field of supply chain management with more than 15 years of professional experience. He specializes in supply chain application advisory services and has achieved results by helping clients to understand, architect, select and implement the right SAP SCM solutions required to run their business. In addition to his various roles (project manager, solution architect, supply chain manager), he has been responsible for providing thought leadership in supply chain strategy, business processes transformation, technology architecture, and business integration. He has worked on numerous full lifecycle SAP Event Management project implementations from discovery phase through implementation phase. Sandeep holds MBA degree from Monash University, Australia. You may contact Sandeep Pradhan via email at *spradhan13@gmail.com*.

Index

U

Unexpected event, 46
Unplanned or unexpected event, 24
Unreported event, 46
User exits, 110

V

Vehicle Management System (VMS), 60
Visibility, 50
Visibility scenarios, 18, 51
Visibility scenario templates, 52

Visibility solutions, 37
VMS and SAP Event Management, 60

W

Web Application Server (AS), 95
Web communication, 169
Web Communication Layer (WCL), 50
Web-Dynpro, 169
Web Dynpro Reporting, 178
Web server, 97
Web status portal, 41
Workflow, 41